Need for a New Paradigm in Education

Burçak Çağla Garipağaoğlu (ed.)

Need for a New Paradigm in Education

From the Newtonian Paradigm to the Quantum Paradigm

PETER LANG

Berlin - Bruxelles - Chennai - Lausanne - New York - Oxford

Library of Congress Cataloging-in-Publication Data
A CIP catalog record for this book has been applied for at the
Library of Congress.

**Bibliographic Information published by the
Deutsche Nationalbibliothek**
The Deutsche Nationalbibliothek lists this publication in the Deutsche
Nationalbibliografie; detailed bibliographic data is available online at
http://dnb.d-nb.de.

Funded by Bahçeşehir University

ISBN 978-3-631-91180-8 (Print)
E-ISBN 978-3-631-91181-5 (E-PDF)
E-ISBN 978-3-631-93074-8 (E-PUB)
10.3726/b22562

© 2025 Peter Lang Group AG, Lausanne
Published by Peter Lang GmbH, Berlin, Germany

info@peterlang.com - www.peterlang.com

Table of Contents

Part 1: Squeezed Between the Two Calls

Dr. B. Çağla Garipağaoğlu

Chapter 1 The Legacies of the Past: Newtonian Paradigm in Education

Abstract: The world is now suffering from a deep educational crisis today. Our education system cannot keep up with our fast-paced world. We witness an increasing decline in confidence and public support for college education. Education and obtaining a college diploma, that once was considered as a taken-for-granted path to wealth and social advancement by most people, is now a source of countless debates. The Newtonian paradigm of schooling that worked so well for so many years is now not up for the job it was once set for. Products of our educational system (i.e. our graduates) no longer fit the needs and demands of the today's labor market. Employers are complaining about the incompatibility between job requirements and employee/graduate qualifications; graduates are complaining about not being able to find a job because the employers either reject their job applications claiming that they are either under-educated or over-educated for the type of employment they have applied for; parents are complaining that "the kind of academic education" that opened so many doors for them no longer works for their children; and some politicians even blame the over-education of young learners as the reason for under-employment among the highly educated young people. Despite the numerous efforts to transform our Newtonian education to cure the very problems it has created, the basic notion of Newtonian schooling remained strictly unchanged over the last century. There are multiple reasons why we cannot transform our Newtonian educational system and shift to the Quantum paradigm. In this chapter, we will pinpoint those reasons and a few major misconceptions why the models of quantum paradigm often struggle to take root in education.

Keywords: Newtonian paradigm, Quantum paradigm, paradigm shift in education

For more than 100 years, the Newtonian-inspired way of reductionist understanding dominated the world's main approach to schooling. The strength of the Newtonian paradigm was that through its method of reductionism it had shown the world that there was only one unique, universal truth that can be revealed by scientific methods – which we now know is not true (Louth, 2011). According to this decades-long entrenched Newtonian rule, our schools have been constructed around an individual teacher leading a group of same-aged pupils through a uniform curriculum (Rose et al., 2022). The authors of "Out of the Box" report called this approach to schooling the "industrial paradigm" as it was mirroring the standardized ways in which factories operated during the industrial era (Rose et al., 2022). Just because our schools were built in a way to reflect the so-called strength of the Newtonian-reductionist way of understanding the world, this approach – in this chapter – will be called the "Newtonian paradigm". However, despite the so-called strength of the Newtonian way of schooling, today, as learners make their way through this paradigm, approximately 66 % end up "disengaged" (Arnett, 2022a) proving that this paradigm no longer benefits the world. While this paradigm significantly increased the world's access to education, it did not necessarily ensure learning. While the parents, educators and politicians keep on uttering their continued testimonies about the value of education to the young generations, worldwide millions of children graduate from the education system without even the most basic skills (World Bank, 2019). Most of them, for example, are simply still struggling to calculate the correct amount of change to return when performing a cash transaction, having a hard time in understanding Ikea's assembly instructions, or reading a transit schedule. Research shows that even those who successfully navigate the system gain only a limited set of academic skills that may or may not align with their individual needs, interests, and strengths (Arnett, 2022a). Plus, as a side effect, learners often develop fixed and narrow mindsets about their potentials and evaluate their value and identity through the narrow framing of academic ranking and sorting systems (Arnett, 2022a). Therefore, almost all parents are in search of a "better" education and "better" schools for their children, while most employers are frantically complaining about the "skill gap" between universities and the business world (Prensky, 2018). Countries and politicians try to make systemwide reforms in education enthusiastically – often in vain – in order to align skills acquired in schools to those of skills needed in the marketplace.

For most of the world, the "American Dream" and what it represents is so much more elusive today (Agarwal, 2017). To begin with, now a university degree costs a lot higher than it cost compared with a mere decade ago, making the first step of the American dream out of many of our youth's reach. Many college-age students are struggling with student loans and more than half of them say that their loans weren't worth it (Hess, 2021). At the same time, more and more employers are complaining that they can't find qualified candidates to fill the job openings. According to Turczynski (2023), about 50 % of employers reportedly say that they have job openings, but they can't find qualified candidates to fill them. This demand for qualified people will keep increasing as economies and jobs get more sophisticated over time. However, our youth are just ill-equipped to launch a fulfilling career because they are lacking the necessary skills and professional knowledge. What's more, there are new jobs emerging that didn't even exist a decade ago. However, our education system cannot keep up with our fast-paced

world. We are not even close to meeting the critical demands of today's learners, employees, and employers. Employers are looking for people "who can get
things done". Yet, the type of schooling – almost all the world's people go through
between the ages of roughly 5 and 21 – offers almost no preparation at all to
thrive in the real world. Our education system cannot keep up with our ever-
changing, digitally driven workplace. We are not even close to meeting the critical demands of today's learners, employees, and employers.

Although it is at odds with the realities of the world we live in today, we must
admit that our schools are doing exactly what they are built to do. The reason
that our education system suffers from a deep learning crisis today is that it was
built for a different age – when the Newtonian paradigm approach to schooling
was considered the most efficient way of education. Yet, with globalization, digital transformations, pandemic, and natural disasters transforming the world,
our schools patterned after the factory-model of the industrial age are no longer
up for the needs of our current realms. We no longer need factory workers who
are merely able to execute repetitive tasks, understand and follow directions and
perform basic numeracy and literacy skills (Rose et al., 2022). What we really
need are innovators, entrepreneurs and creative talents who can change the rules
of the game (Garipağaoğlu, 2013). Our schools require a paradigm shift that
put more emphasis on interdisciplinary mindset, critical thinking, problem-
solving, and communication skills rather than rote memorization of a subject
matter and the mastery of a limited set of academic knowledge (e.g. four operations) and test-taking skills (Zhao, 2012). We must eventually prepare our kids
for the future by integrating real-world problems into our education system.

While creating great challenges for learners, worldwide technological transformations and natural disasters are also creating new possibilities both for
learners and teachers by changing the way we learn and teach (Anderson et al.,
2017). The pandemic has shown the world that we are all interconnected and
highly vulnerable in the face of the unpredictable nature of the future. We must
understand that our current education model was indeed designed for the First
Industrial Revolution. Yet, we no longer live in the First Industrial Revolution.
Fueled with globalization and technology, the Fourth Industrial Revolution has
already arrived, and the Fifth one is at the door. Apparently, our strongest competitive advantage that will single out our nation and people in the Fourth &
Fifth Industrial Revolution will be our ingenuity and entrepreneurship of our
next-gen. Therefore, it is in our best interest to re-design our education system
to meet the dynamic needs of the fourth industrial revolution and get prepared
for the fifth Industrial Revolution by equipping our kids with the skills required
for the 21st century workforce. Indeed, every part of K-12 and higher education

needs to redesign its approach and outcomes to increase voice and choice of students and foster entrepreneurial mindsets in our young people (Prensky, 2014).

Challenges of Shifting from Newtonian Paradigm to Quantum Paradigm

Despite numerous efforts to transform Newtonian education, the basic notion of Newtonian schooling remained strictly unchanged over the last century. There are multiple reasons as to why we cannot transform Newtonian school systems into learner-centered systems defined by the Quantum paradigm.

The first reason is that changing anything that is so established and ubiquitous is never easy (Horn & Staker, 2017). Our education structure is massive, and the system is not designed to allow for a smooth paradigm shift (Rose et al., 2022). Neither school principals nor the individual teachers are able to design the education system of the future while also managing requirements of the conventional education system of today (Christensen et al., 2013). Indeed, a few sectors ask their practitioners on the ground to create something new and different as a part of their daily job (Horn, 2022). It wasn't the doctors, for instance, who developed antibiotics, nor someone from a ship crew who designed a submarine (Rose et al., 2022). As argued by Horn (2022), these people might take a sit on the Research and Development teams or Tink-tank teams designing for the next-gen breakthroughs, but none of them can be expected to accomplish such a task as part of their daily duty. First, in our never-ending quest to look successful, most of us tend to focus on daily operational excellence but not on a disruptive or sustaining innovation with the potential to change the whole operation altogether. Second, just because the most urgent and immediate tasks consume all the energy necessary for new innovations, the type of re-engineering or innovation required by the education system can never be realized by individual practitioners (teachers and school principals), especially at the very boundaries of an established school organization (Horn, 2022). As noted by Matheson (2021), the pursuit of operational excellence will always wound any efforts necessary for a long-term transformation. In other words, the short-term, day-to-day routines will always be prioritized over the more important but less urgent work of new innovations (Horn, 2022). Indeed, this is exactly the reason why Christensen (2011) advises established companies to spin out their best ideas into independent startups. To sum up, the paradigm shift in our education system cannot be accomplished without an interdisciplinary mindset and wise strategies accompanied by wise tactics (e.g. spin off schools). So, all we have to do is to recognize the paradox and avoid it by creating a new reality outside of our current operational boundaries. As famously stated by Sun Tzu –the ancient Chinese military strategist (also the author of one of the most influential and epic documents in the history of warfare strategy-The Art of War): "Strategy without tactics is the slowest route to victory. Tactics without strategy are the noise before defeat" (Tzu, 2010). We must always keep that in mind: Fixation on operational excellence can kill any effort for innovation yet any deviation or failure of operational excellence can make you vulnerable and endanger your financial structure or upset your value networks (Hamel & Prahalad, 1994). Thus, to successfully navigate through this dilemma we have to find ways to be more resourceful with the help of wiser strategies and tactics.

Second, another reason why established schools are having trouble in changing their instructional models is that today's schools are structured, designed, and built with a one-size-fits-all mentality (Rose et al., 2022). Our education system is patterned after the dominant industrial model of the era and operated as if all students who are at the same age learn at the same pace and have the exact same learning needs. The education system we have today is, in many ways, built as a ranking system. Those students who can't keep up with the pace are kicked off from the system at various stages – an arrangement that worked fine for many decades in the past, but no longer today. As most famously pointed out by Senge (2004) this is a typical example of the learning disability which is called "today's problems come from yesterday's solutions". Because the majority of people still think that "mastering the subjects of math, language arts, science and social studies is what education is all about, our curricula was simply oriented around these four core subjects" (Prensky, 2014, p. 23). Therefore, although curricular innovations for skills like emotional intelligence, negotiation, entrepreneurship, reflexivity, empathy, creativity, problem solving, agency, community service, technology literacy are more laudable today, these skills were never at the core but a rainbow surrounding the real core or simply provided as adds-on (Prensky, 2014). Plus, most of those popular curricular innovations are merely created and funded by some special-interest groups with a limited usage and scope (Prensky, 2014).

Third reason as to why learner-centered curricular innovations often fail to take root is often the "Don't experiment with my kid!" attitude (Prensky, 2016, p. 23). Anyone in authority attempts at a comprehensive curricular change is usually destined to meet with this attitude. The primary reason for this attitude is often the belief that the things that worked for too many years should work again. So, it is all about our tendency to stick to the well-known, familiar, taken-for-granted recipe (Garipağaoğlu, 2023). Just because we see new ideas as unnecessary distractions that interfere with our day-to-day business, we tend to perpetuate the past practices reflexively by over-valuing conformance more highly than creativity and by turning our long-tenured nostrums into sacred truths (Hamel, 2001). This is also famously known as "success is an innovation killer" syndrome. Because of this syndrome, the educational visions we set for our young people are generally limited to what is most familiar. Even when school communities articulate bold visions, they rarely have the capacity to design and build what it takes to actualize those visions (Rose et al., 2022). As such, they are compelled to resort to short-term ineffective solutions within the frames of the old Newtonian paradigm, rather than shifting to Quantum mindset for more effective and long-term solutions. So, as stated by Prensky (2016), we can conclude that not experimenting to find better ways to educate our young minds would be "being irresponsible and reckless". We must understand that the most responsible thing to do is never to let things go as they are but to experiment and dare to go beyond our old Newtonian paradigm in order to find and pursue fundamentally better ways to change our education system. Although our instincts tell us to stick to the familiar solutions or apply "best practices" to every single problem we face, we should learn to avoid this trap by thinking "out of the box".

The fourth reason is that all the real, down-to-earth solutions for schools aiming for a paradigm shift are just risky and come with a huge cost. Therefore, we tend to settle down with the easiest, temporary yet low-leverage solutions. This is pretty much like focusing on symptoms rather than the true disease. Schools regularly enjoy an illusion of "taking charge" (Senge, 1990) by finding quick fixes to their problems. They make reforms to their curricula, update their professional training programs, revise their elective courses, employ new technologies and improve their value propositions. However, all these marginal improvements only serve to reinforce the established organizational models and turn out to be tomorrow's problems. While the low-leverage solutions fit perfectly well with our education system by reinforcing the deeply entrenched value propositions of the existing system, down-to-earth innovations prove to be too difficult or too risky to adopt as they risk upsetting the existing financial structure or value networks. In a similar vein of thinking, for schools to purchase and adopt many products such as better textbooks, interactive whiteboards, or an electronic gradebook at a scale, they must be effective in addressing the exact needs of the Newtonian paradigm. Because only then the investments may fit inside the conventional design of a typical school and the act can be welcome, accepted unquestionably and considered legitimate by the stakeholders. As a result, these solutions and the money invested in them typically help reinforce, rather than challenge the Newtonian type of schooling. It is indeed a very typical example of path dependency – the tendency to rely on past practices, decisions, and actions as a short-cut for the sake of efficiency rather than effectiveness (Garipağaoğlu, 2023). Yet, it must be kept in mind that although path-dependency can save time and money by providing short-cuts and offering incremental developments for the system at hand, it does not necessarily offer the much-needed cure for the persistent problems of the system in play. In other words, sticking to a conventional path is not always and necessarily the ideal strategy as it inhibits the much-needed paradigm change required to solve the perennial problems of our current educational system.

The fifth reason is that the educational landscape itself has fortified the Newtonian paradigm by developing a bunch of standards, regulations, procedures, and practices designed to manage the often-conflicting demands of various constituencies. Because they must be immediately implemented within today's system and require immediate results, they have an impact of enhancing the Newtonian paradigm's constraints, making it harder for innovative educators to go beyond the existing boundaries. As most famously put by Senge (1990) this is a typical example of a learning disability which is called "the easy way out usually leads back in". According to the theory of institutionalization, it is critical for institutions to establish legitimacy and preserve it to respond better to intense competition, increased public expectations, and changing technologies (March & Olsen, 1989; Meyer & Rowen, 1977). To achieve this, they design their structures and processes through laws and regulations by adopting long-tenured nostrums (Clegg, 2010; DiMaggio & Powell, 1983; Powell & DiMaggio, 1991). Clearly, there is a tension between what is mandated by the realities of today, and what has worked in the past (Anderson et al., 2017). The conventional mindset that enables efficient execution in the face of an uncertain environment merely serves to encourage marginal progress but stifles the organization's ability to learn, create and innovate (Gyau & Stringer, 2011). The narrow, strong and collective focus on getting things done forcefully merely inhibits the experimentation and reflection that are vital to sustainability in an unpredictable and evolving environment. This syndrome can be best explained with a picture of Japan that keeps on preparing Samurai swordsmen for war. So, if we continue to fixate on the exact wrong things at the exact wrong time by miscalculating our real priorities and fail to re-arrange our priorities soon enough, we will lag behind in transforming our educational system and soon face to our own defeat brought upon us by our ignorance and miscalculations. Kılıçoğlu and Yılmaz-Kılıçoğlu (2021) advocate that contradictions between the real deeds of the organizations and professed calls for a fundamental reform in education are bound to happen when schools have to comply with the standards, policies, practices, and priorities of the conventional system. Brunsson (1989) argues that given the often-contradictory demands organizations face from the institutional environment, compliance instead of innovation will surpass the fight just because the organizations must ensure the support of their environment for mere survival. However, as we have said repeatedly before, we are facing a learning crisis, and our education system is at a crossroads, and we have no luxury to pamper our institutional environments by endangering our future generation. We can no longer let our fixation on past practices and our institutional environment blind us to the current needs of our young minds and distract us from our rightful efforts to innovate an education system aligned with the Quantum paradigm.

Lastly, a system's value network can become a constraint for an innovation to take root, because even if the need for a new model is acknowledged, efforts for such a reform are more likely to get nullified by the conflicting priorities of the existing value networks of our conventional educational system. Priorities of any system are determined by its value network and different value networks that set divergent priorities. For example, while public schools are supposed to serve all students in a region in the same way regardless of the conflicting priorities of various stakeholders, private schools are more flexible to build their own value networks with a particular vision in their mind. This vision might reveal itself with a strong emphasis on rigorous college preparation or with an emphasis on sports, language, or STEM (Science, Technology, Engineering and Math) (Arnett, 2022b). Funders, teachers, students, and parents who share the same vision come together, and others who don't share it are discouraged to go elsewhere, unite together and form their own value network (Arnett, 2022b). If a value network starts to produce a set of divergent goals, the system gets stuck with politics. And instead of actualizing a particular vision exceptionally well, it eventually ends up being a jack of all trades and master of none. Yet, according to Arnett (2022b), this doesn't mean that private schools are inherently more innovative than their public counterparts. Some private schools are pretty much like their counterparts because their value networks are pretty much similar to those of public schools. On the contrary, some public schools may even be distinctively more innovative than their private counterparts. Public or private, generally, all school systems have to navigate through the divergent priorities of their value network and engage in politics that drains all the energy of the system away from the efforts that must be targeting innovative pursuits (Arnett, 2022b).

To sum up, innovative models and new ideas can get attention only if they're aligned with the distinctive priorities of a different value network (Arnett, 2022a). The value network of a system consists of individuals, other institutions, and regulations that the system interfaces with (Arnett, 2022a). Any new model is doomed to regress back to the conventional model if it has to operate within the value network of the conventional model (Arnett, 2022a). Value networks of an education system often include local, and national regulatory bodies; funders, donors, and investors; learners, teachers, and parents; employees and unions; policymakers and taxpayers; the upper educational stage and the labor market; teacher preparation institutes and other vendors; and the larger community (Arnett, 2022a). Because schools do not live in isolation, they have to manage the perceptions of their multiple stakeholders and please them by meeting their expectations. In an effort to meet those expectations, schools generally exhibit isomorphic tendencies and embrace structures, standards and policies that help them look legitimate without really caring about the true effectiveness of those standards and structures (Beckert, 2010, DiMaggio & Powell, 1983; Lai et al., 2006). Perennial organizations' motivation and ability (i.e. Newtonian schools) to create something new and different relies on first; the fit between the innovation and the existing system and second, the welcoming attitude of organization's value networks towards that particular innovation (Arnett, 2022a). An organization's value network is indeed what determines its priorities. This is exactly the reason why many learner-centered systems fail. They simply fail because they do not fit well with the expectations of the organization's existing value network.

Few Major Misconceptions Why Quantum Models Often Struggle to Take Root in Education

The first misconception is that there is a lack of promising educational models. The reason for the limited adoption of new innovative models is definitely not the lack of promising learner-centered models. Indeed, there are many noteworthy models in the world created and funded by some special interest-groups, think-tank institutes and thought leaders in the field of education. Since they have generously shared their visions, the most recommended models, resources, and processes openly, we indeed know what learner-centered education models are and how they can be put into practice as long as a new value network can be formed to support that vision. Without the support and the protection of a strong value network, no innovative model or curricula can flourish or have widespread usage. So, the real problem is never the lack of promising learner-centered education models but the difficulty of forming a new, strong, and supportive value network independent from old ones.

Second, although most school principals generally assume that designing a learner-centered model or more personalized education is just a matter of making some reforms on the old curricula and the learning strategies, the problem goes beyond the scope of curricula or learning strategies. The problem lies in the fact that shifting to a new model requires more than just changing the content, resources, technologies, partners, or professional training programs, it also requires a drastic change in the value networks. Just as "you can't build an airplane by merely putting wings and a jet engine on a car", school systems can't make the transformation desired for the new age by merely swapping the Newtonian curricula and schedules for learner-centered alternatives and training their staff on learner-centered practices (Arnett, 2022a). The new models need to be designed from the ground up in line with the priorities of the value networks of learners, teachers, parents, and regulatory bodies.

Third, the problem is not the lack of inspiring leadership or lack of effective communication either. Even though most organizational change is a matter of employing effective leadership and communication strategies by building consensus among the wide range of competing stakeholders, new models require completely new value networks with completely new priorities. When it comes to a perennial paradigm change, reducing the matter down to mere effective leadership or communication would be naïve. When there is a call for new models – not just upgrades–, trying to adjust established value network of a Newtonian paradigm to the those of Quantum paradigm and then mobilizing the action surely cannot be merely the matter of effective leadership or communication. Change does not happen without the buy-in of at least a critical mass of the key stakeholders (Arnett, 2022a). All these requirements put significant constraints on the extent to which new models of education are adopted. Competing stakeholders often pull schools in many diverging directions. Most school leaders got into the profession with idealistic intentions in mind, but to keep their jobs and satisfy the divergent needs and wants of their stakeholders, they eventually have to engage in politics, make compromises, persuade key influencers in the value network, and maintain a good public image by sacrificing their idealistic intents (Arnett, 2022a). This often leads to strong inertia in the status quo and dilutes and undermines any efforts and will to change. Departing from the status quo goes beyond rallying diverse array of stakeholders around a shared vision, it is simply about constituting a new value network with new priorities. To sum up, the problem is not the lack of effective school leadership but politics.

Fourth, the problem isn't a lack of desire. Most educational leaders and teachers agree that their students' voices are important, and most superintendents keep on professing the value of hearing students' and teachers' feedback. So, indeed, a greater number of leaders in the system of education welcome student opinions and understand the importance of more innovative curriculum and pedagogy than the ones who are satisfied with the existing system. Indeed, no one seems to celebrate the existing system and most of the leaders seem willing to embrace all the possibilities for a paradigm change in education. Nowadays the world fiercely calls for education at all levels to re-imagine its values and promises. People are talking about the idea that education should transform all learners in a way to help them realize their potential regardless of their background, race, color, and gender. Today, students are talking about democratizing education at all levels and calling for an education where they are more engaged, driven, and have autonomy over their education. Employers raise concerns about school graduates lacking the skills that they need. UNESCO (2021) notes that parents want drastic changes in education such as more experiential learning, personalized learning, and attention to learners' emotional wellbeing. Influential think-tank groups, school leaders and world leaders, all call for a drastic change in education describing a vision for learner-centered education. So, there's already a growing demand for change. However, there's also a growing hypocrisy accompanying it. People are pointing out the huge discrepancy between what people want from education and what our schools deliver; they advocate for the change; but still expect schools just to layer those changes on top of the existing model without dismantling the systems old value propositions. So, the problem is not the lack of desire but hypocrisy.

Conclusion

Practices such as separation of learners by age, class, and academic discipline; ranking and sorting students based on their academic achievement; teacher-led and single-paced instruction don't go hand in hand with many of the practices that play well with the learner-centered education system. Newtonian schooling prioritizes covering content during a fixed period of time within the confine of predetermined academic calendar and uses standardized tests to measure student achievement, whereas learner-centered Quantum models prioritize competency-based learning, interdisciplinary mindset, off-campus projects, flexible learning schedules, and learner's agency. Quantum models also measure success in terms of life outcomes, such as fulfilling career and success in upcoming educational pursuits. Shifting from Newtonian paradigm to Quantum paradigm usually requires three enablers: a new technology, a new organizational model, and a congruent value network (Christensen, 2011). Technology is often the easiest to recognize and attain. However, in order to leverage the enabling technology, we need new organizational models with distinctive value propositions. Although the "enabling technology" is the one that gets the most attention, it is not the problem. The problem is the firmly established value networks reinforcing the Newtonian approach to schooling, and the difficulty of establishing new ones.

Quantum paradigm requires new organizational models emerge from different value networks than those created the old models. Trying to create new models in tune with Quantum paradigm with reformed practices is akin to the colloquial definition of insanity: doing more of the same thing and expecting different results. Quantum paradigm requires new value networks that are congruent with the new value propositions of quantum paradigm. It requires new value networks who are willing to bet on small, new schools (e.g. microschools or practical, flexible solutions that build on massive open online courses (MOOCs) – educating millions of learners for free) without expecting immediate and drastic growth in profits. Trying to reproduce new models within the value networks of an incumbent system will eventually mean that all the genuine efforts aiming to bring about the desired change will fail while it tries to compromise the old system.

In a nutshell, to develop new models for Quantum age, new value networks that can truly prioritize distinctive value propositions must be created and the vision and talents of the best learning institutions and companies in the world must be utilized. Educational policies must first start validating nontraditional micro-credentials for teachers, students, academics, and school leaders to enable greater entry into, and advancement in the education system. Our education system must invest in developing talent. Universities must embrace open online learning in order to democratize the educational system. Learners must pursue education as a lifelong journey and challenge themselves consistently to learn in order to keep up with the change in life. Policymakers must support education policy that invests in technology-based learning and alternative education credentials.

References

Agarwal, A. (2017, January 4). *Companies are complaining about the skills gap: Here's how we get closer to solving it.* The Education Commission. https://educationcommission.org/in-the-media/anant-agarwal-skills-gap-huffington-post/

Anderson, M., Hinz, B., & Matus, H. (2017, November). *The paradigm shifters: Entrepreneurial learning in schools.* Mitchell Report. The Paradigm Shifters: Entrepreneurial Learning in Schools – Research Report (vu.edu.au)

Arnett, T. (2022a, November 14). *K-12 value networks: The hidden forces that help or hinder learner-centered education.* Education Reimagined, Christensen Institute. https://www.christenseninstitute.org/publications/value-networks/

Arnett, T. (2022b, November 4). *Predicting innovation trajectories in K–12 education*. Christensen Institute for Disruptive Innovation. https://www.christens eninstitute.org/blog/predicting-innovation-trajectories-in-k-12-education/

Beckert, J. (2010). Institutional isomorphism revisited: Convergence and divergence in institutional change. *Sociological Theory, 28*(2), 150–166. https://doi.org/10.1111/j.1467-9558.2010.01369.x

Brunsson, N. (1989). *The organization of hypocrisy: Talk, decisions, and actions in organizations.* John Wiley & Sons Inc.

Christensen, C. M. (2011). *The innovator's dilemma: The revolutionary book that will change the way you do business.* HarperBusiness.

Christensen, C. M., Horn, M. B., & Staker, H. (2013, May). *Is K-12 blended learning disruptive? An introduction to the theory of hybrids.* Clayton Christensen Institute. https://files.eric.ed.gov/fulltext/ED566878.pdf

Clegg, S. (2010). The state, power and agency. Missing in action in institutional theory? *Journal of Management Inquiry, 19*(1), 4–13. https://doi.org/10.1177/1056492609347562

DiMaggio, P. J., & Powell, W. W. (1983). The iron cage revisited: Institutional isomorphism and collective rationality in organizational fields. *American Sociological Review, 48*(2), 147–160. https://doi.org/10.2307/2095101

Garipağaoğlu, B. Ç. (2013). Leading by becoming a learning organization in the age of quantum. In S. Dulay (Ed.), *Empowering educational leaders: How to thrive in a volatile, uncertain, complex, and ambiguous world* (pp. 115–134). Peter Lang.

Gyau, A., & Stringer, R. (2011). Institutional isomorphism and adoption of e-marketing in the hospitality industry: A new perspective for research. In K. L. Sidali, A. Spiller, & B. Schulze (Eds.), *Food, agriculture, and tourism: Linking local gastronomy and rural tourism: Interdisciplinary perspectives* (pp. 130–139). https://doi.org/10.1007/978- 3-642-11361-1-9

Hamel, G. (2001). Leading the revolution: An interview with Gary Hamel. *Strategy & Leadership, 29*(1), 4–10. https://doi.org/10.1108/1087857011 0367141

Hamel, G., & Prahalad, C. K. (1994). *Competing for the future.* Harvard Business School Press.

Hess, A. J. (2021, April 8). *More than half of older millennials with student debt say their loans weren't worth it.* CNBC: Make it. https://www.cnbc.com/2021/04/08/older-millennials-with-student-debt-say-their-loans-werent-worth-it.html

Horn, M. B., & Staker, H. (2017). *Blended: Using disruptive innovation to improve schools.* John Wiley & Sons.

Horn, M. B. (2022). Only out-of-the-box solutions will tackle the root cause of what ails schools. Clayton Christensen Institute. https://www.christensenin stitute.org/blog/only-out-of-the-box-solutions-will-tackle-the-root-cause-of-what-ails-schools/

Kılıçoğlu, G., & Yılmaz-Kılıçoğlu, D. (2021). Understanding organizational hypocrisy in schools: the relationships between organizational legitimacy, ethical leadership, organizational hypocrisy and work-related outcomes. *International Journal of Leadership in Education, 24*(1), 1–33. https://doi.org/10.1080/13603124.2019.1623924

Lai, K., Wong, C. W., & Cheng, T. C. (2006). Institutional isomorphism and the adoption of information technology for supply chain management. *Computers in Industry, 57*(1), 93–98. https://doi.org/10.1016/j.compind.2005.05.002

Louth, J. (2011). From Newton to Newtonianism: Reductionism and the development of the social sciences. *Emergence: Complexity and Organization, 13*(4), 63–83.

March, J. G., & Olsen, J. P. (1989). *Rediscovering institutions: The organizational basis of politics.* The Free Press.

Matheson, D. (2021, August). *Operational excellence can kill.* SmartOrg. https://smartorg.com/operational-excellence-can-kill/

Meyer, J. W., & Rowan, B. (1977). Institutional organizations: Formal structure as myth and ceremony. *American Journal of Sociology, 83*(2), 340–363. https://doi.org/10.1086/226550

Powell, W. W., & DiMaggio, P. J. (1991). *The new institutionalism in organizational analysis.* University of Chicago Press

Prensky, M. (2014). The world needs a new curriculum. *Educational Technology, 54*(4), 3–15. https://eric.ed.gov/?id=EJ1054984

Prensky, M. (2016). *Education to better their world: Unleashing the power of 21st-century kids.* Teachers College Press.

Prensky, M. (2018, May). *Scientific revolution and education, part I.* SNS: Special Letter. https://marcprenskyarchive.com/wp-content/uploads/2018/05/Pren sky-Scientific-Revolution-Education-SNS2.pdf

Rose, J., Wetzler, J., & Wood, J. H. (2022). *Out of the box: How innovative learning models can transform K-12 education.* New Classrooms Innovation Partners and Transcend. https://www.outoftheboxreport.org/

Senge, P. M. (1990). *The fifth discipline: The art and practice of the learning organization.* Doubleday

Turczynski, B. (2023, December 19). *2024 HR Statistics: Job Search, Hiring, Recruiting & Interviews.* Zety. https://zety.com/blog/hr-statistics

Tzu, S. (2010). *The art of war.* Capstone Publishing.

UNESCO. (2021, November 21). *Reimagining our futures together: A new social contract for education.* UNESCO.https://www.right-to-education.org/sites/right-to-education.org/files/resource-attachments/UNESCO_Reimagining%20our%20futures%20together_social%20contract%20for%20education_Nov2021_EN.pdf

World Bank. (2019, January 22). *The education crisis: Being in school is not the same as learning.* World Bank. https://www.worldbank.org/en/news/immersive-story/2019/01/22/pass-or-fail-how-can-the-world-do-its-homework

Zhao, Y. (2012). *World class learners – Educating creative and entrepreneurial students.* SAGE.

Dr. B. Çağla Garipağaoğlu

Chapter 2   The Call of the Present: Quantum Paradigm in Education

Abstract: Our education system is in its demise. While the other sectors in the world are continually striving to synch with the industrial advancements and technological disruptions, our schools have long been locked into the same, unchanging Newtonian paradigm. While many other sectors have spent the last two decades modernizing their core designs and know-how, our schools continue to bank on the educational model and know-how rooted back in the Industrial Revolution. Our Newtonian-inspired education system still suffers from obsolete methodologies and educational content dating back to the Industrial age. The current "academic" educational system has reached the end of its mainstream usefulness. It does not address our needs. It does not produce the workforce that we need. It is a system essentially to train thinkers – who are not, also, doers (i.e. academic training) or a system to train doers who are not also thinkers (i.e. vocational training for less academically minded). However, what we need now is thinkers who are also doers and doers who can also think. Although most people seem to declare technology as the only savior in the current situation. The truth is far from it. What we need is a true paradigm shift (shift from Newtonian paradigm to Quantum paradigm). Thus, in this chapter, we will suggest "empowerment education" as the true tenet of new paradigm in education and "disruptive forms of education" as a way to accomplish a true transformation. What we need is to (1) adopt a more relevant and meaningful purpose for our schooling, (2) turn our learner into solutionaries and train our teachers to educate our youth to be solutionaries, and (3) avoid using proxies in education and focus more on real-world problems and projects instead.

Keywords: proxies, solutionaries, empowerment education, real-world improving projects, disruptive education

Our Newtonian-inspired education system is characterized by well-established traditions, one-size-fits-all approach, and a blind insistence on addressing the persistent problems of the world with the same mindsets that created them in the first place (Rose et al., 2022). The Newtonian paradigm in schooling emerged during the age of industrialization to educate the masses in order to supply a culturally assimilated, factory-ready workforce for industry (Rose et al., 2022). By simply allowing increased access to education, the system intended to provide the much-needed workforce into industrial or agricultural labor market for a booming economy. The aim is indeed achieved. During the first four decades of the 20th century, while most men found jobs as mechanics, electricians, drivers, machine operators, constructors and assembly-line workers, women worked as administrative assistants, cashiers, and grocery clerks (Fogel, 2000). Providing a high-quality education for all learners regardless of race, gender, color, socio-economic background, language, culture was not the concern of education. With few exceptions, schools were strictly limited to students of dominant culture, faith, and color (Andersen, 1998). Students of ethnicities other than the dominant ethnicity and religions, those with a disability, or those coming from minorities and other marginalized groups such as LGBTQIA+, simply faced alienation (Young, 2017). Students were ranked and windowed out based on their aptitude and achievement in their schools (Rose et al., 2022). But they were also put into different pathways not only based on their individual ability or achievement but on their wealth, race, ethnicity, family connections or social positions (Braga, 2017). Immigrant education, on the other hand, was focused mostly on cultural and national assimilation (Bandiere et al., 2019).

Several studies after WWII revealed how assumptions about people's attitudes and behavior had profound consequences for our Newtonian-inspired industrial design in schooling. The predominant characteristic of the Newtonian-inspired industrial paradigm of education was an emphasis on the pessimistic view of human nature. Although it was true to some extent, it also overlooked the more positive aspects of human nature. Unfortunately, Newtonian-inspired industrial paradigm of schooling was clouded by the misconception that all students and teachers were inherently lazy and unless they were forced to study and work hard or supervised closely, they would avoid taking the responsibility of their own learning. It was also assumed that students were not naturally and intrinsically motivated to achieve their true potential out of their instinct and tendency to "take it easy" (Taylor, 1985). This assumption led to close supervision and strict control mechanisms in schools by reinforcing a pattern of suspicion and mistrust that shaded teacher-student and teacher-administrator relations for decades.

The Newtonian paradigm of education copied and borrowed Ford and Taylor's legacy of Scientific Management. To fulfill its core purpose of suppling factory-ready workforce for the economy, design of the schools relied on the top-down, command-and-control approaches, standardization, departmentalization by academic disciplines, teacher specialization, and division of students according to their ages (Rose et al., 2022). Based on those fixed design elements of the Newtonian paradigm, since the middle of the 19th century, our schools oriented around the following ten tenets:

(1) Students of the same age would be batched together and engaged in the same curriculum at the same pace even though this would hold some students back from more advanced learning while keeping others behind.

(2) Teachers would transfer the content; set and reinforce the desired behavior patterns for students without taking their strengths, weaknesses, preferences, interests, and goals into account.

(3) Learning would happen inside the walls of a psychical environment with a fixed timeline.

(4) Well-trained teachers who excelled in a specialized field/discipline (e.g. math, literature, science, etc.) would teach/tell/deliver/explain the course material directly to students with no need or desire to connect it to other disciplines.

(5) Students and teachers would follow a specific set of instructions outlining the "one best way to do a task" to complete any given task

(6) Both student and teacher performance would be assessed based on specific performance indicators.

(7) Teachers would have covered specific content during a specified set of time.

(8) The system would value efficiency and predictability over innovation and flexibility.

(9) The system would spur both teachers and students to teach and learn faster and harder but not better.

(10) It was also believed that both students and teachers would respond "rationally" to rules, chains of authority, and material incentives.

Followers of the Newtonian-inspired paradigm believed that it was possible to scientifically analyze tasks performed by individual students and teachers. They also believed that the best way to perform any task could be best determined by means of scientific analysis. Moreover, there was a scientifically proven best way to perform a task that would allow students to learn at a peak efficiency. This transparency and certainty eventually combined with an emphasis on control and inspection, thereby making fear a reasonably good tool to motivate both students and teachers. According to the assumptions of the Newtonian-inspired industrial paradigm, an average student was lazy, disliked working hard, and would try to do as little as possible. Moreover, it was also believed that students had little ambition to learn more and would have wished to avoid taking responsibility for their own learning. Therefore, to ensure high-level student-learning, teachers would have to supervise students closely and shape their behavior by means of "the carrot and stick" mechanisms. Meanwhile, learners would be expected to absorb what has been taught by their teachers and model the behaviors expected from them through extrinsic rewards and punitive mechanisms (Rose et al., 2022). Therefore, schools were designed in a way to maximize the supervisors' (teachers' and school superintendents') control over students' behaviors and minimize any deviation from the standard. Whether through a fear of teacher sanction or loss of material rewards like grades or fear of failure, teachers would be able to coerce and intimidate students to ensure efficiency and standardization. Student success would strictly hinge on compliance with teachers' one-size-fits-all instructions. Even if there were costs to this approach, those costs were not in plain sight.

In Newtonian paradigm, we began to put students together with a "curriculum" and a "supervisor/teacher" (Prensky, 2016). The "content" was then reduced into smaller pieces to make it more teachable and easier to convey. Students were provided with tasks aiming to teach those "contents" that were no longer connected to their actual contexts. Advantages of these detached, small, repetitive, and often the context-free tasks were many: Since this type of reductionism also enabled increased transparency, the job of monitoring, measuring, and assessing the tasks of both students and supervisors were easier and simpler. Such a devotion to efficiency, standardization and productivity in learning and teaching gradually undermined the importance of effectiveness and resulted in two major legacies: (1) a basic distrust of the student leading to close supervision and inspection and (2) de-valuation of creativity in the education system. To ensure that the students did their tasks according to specified instructions, objective measurements of individual student performance were determined. Later, teachers assessed their students based on those predetermined objective criteria. The same mindset was in play for teacher evaluations as well. Administrators would use pre-determined specified objective criteria to assess teachers' performance too. And, for the most part, students and teachers who tried harder performed better. Yet, the specialized, simplified tasks were often monotonous and repetitive, and many students and teachers became dissatisfied with their experience. In such a design like the one created by Ford for the industrial age, opportunities for both student and teacher creativity were very limited. Those students who were better at accomplishing given tasks by the pre-determined "one best method" were called as "good" students and those teachers and supervisors who were better able to teach and supervise well-designed and well-executed repetitive individual tasks by the pre-determined "one best method" were called "good" teachers and "good" supervisors.

Practically, many of the tenets of the Newtonian paradigm have had tremendous influence on education. First, the expectations set for students and opportunities offered for them were determined at a very young age. They were mostly based on the factors based on students' family wealth and background. They were also average for most learners, disproportionately below-average for some, and too high for others (Rose et al., 2022). So, schools eventually ended up ranking students, thus sorting out those who cannot keep up with a standardized, one-size-fits-all approach. Second, schools merely put the cognitive dimension of learning at the heart of the system and left the rest to after-graduation. Third, the schools mostly engaged students in rote memorization and assessed students primarily based on their ability to recall a broad array of content. Fourth, learning that took place in schools was mostly disconnected from young people's preferences, needs, and real-life experiences. Fifth, learners from minorities such as people of color, LGBTQIA+, and those living in poverty, or those with a disability are forced to either blend into the dominant power, outcasted or faced with discriminatory and exclusionary policies and practices (Rose et al., 2022). Sixth, the schools implicitly and explicitly reinforced the status quo. Seventh, schools prioritized competition over collaboration; specialization over cross-disciplinary work; and inspection over total quality management. Lastly, the design and the value network of schools severely constrained the possibility of any breakthroughs that took place in cognitive research or advanced technologies to be leveraged in the education system as they wouldn't reasonably fit within the framework of Newtonian-inspired industrial paradigm.

Apparently, some of the most basic tenets of this paradigm were to ensure control, eliminate variance, focus on expertise/specialization and reward conformance. Needless to say, all of those also hinder collaboration and meaningful learning. Yet, what we require in the 21st century is collaboration and meaningful learning. The twenty-first-century problems and challenges must be dealt with a new and more innovative paradigm in schooling. Since expertise is becoming an increasingly moving target almost in every sector, to keep up with developments, people must learn to become lifelong learners, and work together across disciplines (Edmondson, 2012). It is no secret that our education system calls for cross-disciplinary teamwork. Students must absorb, and sometimes create new knowledge while performing the task. They need to acquire and master new skills and envision novel possibilities (Edmondson, 2012). To sum up, to prosper especially at the BANI (Brittle, Anxious, Nonlinear, and Incomprehensible) phase of our VUCA (Volatile, Uncertain, Complex, and Ambiguous) environment, we must all learn how to work and learn collectively, take more ownership for our own learning, and rely on each other. The implications of this new reality are enormous for educational leaders, and professionals. Insisting on the industrial paradigm of schooling, however, means that even the most successful students, led by great teachers, will have to face failure when they confront complex and dynamic contexts.

Empowerment Education and Educating a Generation of Solutionaries

Our Newtonian paradigm of schooling is now at a crossroads. The current educational system falters in the light of the fourth industrial revolution (Bharti, 2022). Quantum paradigm is now presented as the anti-thesis of Newtonian paradigm. UNESCO (2021) reports that our education system is facing a dual challenge of ensuring high quality education for every child and creating societies who are committed to the principles of non-discrimination, social justice, respect for life, human dignity, and cultural diversity. Nyerere (1967) argues that our education must cultivate a sense of commitment to human rights and sustainability. To do this, however, "we need a new social contract for education that can level out injustices while transforming the future altogether" (UNESCO, 2021). As put in the report, we have to re-imagine the purpose of our education system. The fundamental purpose of education must be to cultivate more fair and humanitarian grounds in society that help people live and work together in peace and harmony for the common good. The purpose must be to let our young generation to actively participate in the development of a society so that they can truly understand and appreciate their role in the good or bad fortune of their community fairly and take responsibility for a brighter future (UNESCO, 2021). This can be achieved only when we focus on teaching the youth about the interconnectedness of environmental preservation, human rights, and animal protection. The goal of education must be to provide students with the knowledge, skills, and motivation to be conscientious choice-makers and engaged change-makers for a better regenerative world for people, animals, and the environment (Weil, 2021).

Devastating losses in learning, constant decrease in teacher satisfaction, growing number of teachers who are contemplating quitting the job, accelerating number of students reporting being bored at school grounds, and high levels of stress symptoms demonstrated by every single stakeholder of the educational system wants a dramatic change in the educational system. In addition to all these reported problems, parents demand greater levels of personalization and psychological support, and students report that they want to progress at their own pace, and according to their own interests, and needs. School superintendents and labor-markets are also demanding a more relevant, more professional, and real-life related educational system. Addressing all of those needs and reported problems goes beyond the abilities of what the Newtonian-inspired industrial paradigm was ever designed to do. So, we can either assume that the best way of delivering education is embracing the conventional Newtonian paradigm and focus on optimizing what we have already been delivering so far or we can try to transform the Newtonian paradigm itself. It is quite clear that the Newtonian paradigm undermines the impact of all well-intended reform efforts aiming for "better and more meaningful teaching & learning" (Rose et al., 2022). Transcending these inherent limitations requires contemplating a new paradigm that fundamentally re-imagines the educational system.

Unlike its Newtonian counterpart, Quantum paradigm does not advocate Ford and Taylor's legacy of ranking and sorting system but a more student-oriented design. It advocates genuine cooperation between students and teachers based on mutual trust (empowerment education). Instead of putting students together with "content", recently evolving Quantum paradigm advocates to put them together with problems (Prensky, 2016). Not with problems made up by educators, but with the problems that our children themselves actually experience in their own world. Schools then become "about finding and implementing solutions to those real-world problems in ways that fully apply the strengths and passions of each child" (Prensky, 2016, p. 3). That way we produce an empowered young generation – as named by Weil (2021) "Solutionaries" – who are able to craft world-bettering solutions to real-world problems for the rest of their lives. Children need to be educated in a way that they commit to identify any unjust, inhumane, and unsustainable conduct and equipped with the tools, knowledge, awareness, and enthusiasm to change them. So, the educational transformations that need to be undertaken must ensure that "a generation of solutionaries" be educated and empowered to create a future that will promote to live in the most intelligent and humane way (Weil, 2021).

Considering the fact that the world changes in so many ways, so must the tenets of our educational system (Prensky, 2014). Our education system is not preordained. On the contrary, it is man-made and subject to change. Over-reliance on control, fear, plans, details, roles, budgets, and schedule as the tools of certainty and predictability that worked well for the factory workers and the organization-man during the age of industrialization is no longer competitive in today's knowledge-based economy and turbulent work environment. Collective learning is the only reliable way to cope with tomorrow's world. Just as the business world underwent a profound change in how they thought about the way the work should get done, our approach to schooling requires a new mindset but not new slogans (Edmondson, 2012). It requires a new way of thinking and becoming.

People around the world are recognizing that there are other, more effective ways to raise our next generations than the way we have been forced to accept for decades (Prensky, 2014). What we need is not reforms but a brand-new system that is not based on the four "core" subjects of math, language arts, science, and social studies but rather the principles of "Effective Thinking, Effective Action, Effective Relationships and Effective Accomplishment" (Prensky, 2014, p. 13). Our education system designed in Newtonian paradigm cannot provide what our children need to be successful in the future. "Yet, it does not mean that we have to abandon our past "core". They are just not needed in the same way by every individual and society. Moreover, there are far more important skills required by all people and all societies all around the world" (Prensky, 2014, p. 13). According to Weil (2021), a brand new paradigm is urgently needed in our education system as our earth is about to face an even grimmer future in which rainforests, coral reefs and glaciers will gradually exhaust and half of all species are at a high risk of extinction. During these times of great threats, it has become more and more evident that the problems of today cannot be solved by the same kind of thinking that was created by them. Ethical, planetary, technological, and sustainability demands during these very complicated times and serious shortcomings in natural resources requires a dramatic shift in our school programs and concentration on the development of totally different set of values and skills in our youth in order to promote more peaceful, humane and sustainable world.

For decades, we have used "mathematics, language, science, and social sciences as "proxies" for teaching and acquiring many of the truly needed skills: the ability to think effectively, act effectively, relate to others effectively and accomplish useful things effectively" (Prensky, 2014, p. 13). Yet, most of the time, our students never even understand what those skills actually are, neither did we ever bother to communicate what those skills are. Even worse, we do not even have "proxies" for many important skills (Prensky, 2014). Because we've been teaching the same core proxies with the same strategies for so long, we eventually come to accept it as what "education" is truly about (Prensky, 2014). However, there are more direct ways for teaching those four underlying skills and equating "education" with the learning of widely accepted core studies is false, deceitful, and extremely harmful (Prensky, 2014). Instead of teaching truly desired skills (i.e. collaboration, self-management, effective communication, and critical thinking) to our young generation indirectly as we were used to in the past, we must concentrate on finding more direct ways to teach our students what they really need to live in peace and harmony in our planet with other people and let go of those "proxies".

To sum up, although the problems with "how to teach" have become obvious much earlier than the problems with "what to teach", the real problem is not "how" we teach but, rather, "what" we teach (Prensky, 2014). The fundamental reform needed to make education more effective for our children is to reform the world's core curriculum (Prensky, 2014). Because the world has changed in so many diverse ways, our educational goals must change as well in order to align with the world's new dynamics. We can never keep up with the changes occurring all around us with the same educational paradigm we embraced decades ago. The entire world today is in desperate need of a wholly new education "core" and set of new "fundamentals". Obviously, merely delivering the old formula in a "better" way through new pedagogy and new technology is not – by itself – a solution but a waste of time and money. Just because changing the "core" and the "fundamentals of what we teach" brings about so many complexities; policymakers, and practitioners, so far, preferred merely to make reforms on "how to teach" aspect of the education rather than the "fundamentals of what we teach". Prensky (2014, p. 8) argues that although there is a huge resistance to changing "how to teach" aspect of education (i.e. pedagogy and technology) as well, changing this specific aspect is still far easier. Experts seem to have already reached an agreement on the best ways to improve "how" we teach. Student-centered learning, problem-based learning, flipping, partnering are all "brand names" with almost the same essence aiming to change what we teach to our young people.

Our current education system wastes human beings' arguably the most curious and creative time of their lives by systematically numbing their curiosity and creativity. It is not only tragic for our children, but also for our world. Prensky (2014) argues that we waste our learner's valuable attention, during their most "influence-able" years, on the subjects of mathematics, language arts, science and social which are nowhere "ordained" that they are the "right" cannons to build our entire education. And merely adding on a few "21st century skills" on top of those cannons will not fix the underlying problems of the education system. First, our curricula are already overcrowded and occupy much more time than we are supposed to spare, so, there's "No Room to Add, Unless We Delete" (Prensky, 2014, p. 10). Second, many teachers are not well-versed to teach these additional skills or merge them well with the original "core" (Prensky, 2014). Third, many teachers still do not consider those skills as important as the original core – math, language arts, science and/or social studies (Prensky, 2014). Yet, the far bigger and more important problem with the "add-on" approach is that what we need is not to find new ways to educate our young people with the old content better but, rather, to find new ways to make our education more relevant to our real–world problems and expose our kids much earlier to real world problems (Prensky, 2014). We should prioritize making learning more connected to the real professional, personal, and societal problems that young people might encounter in life and let them experiment their solutions to real, world-improving problems. Our new education system should also focus more on the customization of learning by taking advantage of improved technology, and tools to support students' physical and psychological health (Prensky, 2014). So, since the new concern of the education system is no longer to train factory-workers but to educate a generation of "solutionaries", both the "content" and the "pedagogy" in education must change fundamentally.

Disruptive Education

Disruptive education refers to an innovative approach to teaching and learning that challenges traditional educational models and seeks to generate new and more effective ways of teaching and learning with a profound transformation of educational environments. It breaks away from conventional methods and embraces new technologies and personalized learning experiences to empower students and improve learning outcomes. Disruptive education not only requires the introduction of technology in classrooms but also calls for comprehensive work that changes the educational objectives, processes, and methodologies with the involvement of the entire educational ecosystem to achieve an effective shift towards a more customized and independent learning that is in line with the demands of our current realms. We are currently going through a disruptive period marked by the following milestones: Practice over theory, interdisciplinary learning, life-long learning, commitment to early training, digital innovation, artificial intelligence, gamification, customization of learning, commitment to digital literacy, collaboration with the job market, and cooperative competition (Co-opetition).

It must be understood that business and economic theories have a lot to offer schools in their search for transformation (Horn, 2014). Current disruptions happening throughout education already gave us an opportunity to revisit how we educate our children (Sudhakar, 2018). Hopefully, those disruptions helped us see if there is a better way to educate our children and make them more prepared and equipped for a more sustainable future given what we now know today. Indeed, through disruptive innovation, we may make education fundamentally more affordable (i.e. MOOCs, micro-schools, and Artificial Intelligence-AI) and therefore allow more people to access it. Judging from years of prevalence and no non-consumption of education in the world no matter how ineffective it is, one might think that disrupting our K–12 schools or higher education is impossible; yet it is far from the truth (Horn, 2014). We can still leverage disruptive innovations to better our education system for the good of all of us. One misreading of disruption theory has been that disruptive innovations tend to focus on new technologies: artificial intelligence, teleconferencing, virtual reality etc. However, the true promise of a disruption does not come from the technology itself, but from the designs those technologies facilitate (Horn, 2014). In fact, disruptions may enable some of the most fundamental shifts in the core processes of an organization by changing the core value propositions of the schooling. Apart from changing the nature of learning experience (i.e. gamification), disruptions change the fundamental roles of teachers and students as well. They help students learn through more customized paths more suitable to their goals and interests at their own pace. They also encourage teachers to guide students more effectively on their personalized learning journeys by shifting their focus from classroom management to providing learning experience (Arnett, 2023). Disruptive innovations can also change the fundamental cost structure of schooling (Arnett, 2023). For instance, micro-schools don't need to build, buy, or rent large school facilities (Arnett, 2023). Or they don't need to hire teachers for each grade level and subject area. This ability to operate at a small scale with a low budget reduces the start-up barriers for micro-schools thereby making education more affordable for families who can't afford the conventional systems and let many new players enter the field increasing both the competition for quality (Arnett, 2023).

Conclusion

Currently, the world's mainstream education still reflects the assumptions of the old, Newtonian paradigm. Even with its many reform initiatives, we are still locked in a period of the "old, Newtonian" education, "progressing" only by innovating incrementally within the confines of the prevailing worldview of kids as "unempowered, helpless and incapable". In our increasingly differentiated world, the old Newtonian core of the curriculum is no longer important for all students in the same way. Instead of incrementally improving the old "core" while strictly remaining within the framework of Newtonian design, we should gear all our efforts to re-think and re-design our fundamentals. Teachers should no longer be expected to instruct students but empower them with real-world improving projects. We should learn to live symbiotically with technology, use it to empower our kids, and educate "solutionaries" who have learned to use their skills, knowledge, and talents in service of a more just, humane, and sustainable world. Our schools should no longer be stress-inducing, unfriendly, and status-quo reinforcing places. Our education system should never be felt like an endurance test or a battleground. Educational institutions should be joyful places fostering learner's interests, curiosity, and creativity to meet the challenges of our increasingly hyperactive and hyperconnected world.

With all that being said, it should be noted that disruptive innovations which can pave the way for fundamental changes in education take courage, talent, and heart, only a few people can dare. The task of designing and executing a brand-new education system is one thing most educators cannot really dare to take on. Even if all stakeholders in the educational system articulate bold visions, and demand a fundamental change in education, we should never forget the fact that very few can dare to risk their interdependencies. Therefore, promoting a disruptive form of education that puts teaching and learning in a new light without falling into the trap of operating within the confines of deeply ingrained old interdependencies is vitally essential to break with the established model. It is clear that, merely the educational disruptions happening throughout the world may provide us with an opportunity to revisit how we might educate our next gen for a fundamentally better future.

References

Anderson, J. D. (1998). *The education of blacks in the south*. The University of North Carolina Press.

Arnett, T. (2023, January 10). *Is 2023 the year of the microschool?* Christensen Institute. https://www.christenseninstitute.org/blog/is-2023-the-year-of-the-microschool/

Bandiera, O., Mohnen, M., Rasul, I., & Viarengo, M. (2019). Nation-building through compulsory schooling during the age of mass migration. *The Economic Journal, 129*(617), 62–109. https://doi.org/10.1111/ecoj.12624

Bharti, A. (2022, July 28). *11 Challenges in education industry (With solutions)*. DataToBiz. https://www.datatobiz.com/blog/challenges-in-education-industry

Braga, B. (2017). *Wealth inequality is a barrier to education and social mobility*. Urban Institute.

Edmondson, A. C. (2012). *Teaming: How organizations learn, innovate, and compete in the knowledge economy*. John Wiley & Sons.

Fogel, R. (2000). *The fourth great awakening and the future of egalitarianism*. The University of Chicago Press.

Horn, M. B. (2014, July 2). *Disruptive innovation and education*. Christensen Institute. https://www.christenseninstitute.org/blog/disruptive-innovation-and-education

Nyerere, J. K. (1967). *Education for self-reliance*. GovernmentPinter.

Prensky, M. (2014). The World Needs a New Curriculum: It's time to lose the "proxies," and go beyond "21st century skills" – and get all students in the world to the real core of education. *Educational Technology, 54*(4), 3–15. http://www.jstor.org/stable/44430282

Prensky, M. (2016). *Education to better their world: Unleashing the power of 21st-century kids*. Teachers College Press

Rose, J., Wetzler, J., & Wood, J. H. (2022). *Out of the box: How innovative learning models can transform K-12 education*. New Classrooms Innovation Partners and Transcend.

Sudhakar, J. (2018, March 1). *Disruptive educational transformation is marvelous!!! Move a few steps forward!* Linkedin. https://www.linkedin.com/pulse/disruptive-educational-transformation-marvelous-move-few-sudhakar/

Taylor, F. W. (1985). *Principles of scientific management*. Hive.

UNESCO. (2021, November 21). *Reimagining our futures together: A new social contract for education*. UNESCO. https://www.right-to-education.org/sites/right-to-education.org/files/resource-attachments/UNESCO_Reimagining%20our%20futures%20together_social%20contract%20for%20education_Nov2021_EN.pdf

Weil, Z. (2021). *The world becomes what we teach: Educating a generation of solutionaries*. Lantern Publishing & Media.

Young, J. G. (2017). Making America 1920 again? Nativism and US immigration, past and present. *Journal on Migration and Human Society, 5*(1), 217–235. https://journals.sagepub.com/doi/pdf/10.1177/233150241700500111

Part 2: A New Social Contract for Education

Dr. K. Selçuk Tuzcuoğlu

Chapter 3 Understanding That Schools Indeed Have Economic and Business Models

Abstract: This article aims to shed light on the often overlooked economic and business aspects of educational institutions. While schools are primarily associated with the dissemination of knowledge and the cultivation of young minds, they also operate within complex economic frameworks. This paper explores the various dimensions of the economic and business models that underpin educational institutions, from funding sources and financial sustainability to marketing strategies and organizational structures. By examining these aspects, we gain a deeper understanding of the intricate relationship between education and economics, highlighting the critical role of economic sustainability in the success of educational institutions.

Keywords: financial and economic sustainability of educational institutions, marketing of educational institutions

Schools, like other businesses, are enterprises that have to manage their limited resources efficiently, aim to maintain positive relationships with their stakeholders, and aim to find new students in terms of sustainability. For this reason, schools need to be managed in accordance with certain business models. Departments such as finance, marketing, sales, product development, accounting, innovation, and IT, which are considered indispensable for a business, should all have their counterparts in school organizations. In increasingly competitive conditions, schools, like other commercial institutions, have to create and strengthen their brands and gain features that will provide competitive advantage. Since brand new technologies are emerging in the field of education every day, it has become a necessity for school administrators to constantly renew themselves and adapt their institutions to technological and social changes.

Educational institutions play a pivotal role in society, serving as the foundation for knowledge acquisition, skill development, and personal growth. However, it is essential to recognize that schools are not exempt from the economic realities that govern most organizations. This article seeks to explore and analyze the economic and business models that schools operate within, emphasizing the significance of these models in achieving educational goals and ensuring the sustainability of educational institutions.

Economic and Business Models of Achools

Economic and business models of schools can vary significantly depending on the type of institution, its location, funding sources, and educational philosophy. Here are some common economic and business models of schools (Perepelytsia, 2023).

i. **Public Schools:**
   a. Funded primarily by government sources, such as local, state, and federal taxes.
   b. Generally, provide free education to all students in their designated district.
   c. Funding allocation can vary based on factors like enrollment, special education needs, and socio-economic status of students.
   d. May also receive grants, donations, or engage in fundraising activities to support extracurricular programs or special projects.

ii. **Private Schools:**
   a. Tuition fees paid by students and their families are the primary source of revenue.
   b. May also receive donations, endowments, and grants from private individuals, foundations, or businesses.
   c. Business models can vary, with some schools aiming for exclusivity and charging high tuition fees, while others focus on affordability and financial aid.

iii. **Charter Schools:**
   a. Publicly funded but often operate independently, allowing for more flexibility in curriculum and teaching methods.
   b. Receive per-pupil funding from the government, similar to traditional public schools.
   c. May supplement funding with donations or grants, especially if they have specific educational goals or programs.

iv. **Online Schools:**
   a. Typically operate with lower overhead costs compared to physical schools.
   b. Revenue comes from tuition fees, often lower than traditional private schools.
   c. May offer a variety of courses, including K-12, college, or specialized training programs.

v. **International Schools:**
   a. Often serve expatriate or international communities and charge tuition fees, which can be substantial.
   b. May receive additional funding from the home country's government or organizations.
   c. Business models can vary based on the demographics and economic status of the community they serve.

vi. **Montessori and Waldorf Schools:**
   a. Typically, independent and charge tuition fees.
   b. May emphasize alternative educational philosophies and methods.
   c. Often rely on dedicated parent involvement and donations to support their programs.

vii. **For-Profit vs. Non-Profit:**
   a. Schools can be for-profit or non-profit entities, impacting their financial goals and practices.
   b. For-profit schools aim to generate profit for their owners or shareholders, while non-profit schools reinvest any surplus funds into improving education and facilities.

viii. **Specialized and Vocational Schools:**
   a. May focus on specific industries or vocational training.
   b. Funding sources can include tuition fees, government grants, and partnerships with businesses or industry organizations.

It's important to note that the economic and business models of schools can evolve over time, and individual schools may employ a combination of funding sources to meet their operational needs and educational goals. Additionally, the regulatory environment, local policies, and societal factors can influence how schools generate and allocate their resources.

Funding Sources of Schools

Funding sources for schools are crucial to sustaining their operations and providing quality education. These sources can vary depending on the type of school and its location. Here are some common funding sources for schools (Lafortune & Herrera, 2022; Owings & Kaplan, 2019; OECD, 2017):

i. **Government Funding:**
   Public Schools: Public schools receive the majority of their funding from government sources, including local, state, and federal taxes. Funding

allocation often depends on factors like enrollment, student demographics, and specific educational programs.

ii. **Tuition Fees:**

Private Schools: Tuition fees paid by students and their families are the primary source of revenue for private schools. These fees can vary widely, with some schools charging high tuition for exclusivity, while others focus on affordability.

iii. **Grants and Donations:**

Schools, both public and private, often seek grants from government agencies, foundations, and nonprofit organizations to support special projects, research, or infrastructure improvements. Private schools may rely on donations from alumni, parents, and philanthropic individuals or organizations to supplement their budgets.

iv. **Endowments:**

Some prestigious private schools and universities have significant endowments. These endowments are invested funds that generate income, and a portion of that income is used to support the institution's operations and financial aid programs.

v. **Parent and Community Fundraising:**

Many schools, especially public and nonprofit ones, engage in fundraising activities like bake sales, auctions, and donation drives to supplement their budgets. Parent-teacher associations (PTAs) often play a role in organizing these efforts.

vi. **Tuition Assistance and Scholarships:**

Schools may offer tuition assistance or scholarships to students based on need or merit. These programs can be funded through a combination of tuition revenue, donations, and grants.

vii. **Special Education Funding:**

Schools that provide special education services often receive additional funding from government sources to support students with disabilities.

viii. **Charter School Funding:**

Charter schools are publicly funded and typically receive per-pupil funding from the government. Some may also receive additional funding through grants or donations.

ix. **Corporate Sponsorships and Partnerships:**

In some cases, businesses and corporations may sponsor or partner with schools to support specific programs, such as STEM initiatives or extracurricular activities.

x. **International Student Tuition:**
    International schools often generate revenue by charging tuition fees to students from different countries. These schools may also receive support from foreign governments or organizations.

xi. **Online Course Fees:**
    Online schools generate revenue through tuition fees paid by students taking virtual courses. These fees can vary depending on the level of education and the institution.

xii. **Taxes and Levies:**
    Some regions may pass specific taxes or levies to fund education, such as property taxes that directly contribute to local school district budgets.

It's important to note that the mix of funding sources can vary greatly depending on the specific school's circumstances and goals. Additionally, changes in government policies, economic conditions, and shifts in enrollment can impact a school's financial stability and funding sources.

Financial Sustainability

Financial sustainability is a critical aspect of a school's long-term success and ability to provide a quality education (Demirbilek, 2022; Hanushek, 1986; Morgan & Prowle, 2005). Schools, whether public or private, need to manage their finances wisely to ensure they can continue operating effectively (Baker, 2016; Vicente et al., 2023). Here are key factors and strategies related to financial sustainability for schools (Baker, 2018; Dedman, 2014; Dobbie & Fryer, 2018; Eskinat & Teker, 2023; National Audit Office, 2016).

i. **Budget Management:**
    Developing and maintaining a balanced budget is fundamental to financial sustainability. Schools should track income and expenses carefully, ensuring that expenditures do not consistently exceed revenue.

ii. **Diversification of Funding Sources:**
    Relying on a single funding source can make a school vulnerable to fluctuations in that source. Diversifying funding sources by seeking grants, donations, tuition, and other revenue streams can enhance financial stability.

iii. **Reserve Funds:**
    Building and maintaining reserve funds (e.g. rainy-day funds) can help schools weather unexpected financial challenges, such as drops in enrollment or unforeseen expenses.

iv. **Long-Term Financial Planning:**
Schools should engage in long-term financial planning to anticipate future needs, including facility maintenance, infrastructure upgrades, and program expansion. This planning can help allocate resources effectively.

v. **Efficiency Measures:**
Implementing cost-saving measures and improving operational efficiency can free up resources for educational programs. This may involve energy-efficient infrastructure, streamlining administrative processes, and optimizing staff allocation.

vi. **Fundraising and Development:**
Schools, especially private and nonprofit institutions, should actively engage in fundraising and development efforts to secure additional financial support from alumni, parents, community members, and philanthropic organizations.

vii. **Endowment Growth:**
Building and growing an endowment fund can provide a stable source of income over the long term. Schools can invest endowment funds and use the generated income to support operations and scholarships.

viii. **Tuition Strategy:**
Private schools need to strike a balance between setting tuition fees at a level that covers costs and remains competitive in the market. Offering financial aid and scholarships can attract a diverse student body.

ix. **Grant Writing and Management:**
Schools can seek grants from government agencies and private foundations. Effective grant writing and management are essential to secure and effectively use grant funding.

x. **Continuous Enrollment Management:**
Schools should actively manage student enrollment to maintain stable revenue streams. This may include marketing efforts, retention strategies, and understanding demographic trends in the area.

xi. **Financial Transparency:**
Maintaining transparency in financial matters, including budgeting and spending, helps build trust with stakeholders, such as parents, donors, and the community.

xii. **Strategic Partnerships:**
Collaborating with other educational institutions, nonprofits, or businesses can lead to cost-sharing opportunities, shared resources, and revenue-generating partnerships.

xiii. **Adaptability and Innovation:**
   Being adaptable and open to innovation can help schools respond to changing educational needs and economic conditions while remaining financially sustainable.

Financial sustainability is an ongoing process that requires careful planning, prudent financial management, and a commitment to the long-term goals and mission of the school. It involves balancing short-term financial stability with the ability to invest in the future to provide the best possible education for students.

Organizational Structures

The organizational structure of a school refers to how it is organized and managed, including how decision-making authority is distributed, roles and responsibilities are defined, and communication flows within the institution. The specific structure can vary based on the type of school, its size, and its educational philosophy. Here are some common organizational structures for schools.

   i. **Traditional Public Schools:**
      a. **Centralized Structure:** Typically, traditional public schools have a hierarchical and centralized organizational structure. The district superintendent oversees all schools within the district, and decisions are made at the district level and then filtered down to individual schools.
      b. **School-Based Structure:** Some public schools, particularly charter schools, operate with more autonomy and decentralized decision-making. Each school may have its own governing board or principal with significant authority.
   ii. **Private Schools:**
      a. **Board of Trustees or Directors:** Private schools are often governed by a board of trustees or directors responsible for setting policies, approving budgets, and overseeing the overall direction of the school.
      b. **Head of School/Principal:** The head of school or principal is responsible for the day-to-day management and operations of the school, including academic programs, faculty, and student affairs.
   iii. **Charter Schools:**
      a. **Charter Authorizers:** Charter schools are granted a charter by an authorizing entity (which can be a school district, university, or state agency). The charter outlines the school's mission, goals, and governance structure.
      b. **School-Based Governance:** Some charter schools operate with their own governing boards or councils, which have a high degree of autonomy in decision-making.

iv. **International Schools:**
  a. **Governing Board:** International schools often have a governing board composed of representatives from the international community, parents, and educational professionals.
  b. **Head of School:** Similar to private schools, international schools typically have a head of school or principal responsible for day-to-day operations.
 v. **Montessori and Waldorf Schools:**
  a. **Flat Hierarchical Structure:** These alternative education schools often have a flatter organizational structure. Teachers have significant autonomy in the classroom, and decision-making may be collaborative among staff members.
vi. **Online and Virtual Schools:**
  a. **Centralized Administrative Structure:** Online schools often have centralized administrative offices responsible for curriculum development, technology support, and enrollment management.
  b. **Virtual Learning Coordinators:** These schools may employ virtual learning coordinators or teachers who facilitate online instruction and provide support to students.
vii. **Specialized and Vocational Schools:**
  a. **Departmental Structure:** These schools often have departmental structures, with different departments focused on specific vocational or technical disciplines.
  b. **Advisory Boards:** Some vocational schools may have advisory boards comprised of industry professionals who help shape the curriculum and provide guidance.
viii. **Independent Schools:**
  a. **Varied Structures:** Independent schools can have diverse organizational structures, ranging from traditional to innovative, depending on their educational philosophy and goals.
ix. **Nonprofit vs. For-Profit:**
  a. Whether a school is nonprofit or for-profit can also influence its organizational structure, with nonprofit schools often prioritizing mission and educational goals over profitability.

It's important to note that there is no one-size-fits-all organizational structure for schools, and each institution may adapt its structure to meet its unique needs and goals. Factors such as the school's size, mission, governance model, and educational philosophy will all play a role in determining its organizational structure. Additionally, effective communication and collaboration among staff, faculty, and stakeholders are essential regardless of the specific structure in place.

Marketing and Enrollment Strategies

Marketing and enrollment strategies are essential for schools to attract students, maintain healthy enrollment numbers, and ensure financial sustainability. These strategies can vary based on the type of school, its target audience, and its location. Here are some common marketing and enrollment strategies used by schools (Finalsite, n.d.).

i. **Branding and Positioning:**
   Develop a strong brand identity and clearly define the school's unique selling points (USPs) to differentiate it from competitors. Highlight the school's mission, values, academic programs, extracurricular activities, and any specialized offerings.

ii. **Online Presence:**
   Create and maintain a professional, user-friendly website that provides comprehensive information about the school. Use social media platforms to engage with the school community, share updates, and showcase student achievements.

iii. **Search Engine Optimization (SEO):**
   Optimize the school's website for search engines to ensure it ranks well in online searches for relevant keywords (e.g. "best private schools in [city]").

iv. **Content Marketing:**
   Produce high-quality content, such as blog posts, videos, and infographics, to educate and inform prospective families about the school's programs and values.

v. **Open Houses and Campus Tours:**
   Organize open houses and campus tours to allow prospective students and parents to experience the school environment firsthand.

vi. **Community Engagement:**
   Foster positive relationships with the local community through outreach programs, partnerships with local businesses, and participation in community events.

vii. **Parent Ambassadors:**
   Recruit enthusiastic parents or alumni to serve as ambassadors who can share their positive experiences and advocate for the school within their networks.

viii. **Targeted Advertising:**
Use targeted online advertising through platforms like Google Ads and social media to reach parents and students in the school's demographic area.

ix. **Email Marketing:**
Build and maintain an email list to send newsletters, updates, and event invitations to current and prospective families.

x. **Scholarship and Financial Aid Programs:**
Offer scholarships and financial aid programs to attract a diverse student body and make education more accessible to a wider range of families.

xi. **Referral Programs:**
Implement referral programs that reward current families for referring new students to the school.

xii. **Alumni Engagement:**
Engage with alumni and leverage their success stories to showcase the value of a school education.

xiii. **Public Relations:**
Work with local media outlets to get coverage of school achievements, events, and community involvement.

xiv. **Data Analytics:**
Use data analytics to track the effectiveness of marketing campaigns and enrollment efforts, allowing for adjustments and improvements.

xv. **Retention Strategies:**
Focus on retaining existing students by providing a high-quality educational experience, addressing concerns promptly, and involving parents in their child's education.

xvi. **Admissions Process:**
Streamline the admissions process, making it easy for families to apply, submit required documents, and schedule interviews or assessments.

xvii. **Crisis Communication Plan:**
Develop a plan to manage any negative publicity or crises that may arise, ensuring that the school's reputation remains intact.

xviii. **Feedback Collection:**
Seek feedback from current and past families to identify areas for improvement and make necessary adjustments.

Effective marketing and enrollment strategies are ongoing efforts that require adaptability and a deep understanding of the school's target audience. Schools should continuously assess and refine their strategies to meet enrollment goals and maintain a positive reputation in the community.

Cost Benefit Analysis

Cost-benefit analysis (CBA) is a valuable tool that can help schools assess the financial implications of various decisions and initiatives. It involves comparing the costs associated with a particular project, program, or policy against the anticipated benefits or returns it is expected to generate. Here's how cost-benefit analysis can be applied in the context of schools (Woodhall, 2004; Gilead, 2014):

i. **New Programs or Curriculum Changes:**
   Before implementing a new academic program or making significant changes to the curriculum, schools can conduct a cost-benefit analysis. This would involve estimating the costs of developing and maintaining the program versus the expected educational benefits, such as improved student outcomes, increased enrollment, or enhanced reputation.

ii. **Facility Upgrades and Maintenance:**
   Schools can use CBA to evaluate whether investing in facility upgrades, maintenance, or expansion is financially justified. It considers the costs of construction or renovation, ongoing maintenance expenses, and potential benefits like improved learning environments or increased enrollment.

iii. **Technology Investments:**
   Assessing the cost-effectiveness of technology investments, such as purchasing and maintaining computers or tablets for students, involves comparing the upfront and ongoing costs with the anticipated benefits, such as enhanced educational outcomes and improved efficiency.

iv. **Teacher Professional Development:**
   Schools may invest in teacher professional development programs. A cost-benefit analysis can help weigh the costs of training against expected benefits, such as improved teaching quality, student performance, and teacher retention.

v. **Extracurricular Activities and Athletics:**
   When considering offering extracurricular activities or sports programs, schools can analyze the costs involved (coaches, equipment, facilities) and compare them to the expected benefits, such as student engagement, improved school culture, or potential revenue from sports events.

vi. **Safety and Security Measures:**
   Schools can assess the cost-effectiveness of implementing security measures like surveillance systems, access control, or security personnel. This analysis considers the costs and potential benefits in terms of student safety and reduced security incidents.

vii. **Transportation Services:**
   If a school provides transportation services for students, a cost-benefit analysis can help evaluate whether the expenses associated with maintaining a transportation fleet are justified by the benefits of improved student attendance and convenience.

viii. **Enrollment Strategies:**
   When developing enrollment strategies or marketing campaigns, schools can estimate the costs of advertising, outreach, and recruitment efforts and compare them to the expected benefits in terms of increased student enrollment and tuition revenue.

To conduct a cost-benefit analysis effectively, schools should consider both quantitative and qualitative factors. Quantitative data might include actual cost figures, projected revenue, and measurable outcomes (e.g. test scores, retention rates). Qualitative factors may encompass intangible benefits like improved reputation, student satisfaction, or community engagement. It's important to note that while CBA is a valuable decision-making tool, it may not capture all the intangible or long-term benefits of education. Therefore, schools should use CBA as one of several tools to inform their decisions, taking into account their unique missions, values, and educational goals. Additionally, involving stakeholders, including teachers, administrators, parents, and community members, in the analysis process can provide valuable perspectives and insights.

Challenges and Future Considerations

Challenges and future considerations in the field of education are complex and multifaceted, and they evolve over time in response to societal, technological, and economic changes. Here are some key challenges and future considerations for schools and the education sector:
   Here are some key challenges for schools (Ofsted, 2020; Montgomery, 2022):

i. **Digital Divide:** The digital divide, which represents disparities in access to technology and the internet, remains a significant challenge, as not all students have equal access to online learning resources and opportunities.

ii. **Equity in Education:** Ensuring equity in education, which includes addressing disparities in resources, opportunities, and outcomes among students of different backgrounds, remains a critical challenge.

iii. **Teacher Recruitment and Retention:** Many regions face difficulties in recruiting and retaining qualified teachers, especially in underserved areas or for certain subject areas, such as STEM (Science, Technology, Engineering, and Mathematics).

iv. **Mental Health and Well-being:** Schools are increasingly recognizing the importance of addressing students' mental health and well-being, but there are challenges in providing adequate support and resources to meet these needs.

v. **Assessment and Standardized Testing:** The use of standardized testing for assessment and accountability purposes continues to be a topic of debate, with concerns about overemphasis on testing and its impact on teaching and learning.

vi. **Future of Work:** Preparing students for the rapidly evolving job market and the integration of technology into the workforce poses a challenge. Schools must adapt their curricula to teach critical thinking, problem-solving, and digital literacy.

vii. **Diversity and Inclusion:** Promoting diversity and inclusion in schools and addressing issues related to bias, discrimination, and bullying are ongoing challenges.

viii. **Financial Sustainability:** Many schools face financial challenges, including budget constraints, resource allocation, and managing the costs of facilities, staff, and programs.

ix. **Parental Engagement:** Encouraging meaningful parental engagement in students' education and creating strong home-school partnerships can be challenging, especially for underserved populations.

Here are some future considerations for schools (OECD, 2001; Pouncey et al., 2013; Reschovsky & Imazeki, 2001).

i. **Technology Integration:** Schools will need to continue integrating technology effectively into teaching and learning, leveraging online resources, personalized learning platforms, and digital tools for instruction.

ii. **Hybrid Learning:** Hybrid and blended learning models that combine in-person and online education may become more prevalent as schools explore flexible approaches to accommodate diverse student needs.

iii. **Social and Emotional Learning (SEL):** A growing emphasis on SEL programs to support students' emotional and social development will continue, with a focus on building resilience, empathy, and emotional intelligence.

iv. **Innovative Pedagogies:** The adoption of innovative teaching and learning approaches, such as project-based learning, flipped classrooms, and experiential education, will likely expand.

    v. **Professional Development:** Ongoing professional development for educators to stay updated on best practices, technology, and pedagogical advancements will remain a priority.

    vi. **Global and Cultural Competency:** Preparing students for a globalized world will involve promoting cultural competency, global awareness, and proficiency in multiple languages.

    vii. **Sustainable Practices:** Sustainable practices in education, such as eco-friendly facilities and curriculum integration of environmental awareness, will gain importance.

    viii. **Adaptive Assessment:** Assessment methods will evolve to include adaptive and formative assessment techniques that provide timely feedback to guide instruction and support individual student needs.

    ix. **Career and Technical Education (CTE):** Expanding CTE programs to prepare students for diverse career pathways will be crucial, particularly in addressing workforce demands.

    x. **Education Policy Reform:** Ongoing education policy discussions and reforms will shape the future landscape of education, influencing funding, standards, accountability, and curriculum decisions.

Addressing these challenges and embracing future considerations in education requires collaboration among educators, policymakers, parents, and the broader community. Schools must remain adaptable, forward-thinking, and responsive to the changing needs of students and society to provide a high-quality and equitable education.

Conclusion

In conclusion, the field of education faces a range of challenges and exciting future considerations. These challenges include addressing equity and the digital divide, recruiting, and retaining qualified teachers, promoting student well-being, and adapting to the changing job market. Future considerations encompass technology integration, hybrid learning models, social and emotional learning, innovative pedagogies, and sustainability.

Education is a dynamic and evolving sector, and schools must continue to adapt to meet the diverse needs of students, foster inclusion, and prepare learners for a rapidly changing world. Collaboration among educators, policymakers, parents, and the community will be essential in addressing these challenges and harnessing the opportunities of the future to provide a high-quality and equitable education for all.

References

Baker, B. D. (2016). School finance & the distribution of equal educational opportunity in the post-recession U.S. *Journal of Social Issues, 72*(4), 629–655. https://doi.org/10.1111/josi.12187

Baker, B. D. (2018, July 17). *How money matters for schools.* Learning Policy Institute. https://learningpolicyinstitute.org/sites/default/files/product-files/How_Money_Matters_REPORT.pdf

Dedman, C. (2014). *Financing of inclusive education.* UNICEF. https://www.unicef.org/eca/sites/unicef.org.eca/files/IE_Webinar_Booklet_8.pdf

Demirbilek, M. (2022). Investigation of school principals' views on financial sustainability of primary schools using Delphi technique. *Education & Youth Research (EYOR), 2*(1), 9–23.

Dobbie, W., & Fryer, R. G. (2018). Charter schools and labour market outcomes. *Journal of Political Economy, 38*(4), 915–957. https://doi.org/10.1086/706534

Eskinat, A., & Teker, S., (2023). Financial sustainability of higher education system. *Press Academia Procedia (PAP), 18*(12), 71–72. http://doi.org/10.17261/Pressacademia.2023.1854

Finalsite. (n.d.). *8 smart marketing strategies for schools.* https://www.finalsite.com/blog/p/~board/b/post/smart-school-marketing-strategies

Gilead, T. (2014). Education and the rationale of cost-benefit analysis. *British Journal of Educational Studies, 62*(4), 373–391. http://www.jstor.org/stable/43896236

Hanushek, E. A. (1986). The economics of schooling: Production and efficiency in public schools. *Journal of Economic Literature, 24*(3), 1141–1177. http://www.jstor.org/stable/2725865

Lafortune, J., & Herrera, J. (2022, May). *Understanding the effects of school funding.* Public Policy Institute of California. https://www.ppic.org/publication/understanding-the-effects-of-school-funding/

Montgomery, K. (2022, March). *The biggest challenges facing the education sector.* Aim a Little Higher. https://www.aimalittlehigher.com/blog/the-biggest-challenges-facing-the-education-sector

Morgan, E., & Prowle, M. (2005). *Financial management and control in higher education.* Routledge.

National Audit Office. (2016). *Financial sustainability of schools.* https://education-uk.org/documents/pdfs/2016-nao-financial-sustainability-schools.pdf

OECD. (2001). *What future for our schools?* https://www.oecd.org/education/school/1840089.pdf

OECD. (2017). *The funding of school education: Connecting resources and learning*. OECD. http://dx.doi.org/10.1787/9789264276147-en.

Ofsted. (2020). *Making the cut: How schools respond when they are under financial pressure* (No. 200003). https://assets.publishing.service.gov.uk/government/uploads/system/uploads/attachment_data/file/870295/Making_the_cut_how_schools_respond_when_they_are_under_financial_pressure.pdf

Owings, W. A., & Kaplan, L. S. (2019). *American Public School Finance* (3rd ed.). Routledge. https://doi.org/10.4324/9781351013796

Perepelytsia, D. (2023, March 26). *Exploring target markets and business models in EdTech*. eLearning Industry. https://elearningindustry.com/exploring-target-markets-and-business-models-in-edtech

Pouncey, W. C., Ennis, L. S., Woolley, T. W., & Connell, P. H. (2013). School funding issues: State legislators and school superintendents – Adversaries or allies? *Sage Open, 3*(2). https://doi.org/10.1177/2158244013486492

Reschovsky, A., & Imazeki, J. (2001). Achieving educational adequacy through school finance reform. *Journal of Education Finance, 26*(4), 373–396. http://www.jstor.org/stable/20764015

Vicente, R. S., Flores, L. C., Almagro, R. E., Amora, M. R. V., & Lopez, J. P. (2023). The best practices of financial management in education: A systematic literature review. *International Journal of Research and Innovation in Social Science (IJRISS), 7*(8), 387–400. https://dx.doi.org/10.47772/IJRISS.2023.7827

Woodhall, M. (2004). *Cost-benefit analysis in educational planning* (4th ed.). UNESCO.

Dr. K. Selçuk Tuzcuoğlu

Chapter 4 Understanding That Schools Have Value Networks

Abstract: A Value Network represents the interconnected ecosystem of suppliers, distributors, and service providers that collaborate to deliver value to customers within a particular industry, and this structure is the determining factor in whether a business is successful or not. All success criteria such as coping with increasing competition, shortening transaction times, increasing product and service quality, increasing profitability, and increasing customer satisfaction and loyalty are possible with a well-constructed Value Network. Schools, as one of the most important institutions of the 21st century, must create their own Value Networks. For the Value Networks of the Schools to be successful, school administrators must first define the components in this network correctly. Teachers and Educators, Students and Parents, Administrators and Policymakers and Community are the most important components, and they are in close interaction not only with the school but also with each other... Enhancing value networks in schools requires a strategic approach that involves collaboration, communication, and a commitment to improving the overall educational experience. As an advantage Value Networks provide students the advantage of obtaining information from wider sources, families getting to know their children's competencies more closely, teachers improving themselves with better methods, and other institutions working more effectively in closer cooperation with educational institutions. Building strong partnerships, encouraging professional development, promoting inclusivity and diversity, establishing clear communication, and promoting a culture of collaboration are some key strategies for successful Value Networks.

Keywords: Value network, stakeholder management in educational institutions

Porter (1985) emphasizes that for companies not to lose their competitiveness in the market, they must pay attention to creating value at every step taken, in both primary and secondary areas of activity. Porter (1985) argues that the company should aim to create value throughout the entire network, starting from the delivery of the raw materials, intermediate products and inputs required for production to the company, and then to the distribution, marketing, and after-sales services of the produced goods. Porter (1985) advocates that companies should consider all their activities, starting from supply, production, marketing, distribution, and after-sales, within the concept of value network. Only in this way, Porter (1985) says, the company – as a whole – can create a cost advantage. This advantage becomes the company's competitive difference.

In this section, the implementation of the Value Network approach in schools will be discussed, the differences it brings to the classical school approach will be analyzed, the components of the Value Network in the education system will be reviewed, the opportunities and threats in front of Value Network applications will be examined, the advantages of managing schools with the Value Network approach will be emphasized and the Value Network of schools will be emphasized. Suggestions for strategies to be followed to increase their values will be shared.

The Concept of Value Networks

The value network concept has gained prominence in recent years as a way to understand and analyze complex ecosystems, and it has significant relevance within the realm of education. A value network is defined as a strategic network system outlining collaborations, relationships, and interactions between businesses to add value to the end customer (Porter, 1985). Value networks are dynamic and interconnected systems of individuals, organizations, and stakeholders that collaborate to create, exchange, and distribute value within a specific context or industry. It results in creating and delivering value-laced products and services to customers. These networks liaison with organizations to cooperate, interconnect, and share resources for combined success. It is a strong pillar for organizations to forge strong relationships between partners, suppliers, and customers in the hyper-competition scenario.

The emergence of globalization in the 20th century led to a rise in the complexities and interdependence of businesses. However, it started from conventional supply chain management to a wider focus on value creation and collaboration. It primarily functions by having different organizations collaborate. Collaboration may take forms like dissemination of expertise, information, technology, expertise, and promotion within each other. Consequently, network-forming participant organizations offer members unique expertise, resources, and capabilities. Hence, unique, and value-added products are created. It presents certain challenges while being beneficial. The issues include difficulty in communication and coordination, conflict of interest, overlapping objectives, power imbalance, information leakage, and security break-ins.

Value network mapping has multiple implications, like optimized processes, developing innovation, and access to specialized skills. Furthermore, it also provides flexibility to adapt to market demands quickly and effectively to fulfill customer aspirations by addressing their complaints. Investors and analysts benefit from it in market analysis, investment strategies, and risk mitigation.

Moreover, to evaluate businesses' financial wellness and growth potential, it is crucial to comprehend the interconnection and linkages inside value network mapping (Kenton, 2022). In short, it encourages cooperation and resource sharing through coordinated operations amongst companies, improving risk assessment and knowledge of interconnectedness.

In essence, a value network represents the interconnected ecosystem of suppliers, distributors, and service providers that collaborate to deliver value to customers within a particular industry (Christensen, 1997). When disruptors enter established value networks, they often face challenges in disrupting the status quo because these networks tend to be deeply entrenched and resistant to change (Christensen, 1997). Disruptors may find themselves compelled to adapt their business models to fit within the existing structures of the value network, rather than fundamentally altering or challenging them. This adaptation can lead to what Clayton Christensen (1997) termed "co-optation," where the disruptors become assimilated into the existing network rather than instigating transformative change. For example, if a new technology company seeks to disrupt the automotive industry by introducing electric vehicles, they may need to collaborate with existing suppliers of automotive components, distribution channels, and service providers. In doing so, they may find themselves constrained by the established practices and interests of these players, which can limit their ability to enact radical change. However, it's worth noting that successful disruptors often find ways to navigate these challenges by either strategically partnering with certain elements of the value network, finding niche markets to establish themselves before attempting broader disruption, or fundamentally redefining the value proposition to appeal to customers in a way that the existing network cannot match. While entering established value networks can be difficult, it doesn't necessarily guarantee failure for disruptors, but it does require careful navigation and strategic thinking (Christensen, 1997). Stabell and Fjeldstad (1998) declare a value network as one of three ways by which an organization generates value. The others are the value shop and value chain. Their value networks consist of customers, a service that enables interaction among them, an organization to provide the service and contracts that enable access to the service.

One example of a value network is that formed by social media users. The company provides a service, users contract with the company and immediately have access to the value network of other customers. A less obvious example is a car insurance company: The company provides insurance. Customers can travel and interact in various ways while limiting risk exposure. The insurance policies represent the company's contracts and the internal processes. Stabell and Fjeldstad (1998) and Christensen's (1997) concepts address how a company understands itself and its value creation process, but they are not identical. Christensen's (1997) value networks address the relation between a company and its suppliers, and the requirements posed by the customers, and how these interact when defining what represents value in the product that is produced. Stabell and Fjeldstad (1998) value networks emphasize that the created value is between interacting customers, as facilitated by value networks. There are two main categories of value networks – internal value networks and external value networks.

> **Internal:** An internal value network comprises interactions within the organization, and it is the combination of processes and relationships between people working in the organization. It exists when two or more people work together to create a product or service that benefits the organization. Value is created when there are effective interactions between people conducting roles within the business. For example, the R&D department is an internal value network, and it creates value when the R&D personnel interacts with other departments to create new products or services that increase the company's profitability or solve social problems.

> **External:** The external value network, on the other hand, comprises interactions between people who are outside the organization. External networks may include business intermediaries, customers, business partners, stakeholders, open innovation networks, and networks. The participants in the external value network must benefit from the interactions with other people in the network. If one participant does not benefit, the rest of the network will be affected.

Some types of value networks are as follows (Khalid, 2024):

> *Supplier-Centric Value Networks:* These networks place the relationship between manufacturers and suppliers on a high pedestal. Consequently, they optimize the supply chain through increased coordination, efficiency, coordination, and communication among manufacturers and suppliers.

> *Manufacturing-Centric Value Networks:* It focuses on collaborations and processes of manufacturing between different manufacturers. It aims to enhance product quality, production efficiency, and cost reduction.

> *Distribution-Centric Value Networks:* Such networks center around optimizing logistics and distribution processes. Here, collaboration happens between transporters, distributors, manufacturers, and retailers. As a result, customers receive products in timely and efficient delivery.

> *Customer-Centric Value Networks:* Here, the requirements of end-use customers are emphasized to be understood and met. Organizations work

together to create tailored and personalized services and products catering to consumer preferences.

➢ **Innovation-Centric Value Networks:** Organizations working together focus on developing innovation and technological advancements. It leads to newer technologies, products, and services.

➢ *Industry Clusters:* These networks relate to networks of related businesses with a geographic focus within a single industry. Such networks encourage cooperation, knowledge exchange, and shared assets amongst similar businesses.

➢ *Ecosystem Value Networks:* Networks of ecosystem value capture benefits outside of specific industries and support creative business strategies and solutions.

➢ *Cross-Industry Value Networks:* By collaborating and developing distinctive value propositions, these networks bring together industry members to produce cutting-edge goods, services, or solutions.

➢ *Cooperative Value Networks:* Collaborative value networks prioritize common objectives, mutual advantages, and solid connections to improve value creation and trust.

➢ *Virtual Value Networks:* They work around digital spaces that leverage digital platforms and technology for value creation, communication, and collaboration. Its spread considers different industries like platform-based ecosystems, virtual communities, and online marketplaces.

➢ *Global Value Networks:* These networks bring together players from many geographical areas to solve complicated supply chains plus global trade, improve operations, and overcome cross-cultural difficulties.

Value network has certain benefits as follows (Khalid, 2024):

➢ *Shared Resources:* It helps organizations share resources with each network member.

➢ *Collaboration:* It encourages collaboration amongst members, leading to enhanced innovation and problem-solving capabilities. It is due to various stakeholders coming together to bring varied perspectives to the network.

➢ *Effectiveness and Increased Efficiency:* All participants feel the positivity of increased capability and strength due to workflows and process optimization.

➢ *Expansion and Market Reach:* It also enables wider reach to new markets, new consumers, and distribution systems. It happens because the network offers new avenues of expansion, cross-selling, and marketing efforts.

➤ **Risk Mitigation:** Risk gets reduced due to the involvement of many organizations in the network ready to provide deep insights into various product and market segments.

➤ **Cost Reduction:** Value networks provide better tools for pool resources, improved deals with suppliers, and more profit from economies of scale, leading to cost-cutting and more competitiveness.

➤ **Access to Expertise and Specialized Skills:** Every participant in the network brings in new expertise, knowledge, and specialized skills for all. Therefore, participants get access to a larger area of capabilities, assuring all equitable access to the correct resources concerning particular projects and tasks.

➤ **Adaptability:** Members of the network get enough leverage and tools to adapt to dynamic situations, challenges, or opportunities quickly.

➤ **Flexibility:** All members support each other in adapting to different situations like technological progress, dynamic markets, and consumer demands.

➤ **Enhanced Agility:** It helps organizations imbibe quick responses to market changes, making them highly agile.

➤ **Increased Customer Experience:** Network members use the network to fulfill the needs, demands, expectations, and innovation requirements using their network. As a result, the customer experience increases manifolds.

Value Networks in the Context of Education

Value networks in education represent a paradigm shift from the traditional, hierarchical, and linear model of education where knowledge flows unilaterally from teachers to students. In contrast, the concept of value networks acknowledges that education is a complex, multifaceted system where multiple stakeholders collaborate to create, exchange, and distribute value.

Within the context of education, value networks consist of several key components (Bates, 2019).

➤ **Teachers and Educators:** Teachers are at the core of education value networks. They are responsible for delivering content, designing curriculum, and facilitating learning experiences. In a value network, teachers not only impart knowledge but also gather feedback from students, adapt their teaching methods, and collaborate with peers to enhance the educational experience.

➤ **Students and Parents:** Students are active participants in the value creation process. They engage in learning, provide input on their preferences and needs, and contribute to the educational community. Parents, as stakeholders, play a crucial role in supporting their children's education, advocating for their needs, and collaborating with educators to ensure a well-rounded learning experience.

➤ *Administrators and Policymakers:* Educational administrators and policymakers shape the institutional environment in which education occurs. They establish policies, allocate resources, and make decisions that impact the overall educational landscape. In a value network, they engage with teachers, students, and parents to gather insights and align policies with the evolving needs of the community.

➤ *Community and Stakeholders:* The broader community and external stakeholders, such as local businesses, non-profit organizations, and community leaders, also play a role in education value networks. They can provide resources, mentorship opportunities, and real-world experiences that enhance the educational value for students.

Education value networks are characterized by dynamic interactions and value exchanges among these components. Some key functions and interactions include:

➤ *Collaborative Learning:* Students collaborate with peers and educators to co-create knowledge. This may involve group projects, discussions, and peer-to-peer teaching and learning.

➤ *Feedback Loops:* Continuous feedback loops are established, allowing teachers to adapt their teaching methods based on student performance and preferences. This iterative process enhances the quality of education.

➤ *Parent-Teacher Partnerships:* Parents actively engage with teachers to understand their child's progress and provide insights into their learning needs. This partnership fosters a supportive learning environment.

➤ *Policy Adaptation:* Administrators and policymakers collaborate with educators, students, and parents to adjust educational policies and practices based on evolving community needs and educational goals.

➤ *Community Involvement:* Local businesses and community organizations may offer resources, mentorship programs, or internships that enrich the educational experience and prepare students for real-world challenges.

In summary, value networks in education recognize that learning is a collaborative, multidirectional process where value is created through interactions among various stakeholders. Understanding and effectively managing these value networks are essential for schools to adapt to changing educational paradigms and provide a holistic, student-centered learning experience. Subsequent sections of this article will explore the benefits, challenges, and strategies associated with education value networks.

The Historical and Theoretical Background of Value Networks in Education

In this part we will have a closer look to the historical and theoretical background of Value Networks in Education and try to explain these issues.

The Historical Background of Value Networks in Education. The concept of value networks in education did not emerge in isolation but is rooted in the broader evolution of educational philosophies, pedagogical approaches, and societal changes. Understanding the historical context helps us appreciate the trajectory of value networks in education (Alcantara et al., 2020).

➢ *Traditional Pedagogical Models:* Historically, education often followed a one-way transmission model where knowledge flowed primarily from teachers or experts to students. This model prevailed for centuries and was characterized by rigid curriculum structures and a focus on rote learning. Educational institutions, such as schools and universities, were centralized and held a monopoly on knowledge dissemination.

➢ *Emergence of Progressive Education:* The early 20th century marked the emergence of progressive education movements, led by educational philosophers like John Dewey. Progressive education emphasized student-centered learning, active engagement, and the importance of experiential learning. This shift in pedagogical thinking laid the groundwork for more interactive and collaborative educational approaches.

➢ *Technological Advancements:* The advent of technology, particularly the internet and digital tools, brought about significant changes in education. It enabled online learning, open educational resources, and new opportunities for collaboration and knowledge sharing. These technological advancements facilitated the decentralization of education and allowed for the inclusion of diverse voices and resources.

➢ *Community and Stakeholder Engagement:* Over time, there has been a growing recognition of the importance of involving the broader community and stakeholders in education. This shift acknowledges that education does not occur in isolation but is deeply intertwined with societal and economic dynamics. Local businesses, non-profit organizations, and community leaders have increasingly become integral parts of the educational ecosystem.

➢ *Evolving Educational Paradigms:* In recent decades, educational paradigms have continued to evolve. The emphasis has shifted towards personalized learning, competency-based education, and the recognition of multiple pathways to knowledge acquisition. These changes have encouraged a more flexible and adaptable approach to education that aligns with the principles of value networks.

➢ *Value Networks in Modern Education:* The term "value networks" gained prominence as a way to conceptualize and describe the multifaceted, interconnected nature of education in the modern era. The historical evolution of educational philosophies, coupled with technological advancements and a deeper understanding of the importance of collaboration, has paved the way for the emergence of value networks as a fundamental framework for comprehending the dynamics of contemporary education.

Today, educational institutions are increasingly seen as nodes within broader educational ecosystems, where stakeholders collaborate, exchange value, and co-create knowledge. The historical trajectory of education has led us to a point where recognizing and actively managing value networks is essential for providing meaningful and relevant learning experiences in an interconnected world. Subsequent sections of this article will explore the implications and practical aspects of understanding and leveraging value networks in education.

The Theoretical Background of Value Networks in Education. Value networks in education draw upon several theoretical frameworks and concepts that help elucidate their significance and operation within the educational landscape. These theories provide a foundation for understanding how value is created, exchanged, and distributed among various stakeholders in the educational ecosystem.

➢ *Social Constructivism:* Social constructivism, rooted in the work of theorists like Lev Vygotsky and Jean Piaget, posits that knowledge is not a passive acquisition but is actively constructed by individuals through social interactions and experiences. In the context of education, this theory underscores the importance of collaborative learning and the role of teachers and peers in facilitating knowledge construction. Value networks align with social constructivist principles by emphasizing the collaborative nature of education, where students, teachers, and other stakeholders collectively contribute to the creation of knowledge.

➢ *Network Theory:* Network theory, borrowed from sociology and complex systems theory, examines the relationships and interactions among interconnected nodes within a network. In education, value networks can be viewed as networks of actors (teachers, students, parents, administrators, etc.) engaged in various relationships. This theoretical perspective allows us to analyze the structural characteristics of these networks, the flow of information, and the influence of nodes (individuals or institutions) within the network.

➤ *Communities of Practice:* Coined by Jean Lave and Etienne Wenger, the concept of communities of practice highlights the social nature of learning. It posits that learning occurs within communities of individuals who share common goals, practices, and a sense of belonging. In education, value networks can be seen as dynamic communities of practice where educators, students, and other stakeholders collaborate, share expertise, and collectively pursue educational objectives. Understanding value networks through the lens of communities of practice underscores the importance of social engagement and collective knowledge construction.

➤ *Open Education and Connectivism:* Open education and connectivism are contemporary theories that align closely with the concept of value networks. Open education emphasizes the accessibility of educational resources, often made possible through digital technologies and open educational resources (OER). Connectivism, developed by George Siemens and Stephen Downes, posits that learning is distributed across networks of people and technology. In value networks, open education and connectivism converge by emphasizing the importance of diverse resources and connections in the learning process.

➤ *Systems Thinking:* Systems thinking is an interdisciplinary approach that views organizations and systems holistically. It emphasizes understanding the interdependencies and feedback loops within complex systems. When applied to education, value networks are seen as systems where changes in one part of the network can have ripple effects throughout. Systems thinking helps educators and administrators make informed decisions by considering the broader implications of their actions within the value network.

By grounding value networks in these theoretical frameworks, we gain deeper insights into the collaborative, dynamic, and interconnected nature of education. These theories underscore the importance of acknowledging the roles of various stakeholders, the social aspects of learning, and the significance of networks in shaping modern educational practices. As we proceed in this article, we will explore how these theoretical foundations inform strategies for understanding and optimizing value networks in education.

How Value Networks Differ from Traditional Educational Systems

The emergence of value networks in education represents a significant departure from traditional educational systems that have prevailed for generations. Understanding these differences is crucial for grasping the transformative potential of value networks within the realm of education. Differences between Value Networks and Traditional Educational Systems can be gathered under 5 topics:

➢ *Ownership and Centralization.* Traditional educational systems are often characterized by centralized authority, with institutions, curriculum, and resources controlled by a single governing body (e.g. a government, school board, or university administration) and knowledge primarily flows in a unidirectional manner from teachers or experts to students, with limited input from other stakeholders. Value networks, on the other hand, emphasize decentralization and shared ownership and collaboration among various stakeholders, including teachers, students, parents, and community members. Ownership of education extends beyond institutional boundaries. Furthermore, in value networks, knowledge is co-created through interactions and contributions from multiple actors, fostering a more dynamic and inclusive learning environment.

➢ *Focus on Collaboration.* Traditional education tends to have a hierarchical structure, with clear distinctions between teachers, students, and administrators. Teachers, in traditional educational systems, are the primary knowledge holders and decision-makers, while students are passive recipients of information. Value networks, on the other hand, emphasize collaboration and networking among all stakeholders, breaking down hierarchical barriers and unlike teacher-centered traditional education systems, students are active participants in the learning process, with opportunities to contribute, provide feedback, and influence the direction of their education.

➢ *Knowledge Sources and Diversity.* Traditional education relies heavily on textbooks and materials approved by educational authorities, limiting exposure to diverse perspectives and resources and curricula are often standardized and inflexible, providing little room for customization or adaptation. Value networks, on the other hand, encourage the integration of diverse resources, including digital content, open educational resources (OER), community expertise, and real-world experiences. Furthermore, education within value networks is often personalized to meet individual student needs and interests, allowing for a more tailored learning experience.

➤ **Assessment and Feedback.** Traditional systems often rely on standardized tests and grades as primary assessment tools. Moreover, feedback loops between teachers, students, and parents may be infrequent, hindering continuous improvement. Value networks, on the other hand, employ a variety of assessment methods, including formative assessment, peer assessment, and self-assessment, aligning with the principles of personalized learning. Moreover, value networks prioritize ongoing feedback and communication among stakeholders, facilitating timely adjustments to instruction and support.

➤ **Flexibility and Adaptability.** Traditional systems can be inflexible, with fixed schedules, curricula, and classroom structures. Furthermore, changes to traditional systems often require significant time and bureaucratic processes. Value networks, on the other hand, value flexibility and adaptability. They are designed to be adaptable to changing needs and circumstances, accommodating new technologies, teaching methods, and educational priorities. Moreover, educational stakeholders within value networks can quickly adapt to emerging challenges and opportunities, promoting innovation and responsiveness.

Understanding these fundamental differences between value networks and traditional educational systems is essential for educators, policymakers, and stakeholders as they consider the evolving landscape of education. Value networks offer a more dynamic, collaborative, and student-centered approach to learning, fostering a more inclusive and responsive educational experience. Subsequent sections of this article will explore the implications and benefits of embracing value networks in education.

The Components of School Value Networks

In essence, value networks represent a departure from traditional linear models of education, where knowledge and value flow primarily from teachers and educational institutions to students. Instead, they recognize that value creation in education is a multifaceted, collaborative process involving various actors. The concept of value networks acknowledges that each of these stakeholders contributes to and benefits from the educational ecosystem. It emphasizes the bidirectional flow of value, where not only do educators provide knowledge to students, but students also provide feedback and insights to educators. Similarly, parents and community members can influence educational policies, and administrators can shape the educational experience based on their understanding of the community's needs. Furthermore, value networks in education recognize the importance of non-traditional sources of knowledge, such as online resources, peer-to-peer learning, and community-based initiatives. This shift in perspective highlights the need for schools and educational institutions to adapt to a more interconnected and collaborative educational landscape. As this article unfolds, we will delve deeper into the components, functions, and implications of value networks within the context of schools, ultimately illustrating the significance of understanding and managing these networks for the benefit of all stakeholders involved in education.

Teachers and Educators as Key Components of School Value Networks

Teachers and educators are the heart of any school value network. Their roles extend beyond traditional classroom instruction and involve multifaceted interactions with students, parents, administrators, and the broader community. Understanding their functions and contributions is essential for comprehending the dynamics of value networks in education. Teachers and educators are not only knowledge transmitters but also facilitators of the learning process. Their interactions within the school value network are instrumental in shaping students' educational journeys, and their dedication contributes significantly to the overall value created within the educational ecosystem. Recognizing the multifaceted roles of teachers and educators within value networks is essential for promoting effective teaching and learning practices in today's education landscape.

Teachers are responsible for delivering curriculum content, sharing knowledge, and facilitating learning experiences. They serve as subject matter experts and guides in helping students grasp concepts and acquire skills. They are central in transferring knowledge from the curriculum to students. They guide students in acquiring subject-specific knowledge and developing essential skills. Educators are often involved in curriculum development and customization. They select instructional materials, design lesson plans, and adapt teaching strategies to meet the needs of diverse learners. Teachers assess student performance through quizzes, exams, projects, and other assessment methods. Through assessments and continuous feedback, teachers help students understand their strengths and areas for improvement. This feedback loop is critical for student growth. They provide constructive feedback to students, helping them understand their strengths and areas for improvement. Educators create a supportive and engaging classroom environment. They encourage student participation, foster critical thinking, and promote a love for learning. Recognizing that each student has unique learning needs, teachers offer individualized support to address those needs. Teachers contribute to the holistic development of students, including cognitive, social, emotional, and ethical growth. They help students become well-rounded individuals. Educators promote cultural sensitivity and inclusivity by creating a classroom environment that respects and values diversity. They foster a sense of belonging for all students. Teachers often serve as innovators in education. They explore new teaching methods, integrate technology, and adapt to changing educational paradigms to enhance the learning experience. Teacher-student interactions are at the core of the educational process. Teachers engage with students through lectures, discussions, one-on-one sessions, and collaborative projects. They provide guidance, mentorship, and academic support. Moreover, effective communication between teachers and parents is essential for student success. Teachers share information on student progress, behavior, and academic performance. Parent-teacher conferences and regular updates create a strong partnership between home and school. Teachers work closely with administrators to align curriculum with educational goals, implement school policies, and address classroom needs. They also engage in professional development opportunities to enhance their teaching skills. Many schools encourage the formation of PLCs where teachers collaborate with colleagues to share best practices, analyze student data, and collectively improve teaching methods.

Students and Parents as Vital Components of School Value Networks

Students and parents are integral parts of the educational value network, actively participating in the creation, exchange, and distribution of value. Their roles extend beyond the classroom and involve interactions with teachers, administrators, and the broader community. Understanding their functions and contributions is crucial for grasping the dynamics of value networks in education.

Students are at the center of the learning process. Their primary responsibility is to actively engage in classroom activities, absorb knowledge, and develop critical thinking skills. Students provide feedback to teachers and peers through questions, discussions, and classroom participation. They also engage in self-reflection to assess their own progress and areas for improvement. Many educational settings encourage students to collaborate on projects and assignments, fostering teamwork, communication skills, and the exchange of ideas. Students may advocate for their educational needs, seek additional support when necessary, and express their preferences for learning methods or subjects. These interactions form the core of the educational process. Students engage with teachers through questions, discussions, and assignments. They seek clarification, feedback, and guidance from teachers. Students interact with peers through collaborative projects, group discussions, and extracurricular activities. These interactions promote social and cognitive development. Students actively engage in the learning process, absorbing knowledge, developing critical thinking skills, and applying what they learn. They bring diverse backgrounds, experiences, and perspectives to the classroom, enriching discussions and fostering a dynamic learning environment. Through questions, discussions, and assignments, students contribute to the feedback loop that informs instructional decisions, allowing for continuous improvement.

Parents play a crucial role in supporting their children's education by providing a conducive home environment, helping with homework, and offering emotional support. Effective communication between parents and teachers is vital. Parents attend parent-teacher conferences, respond to school communications, and engage in conversations about their child's progress. Parents advocate for their child's educational needs within the school system, addressing concerns and collaborating with teachers and administrators to ensure a positive learning experience. Effective communication between parents and teachers is essential for student success. Parents attend parent-teacher conferences, receive progress reports, and engage in discussions about their child's education. Parents may interact with school administrators to address policy concerns, offer insights, and participate in decision-making processes. Parents provide emotional and academic support to their children, contributing to their holistic development. Parents advocate for their child's educational needs, ensuring that the school environment is conducive to learning and addressing any challenges that may arise. By engaging with teachers and administrators, parents contribute valuable insights and feedback that can help shape school policies and practices.

Administrators and Policymakers as Essential Components of School Value Networks

Administrators and policymakers hold key positions within the educational value network, influencing the management of educational institutions, the development of policies, and the allocation of resources. Their roles extend beyond decision-making and involve interactions with teachers, students, parents, and the broader community. Understanding their functions and contributions is fundamental to comprehending the dynamics of value networks in education. Administrators and policymakers are instrumental in shaping the educational landscape, ensuring that policies align with educational objectives, and managing resources effectively. Their interactions within the school value network influence the overall value created within the educational ecosystem. Recognizing their roles and fostering strong collaboration among all stakeholders is essential for promoting effective educational practices and enhancing the educational experience for all involved. Subsequent sections of this article will explore the broader implications and benefits of managing value networks in schools.

School administrators oversee the allocation of resources, including budgets, staff, and facilities. They ensure that resources are distributed efficiently to support educational goals. Administrators play a central role in implementing educational policies, both at the school and district levels. They interpret policies, communicate them to stakeholders, and oversee their execution. Administrators work with teachers to ensure that the curriculum aligns with educational objectives. They may be involved in curriculum development and modifications. Administrators are responsible for managing school facilities, ensuring that they are safe and conducive to learning. This includes maintenance, security, and improvements. Administrators collaborate with teachers to align curricula with educational goals, provide professional development opportunities, and ensure that instructional practices are consistent with policies and standards. Administrators maintain open lines of communication with parents, addressing concerns, providing updates on school policies, and gathering input on educational initiatives. Administrators often engage with policymakers to share insights from the field, discuss the impact of policies, and advocate for necessary changes. Administrators ensure that resources are allocated efficiently to support teaching and learning. Their decisions impact the availability of materials, technology, and staff. Administrators play a critical role in translating policies into action, ensuring that they are effectively executed within the school setting. Through facility management and safety measures, administrators contribute to creating a conducive and safe learning environment.

Policymakers, often at the district, state, or national levels, develop educational policies that guide schools' operations. They create guidelines, standards, and regulations for curriculum, assessment, and student services. Policymakers influence the allocation of resources by determining funding formulas, grant programs, and budget priorities that affect schools and districts. Policymakers design accountability systems and assessment frameworks to measure student performance and hold schools accountable for achieving educational goals. Policymakers engage in advocacy efforts and may introduce legislation to address educational issues, funding needs, and policy changes. Policymakers work with administrators to implement new policies, provide guidance on compliance, and gather feedback on the effectiveness of policy changes. Teachers may engage with policymakers through teacher associations, providing input on educational policies, curriculum development, and assessment practices. Policymakers may interact with parents through community forums, town hall meetings, and educational advocacy groups to gather input and address concerns. Policymakers shape the overarching educational framework, setting the stage for educational practices and goals within schools. Policymakers influence the distribution of funds, impacting the availability of resources and support services within schools. Policymakers establish accountability systems that guide assessment practices, data collection, and school evaluation.

Community and Stakeholders as Integral Components of School Value Networks

The community and stakeholders play essential roles within the educational value network, connecting the school to the broader world and enriching the educational experience. Their contributions extend beyond the classroom and involve interactions with teachers, students, parents, administrators, and policymakers. Understanding their functions and contributions is crucial for comprehending the dynamics of value networks in education. Community and stakeholders are essential partners in the educational value network, connecting schools to the broader community and enhancing the educational experience for all involved. Their interactions and contributions extend beyond the classroom, creating a richer and more comprehensive educational ecosystem. Recognizing their roles and fostering strong collaboration among all stakeholders is essential for promoting effective educational practices and ensuring that students receive a holistic education that prepares them for success in the modern world. Subsequent sections of this article will explore the broader implications and benefits of managing value networks in schools.

The community may provide resources to schools, such as funding, equipment, and materials. Local businesses, philanthropic organizations, and community members often contribute to educational initiatives. Community members, including professionals and experts, can offer mentorship opportunities, internships, and real-world experiences to students, bridging the gap between classroom learning and practical application. Schools can serve as community hubs, hosting events, workshops, and activities that engage community members and foster a sense of belonging and ownership in the educational process. Schools engage with local businesses, community organizations, and cultural institutions to develop partnerships that enhance the educational experience. These partnerships may involve financial support, mentorship programs, or shared facilities. Schools open their doors to the community, hosting events, workshops, and activities that encourage community members to participate in educational initiatives and connect with students. The community's financial and material contributions enhance the resources available to schools, enabling the provision of a high-quality education. Community members provide students with exposure to real-world experiences, career opportunities, and mentorship, preparing them for life beyond the classroom. Community engagement fosters a sense of belonging and community ownership, reinforcing the school's role as a central hub.

Stakeholders, such as non-profit organizations focused on education, may advocate for educational policies and resources that benefit students and schools. Businesses, non-profits, and government agencies can collaborate with schools on initiatives related to workforce development, career readiness, and community enrichment. Stakeholders often provide valuable input and feedback on school programs, policies, and partnerships, helping to shape the educational direction of the institution. Stakeholders collaborate with schools to develop and implement programs that align with educational goals. This may include career development initiatives, internships, or after-school programs. Stakeholders may advocate for specific policies at the local, state, or national levels that benefit schools and students. They engage with policymakers to influence educational decisions. Stakeholders provide additional support and resources that complement the school's offerings, enriching the educational experience. Stakeholders advocate for policies that benefit students and schools, influencing educational decisions at various levels. Collaboration with stakeholders often leads to innovative educational programs and initiatives that broaden students' horizons and skills.

Interactions of Value Network Components Within the Education Sector

In the education sector, value network components engage in a complex web of interactions that collectively contribute to the creation, exchange, and distribution of value. Understanding these interactions is crucial for appreciating the multifaceted nature of modern education and how each stakeholder plays a vital role in the educational ecosystem.

> **Teacher-Student Interactions:** Teachers engage directly with students to facilitate learning. They deliver instructional content, provide guidance, and

assess student progress. Interactions here are characterized by pedagogical methods, classroom activities, and one-on-one support.

➢ *Teacher-Parent Collaboration:* Effective communication between teachers and parents is essential. Teachers share student progress, offer insights into learning strategies, and seek input from parents to tailor instruction to individual student needs.

➢ *Teacher-Administrator Collaboration:* Teachers collaborate with administrators on curriculum development, policy implementation, and professional development initiatives. These interactions influence the overall teaching and learning environment.

➢ *Student-Teacher Engagement:* Students actively participate in classroom activities, ask questions, and seek clarification from teachers. They provide feedback on instructional methods and the effectiveness of learning materials.

➢ *Peer Interactions:* Students engage with peers through collaborative projects, discussions, and group activities. Peer-to-peer learning fosters knowledge sharing and social development.

➢ *Parent-Student Relationship:* Parents support their children's education by assisting with homework, attending parent-teacher conferences, and advocating for their children's needs. Their involvement is critical for student success.

➢ *Administrator-Teacher Collaboration:* Administrators work closely with teachers to align curricula with educational goals, allocate resources, and ensure a conducive learning environment. They may also provide professional development opportunities.

➢ *Administrator-Parent Communication:* Administrators maintain open lines of communication with parents to address concerns, provide updates on school policies, and gather input on educational initiatives.

➢ *Policymaker-Administrator Engagement:* Policymakers develop and implement education policies. They engage with administrators to gather insights from the field and adjust policies based on evolving needs.

➢ *Community Support:* Local businesses, non-profit organizations, and community leaders contribute resources, mentorship programs, and real-world experiences for students. These interactions bridge the gap between education and the broader community.

➢ *Stakeholder Collaboration:* Various stakeholders collaborate on initiatives that enhance the overall educational experience. Partnerships between schools, businesses, and community organizations can create valuable opportunities for students.

Digital tools and online platforms facilitate interactions among all components of the value network. They enable remote learning, real-time communication, and access to a wealth of educational resources. Technology allows for the collection and analysis of data related to student performance and educational outcomes. This data informs instructional decisions and policy adjustments. These interactions within the educational value network are dynamic and interconnected. They emphasize the importance of collaboration, feedback loops, and the bidirectional flow of value among stakeholders. As the educational landscape continues to evolve, nurturing these interactions and optimizing the value network becomes increasingly essential for providing a holistic and effective learning experience for all students. Subsequent sections of this article will explore the functions and benefits of these interactions in more detail, showcasing their significance in modern education.

Challenges and Opportunities in School Value Networks

School Value Networks sometimes encounter challenges. The most important of these can be summarized under the following headings (FasterCapital, n.d.).

> *Equity and Access:* Ensuring equitable access to quality education remains a significant challenge. Not all students have the same access to resources, technology, and educational opportunities, leading to educational disparities.
> *Data Privacy and Security:* The increased use of technology in education raises concerns about data privacy and security. Protecting student and educator data from breaches and misuse is a complex challenge.
> *Teacher Workload:* Teachers often face heavy workloads, including lesson planning, grading, administrative tasks, and addressing individual student needs. Balancing these demands can be overwhelming.
> *Resource Allocation:* The allocation of resources, including funding, staff, and facilities, can be a source of contention. Limited resources can hinder the implementation of effective educational programs.
> *Policy and Regulation:* The educational landscape is subject to frequent policy changes and regulations that can create uncertainty and administrative burden for educators and administrators.

The opportunities in School Value Networks, on the other hand, can be grouped as follows (Garvie, 2023).

> *Personalized Learning:* School value networks enable personalized learning experiences, where students can access resources tailored to their needs and

learning styles. Technology and data analytics facilitate personalized learning pathways.

➢ *Community Engagement:* Engaging the community and stakeholders in education fosters a sense of ownership and support. Schools can leverage community expertise, resources, and mentorship opportunities to enhance the learning experience.

➢ *Collaboration and Innovation:* Value networks encourage collaboration among educators, administrators, policymakers, and stakeholders. This collaboration can drive innovation in teaching methods, curriculum design, and educational technology adoption.

➢ *Data-Driven Decision-Making:* Value networks collect and analyze data to inform educational practices. Data-driven decision-making can lead to more effective interventions, improved student outcomes, and informed resource allocation.

➢ *Inclusivity and Diversity:* Value networks provide opportunities to promote inclusivity and diversity by accommodating diverse learning needs, fostering cultural sensitivity, and incorporating multiple perspectives into the curriculum.

➢ *Lifelong Learning:* School value networks can promote lifelong learning by connecting students and community members to resources, courses, and opportunities beyond traditional K-12 education.

In navigating the challenges and embracing the opportunities within school value networks, educators, policymakers, and stakeholders must work collaboratively, adapt to changing educational paradigms, and prioritize the needs of students to create a more responsive and effective educational system. By doing so, they can unlock the full potential of value networks to provide high-quality, equitable, and innovative education for all learners.

Why It Is Essential for Educational Institutions to Understand and Actively Manage Their Value Networks

It is essential for educational institutions to understand and actively manage their value networks for several compelling reasons. Managing value networks is not just about providing quality education; it is about optimizing the educational experience for all stakeholders and ensuring that students receive the best possible education in a constantly evolving world. Here's why it's crucial (Arnett, 2023):

➤ *Enhancing Educational Quality.* Understanding value networks allows educational institutions to personalize learning experiences for students, catering to their individual needs, interests, and learning styles. This leads to improved educational quality by making learning more engaging and effective. Furthermore, active management of value networks involves collecting and analyzing data to make informed decisions about teaching methods, resources, and curriculum design. This data-driven approach enables institutions to continuously enhance the quality of education.

➤ *Fostering Innovation.* Value networks help educational institutions stay abreast of evolving educational paradigms and adapt to changing paradigms, such as student-centered learning, technology integration, and competency-based education. This adaptability fosters innovation in teaching and learning methods. Furthermore, collaborative value networks promote the exchange of innovative ideas among educators, administrators, policymakers, and stakeholders. This collective knowledge sharing encourages the adoption of innovative practices.

➤ *Promoting Equity and Inclusivity.* Value networks allow institutions to identify and address disparities in access to educational resources and opportunities. By actively managing value networks, schools can work toward equitable access to quality education for all students, regardless of background or circumstance. Furthermore, understanding value networks helps institutions create inclusive learning environments that embrace diversity and respect different cultural perspectives. This promotes inclusivity and helps students feel valued and represented.

➤ *Strengthening Community Engagement.* Educational institutions play a vital role in their communities. Actively managing value networks involves engaging with community organizations, businesses, and stakeholders to build strong partnerships. These partnerships can provide additional resources and support to enhance the educational experience. Furthermore, active management of value networks includes fostering open communication and collaboration between parents and educators. This involvement strengthens the home-school partnership, which is crucial for student success.

➤ *Data-Driven Decision-Making.* Understanding value networks allows educational institutions to allocate resources effectively. Data-driven decision-making ensures that budgets, staff, and facilities are used efficiently to support educational goals. Furthermore, by collecting and analyzing data on student performance, feedback, and other relevant metrics, institutions can identify areas for improvement and make data-informed decisions to enhance the educational experience.

➤ *Preparing Students for the Future.* Active management of value networks allows institutions to align their educational programs with the skills and competencies needed in the job market. This ensures that students are prepared for the demands of the modern workforce. Furthermore, understanding value networks encourages a culture of lifelong learning, preparing students to adapt to changing career landscapes and pursue further education beyond traditional K-12 or higher education.

In summary, understanding and actively managing value networks in educational institutions is essential for enhancing educational quality, fostering innovation, promoting equity and inclusivity, strengthening community engagement, making data-driven decisions, and preparing students for the challenges of the future. It empowers institutions to provide a well-rounded and effective education that benefits students, educators, parents, and the broader community.

The Potential Benefits of Value Networks for Students, Teachers, Parents, and the Community

How value networks will create an advantage for different partners of schools can be summarized as follows (Arnett, 2023).

➤ *The Potential Benefits of Value Networks for Students.* Value networks enable personalized learning experiences tailored to individual student needs, interests, and learning styles. Students can access a variety of resources, including online courses, digital libraries, and interactive learning platforms, to enhance their educational journey. Exposure to a wide range of viewpoints and cultures fosters tolerance, empathy, and global awareness. Collaborative projects and interactions with peers from diverse backgrounds promote critical thinking and problem-solving skills. Partnerships with community organizations and stakeholders offer students opportunities for internships, mentorship, and hands-on learning experiences. Students can apply classroom knowledge in practical contexts, preparing them for future careers. Value networks support the holistic development of students, including cognitive, social, emotional, and ethical growth. Encouragement of creativity, innovation, and entrepreneurship helps students become well-rounded individuals. Access to a network of resources and opportunities promotes a culture of lifelong learning, empowering students to continue their education beyond formal schooling. Exposure to various learning modalities fosters adaptability and a growth mindset.

➢ *The Potential Benefits of Value Networks for Teachers.* Collaboration with peers, administrators, and policymakers within value networks offers opportunities for professional growth and skill development. Teachers can share best practices, explore innovative teaching methods, and stay updated on educational trends. Value networks can provide access to additional resources, including technology, materials, and funding, to enhance teaching practices. Collaboration with community partners may result in resource-sharing and support for classroom needs. Emphasis on student-centered learning allows teachers to tailor instruction to individual student needs, fostering engagement and academic growth. Collaborative learning and peer interactions enrich the teaching and learning process. Value networks encourage teachers to explore innovative pedagogical approaches, such as project-based learning, flipped classrooms, and blended learning. Integrating technology and educational apps into teaching can enhance instruction and student engagement.

➢ *The Potential Benefits of Value Networks for Parents.* Value networks facilitate open communication between parents and teachers, enabling them to stay informed about their child's progress, challenges, and achievements. Parent-teacher collaboration supports a holistic view of a student's education. Parents can actively participate in their child's education, offering emotional support, homework assistance, and encouragement. Engagement in school activities, parent-teacher associations, and volunteer opportunities strengthen the school-community partnership. Parents can advocate for their child's educational needs within the school system, ensuring that the educational environment is conducive to learning and development. Involvement in parent-led initiatives can shape school policies and practices.

➢ *The Potential Benefits of Value Networks for Community.* Value networks foster collaboration between educational institutions and community organizations, resulting in shared resources, facilities, and expertise. Schools become community hubs, hosting events, workshops, and activities that benefit both students and community members. Community engagement in education promotes a sense of civic responsibility and shared ownership of educational outcomes. Local businesses, organizations, and individuals actively contribute to the educational ecosystem. Collaboration with local businesses and stakeholders helps prepare students for the workforce by offering internships, mentorship, and career guidance. Value networks align educational programs with local industry needs, fostering a skilled workforce. Schools within value networks can promote cultural sensitivity and inclusivity, celebrating diversity and fostering a sense of belonging. Cultural events and partnerships with cultural institutions enrich the community's social fabric.

In conclusion, value networks in education offer a multitude of potential benefits that extend to students, teachers, parents, and the community. These benefits are driven by collaboration, personalized learning, access to resources, and a holistic approach to education, ultimately contributing to the well-being and development of individuals and communities. Recognizing and leveraging the potential of value networks can lead to more effective, inclusive, and responsive educational systems.

Strategies for Enhancing School Value Networks

Enhancing value networks in schools requires a strategic approach that involves collaboration, communication, and a commitment to improving the overall educational experience. Here are practical strategies and recommendations for schools to enhance their value networks.

Build Strong Partnerships

➢ Engage with the Community: Actively involve local businesses, organizations, and community members in educational initiatives. Establish partnerships that support school programs, events, and resource-sharing.

➢ Strengthen Parent-School Relationships: Foster open and regular communication between parents and educators. Encourage parental involvement in school activities and decision-making processes.

➢ Collaborate with Stakeholders: Collaborate with non-profit organizations, government agencies, and other stakeholders to align educational programs with community needs and resources.

Leverage Technology

➢ Utilize Digital Platforms: Implement learning management systems (LMS), online communication tools, and educational apps to facilitate communication and collaboration among students, teachers, and parents.

➢ Provide Access to Technology: Address the digital divide by ensuring that all students have access to necessary technology and high-speed internet at school and home.

➢ Promote Digital Literacy: Offer digital literacy training for students, parents, and educators to maximize the benefits of technology integration.

Embrace Data-Driven Decision-Making

➢ Collect and Analyze Data: Gather data on student performance, attendance, and engagement. Analyze this data to identify areas for improvement and make informed decisions about resource allocation.

➢ Use Assessment Data: Utilize assessment data to personalize learning experiences for students, identify struggling learners, and implement targeted interventions.

➢ Share Data Transparently: Promote transparency by sharing relevant data with parents, teachers, and administrators, allowing for informed discussions and collaborative problem-solving.

Encourage Professional Development

➢ Offer Ongoing Training: Provide teachers and staff with continuous professional development opportunities to keep them updated on the latest teaching methods, technology tools, and educational trends.

➢ Support Collaborative Learning: Foster a culture of collaborative learning among educators, encouraging the sharing of best practices and innovative teaching methods.

Promote Inclusivity and Diversity

➢ Cultivate Inclusive Learning Environments: Implement strategies to create inclusive classrooms where all students feel valued and respected, regardless of their background or identity.

➢ Celebrate Diversity: Incorporate diverse perspectives and voices into the curriculum, highlighting different cultures, histories, and experiences.

Emphasize Student-Centered Learning

➢ Personalize Learning Pathways: Offer opportunities for students to choose their learning pathways and projects, allowing them to pursue their interests and passions.

➢ Encourage Critical Thinking: Foster critical thinking, problem-solving, and creativity by using inquiry-based learning and real-world projects.

Establish Clear Communication

➢ Implement Effective Communication Channels: Use multiple communication channels, including newsletters, emails, parent-teacher conferences, and digital platforms, to keep all stakeholders informed.

➤ Seek Feedback: Encourage feedback from students, parents, teachers, and community members to gauge satisfaction, identify areas for improvement, and make necessary adjustments.

Assess and Adapt

➤ Regularly Assess Value Network Effectiveness: Periodically evaluate the effectiveness of your school's value network, considering the impact on student outcomes, community engagement, and resource allocation.
➤ Adapt to Changing Needs: Be agile in responding to changing educational paradigms, community dynamics, and student needs. Continuously adapt strategies to align with evolving circumstances.

Set Clear Goals and Metrics

➤ Define Clear Objectives: Establish clear, measurable goals for your value network initiatives, such as improving student performance, enhancing community involvement, or reducing educational disparities.
➤ Monitor Progress: Regularly monitor progress toward your goals using relevant metrics and indicators. Adjust strategies as needed to stay on track.

Promote a Culture of Collaboration

➤ Encourage Collaboration: Create opportunities for collaboration among teachers, administrators, parents, and community partners. Recognize and celebrate successful collaborative efforts.
➤ Shared Vision: Ensure that all stakeholders share a common vision for the school's mission, values, and educational objectives, fostering a sense of unity and purpose.

Allocate Resources Wisely

➤ Optimize Resource Allocation: Use data to inform resource allocation decisions, ensuring that resources are distributed equitably and effectively to support educational goals.
➤ Advocate for Additional Resources: Collaborate with stakeholders to advocate for additional resources, grants, and funding opportunities that can enhance the educational experience.

By implementing these practical strategies and recommendations, schools can enhance their value networks, creating a more responsive, inclusive, and effective educational ecosystem that benefits students, educators, parents, and the broader community. Continuous improvement and a commitment to collaboration are key to realizing the full potential of value networks in education.

Conclusion

The success of a business is directly proportional to the success of the Value Network it creates with its stakeholders. As an educational institution with commercial goals, schools must take utmost care to create and develop their value networks. The value networks of educational institutions consist of various stakeholders, and all of them are individually important for the success of the school. One of the most important dimensions of competition between educational institutions is value networks. Educational institutions that aim to stand out in the competition must attach importance to their relations with stakeholders. Since the concept of value network is not yet fully understood even for companies and not much experience has been gained on how to manage it, the threats and opportunities facing schools need to be carefully evaluated.

References

Alcantara, M. C., Braga, M., & van den Heuvel, C. (2020). Historical networks in science education: A case study of an experiment with network analysis by high school students. *Science & Education, 29*(7), 101–121 https://doi.org/10.1007/s11191-019-00096-4

Arnett, T. (2023). *A value network can influence education change.* SmartBrief. https://www.smartbrief.com/original/value-network-education-change

Bates (Tony), A. W. (2019). *Teaching in a Digital Age: Guidelines for designing teaching and learning* (2nd ed.). Creative Commons Attribution. https://opentextbc.ca/teachinginadigitalage/

Christensen, C. M. (1997). *The innovators dilemma: When new technologies cause great firms to fail.* Harvard Business School Press.

FasterCapital. (n.d.). *The challenges of education networks and how to overcome them.* https://fastercapital.com/topics/the-challenges-of-education-networks-and-how-to-overcome-them.html

Garvie, L. (2023). *The benefits of networking – Education.* https://www.linkedin.com/pulse/benefits-networking-education-lorraine-garvie/

Kenton, W. (2022). *Value networks: Definition, benefits and types.* Investopedia. https://www.investopedia.com/terms/v/value-network.asp

Khalid, A. (2024). *Value network.* WallstreetMojo. https://www.wallstreetmojo.com/value-network/

Porter, M. E. (1985). *The competitive advantage: Creating and sustaining superior performance.* Free Press.

Stabell, C. B., & Fjeldstad, O. D. (1998). Configuring value for competitive advantage: On chains, shops, and networks. *Strategic Management Journal, 19*(5), 413–437. https://doi.org/10.1002/(SICI)1097-0266(199805)19:5<413::AID-SMJ946>3.0.CO;2-C

Part 3: Re-Imagining New Pillars of Education

Dr. Seda Gökçe Turan

Chapter 5 New Pedagogies: Pedagogies of Empowerment in the Context of Cancel Culture, Social Media, and Inclusive Education

Abstract: In the contemporary landscape of education, the intersectionality of cancel culture, social media dynamics, and the imperative of inclusive education has significantly influenced pedagogical approaches. This chapter explores the emergence and implementation of empowerment pedagogies within this multifaceted context. The pervasive influence of social media platforms has transformed traditional educational dynamics, providing avenues for both empowerment and vulnerability among learners and educators alike. Cancel culture, with its emphasis on holding individuals and institutions accountable for their actions, has underscored the need for pedagogies that foster critical thinking, empathy, and resilience. Additionally, the push for inclusive education has necessitated pedagogical frameworks that honor diversity, equity, and inclusivity.

By critically examining the intersection of cancel culture, social media dynamics, and inclusive education, this chapter aims to contribute to ongoing conversations within the educational community. It underscores the importance of reimagining pedagogical approaches to empower learners in navigating the complexities of the digital age while fostering inclusivity, empathy, and critical consciousness which are the vital skills for 21st century and for the future.

Keywords: New Pedagogies, New Media, Cancel Culture, Inclusive Education

Public humiliation is not a new phenomenon and has existed for centuries. Throughout humanity, public create the ways of shaming individuals for alleged social and legal infractions such as public flogging, wearing a dunce cap, forced public exposure, and public caning. The concept of cancelling someone is similar to those punishments, but it is specifically designed for the digital age in the midst of hyper sociality which will explained soon (Velasco, 2020). Social media brought so many benefits and risks as well in the pervasiveness of shopping to the spreading and deliberating networked disinformation and fake news. Moreover, due to long time usage of social media online and real life is blurred, individuals mostly stick with their digital persona (Velasco, 2020).

In this part, we have to talk about Manuel Castells who is a great sociologist specialized in digital societies. Castells (2005) describes society in the digital age as a "hyper-sociality". According to him, hyper-sociality is transformation of sociability. He mainly claimed that networked society does not mean a society of isolation. Except for some teenagers, most of the people in the digital environment do not create fake profiles and identity. Castells argued that some teenagers are experimenting with their lives, and it leads to creating fake digital identity. Moreover, according to Castells, people live in various technological forms of communication and with hyper-sociality it begets networked individualism. In the context of society while characterizing "Cancel Culture" we could say that is a form of public shaming which is starting in social media to deprive someone of their usual prestige and social status or attention with the aim of making public discourse more diffused and less monopolized by those in positions of privilege (Velasco, 2020). Moreover, Kato (2021) describes cancel culture much more "dictionary style": society dismisses individuals for behaving outside of perceived social norms.

The raising interaction between society and technology, new forms of collectives emerged. Firstly, social media is not a place for information exchange, it also provides a place for digital participation and movements. Users could share and compete about their culture, knowledge, and ideology. The users build sociability along self-selected communication networks. Consequently, the act of cancelling someone is one of the spontaneous collective practices initiated by social media users without consideration for its possible ramifications and consequences (Velasco, 2020).

In addition to all descriptions, cancel culture is also characterized as a form of intolerance against opposing views (Velasco, 2020). According to Beiner (2020) cancel culture is a manifestation of wokeism which is an ideology that views reality as socially constructed and defined by power, oppression, and group identity. Sailofsky (2021) underlined the woke capitalism in which organizations or brands purport to take a stand against social injustice by removing a person from a job or releasing a statement, without making any substantial changes to the systems that allow those behaviors or beliefs to perpetuate. Beside wokeism there is also another factor that triggers cancel culture: "Celebrity Culture". The term celebrity culture has evolved along with the new developments in social technologies. As result, the public has deployed and stationed new ways of policing misbehaviors, unethical actions, and speech through social media. Cancel culture has significant implications on digital activism and supporting victims (Clarck, 2020). In terms of marginalized people, cancelling is considered as a tool for silencing those people who have adapted earlier resistance strategies for effectiveness in the digital environments.

The culture of cancellation is a highly complicated social movement. One side, it is one of the highest displays of democratizations of discourse. On the contrary, cancel culture is also a force for censoriousness and intolerance for ideas that disagree to the dominant acceptable norms (Velasco, 2020). According to Bangun and Kumaralalita (2022) cancel culture can be a good thing when the public wants to make those who can be a role model are those with positive attitudes and intents. But, on the other hand, cancel culture can be terrifying and dangerous thing when public posits the celebrities as a material commodity and get cancelled easily.

Youngsters Digital Media Participation

Media have a significant impact in shaping who we are today. Due to pervasiveness of social media and digital environments, individuals are bombarded with mediated messages. Moreover, messages from news, websites, television, and other digital platforms have contributed to our cultural discourse. These media have indeed even affected the direction of public discourse on socially significant issues (Bangun & Kumaralita, 2022). While using social media there is another important concept "digital identity" appeared. This part of the chapter we should explain digital identity in depth. According to Subrahmanyam and Greenfield (2008) social media and digital media are highly effective on youths. Moreover, they stated that the physical world and virtual world are psychologically linked to each other. On the other hand, Coleman (2011, cited in Sarıyar, 2019) argued that digital environments were not second "life place", but people could easily change their mind and experience different identities at virtual life means that those places kind of role-playing areas. In terms of "identity" concept, identity is a trait that differentiate individuals, while at the same time it defines concepts such as national identity, gender identity, cultural identity, and individuals' common characteristics with other people (Buckingham, 2008). Youths' identity development process is generally characterized by identity depression, conflicted behaviors, changes in mood and not afraid to risky behaviors or even be enthusiastic about it (Buckingham, 2008). The process of identity construction during adolescence period, youths try to take their new roles, responsibilities; distinguish the consequences of their actions and behaviors (Loh & Lim, 2019). Moreover, during the adolescence period, views and having an attraction for other people are very important for youths. In terms of digital environments, it should be seemed that youths had a chance to be in an environment with audiences where they can present their identities. Unlike mass media, digital media allows users to interact and being an active user instead of passive audiences. In addition, users can present their digital identities to other people as they can produce their own content (Özdemir, 2015).

As a developmental characteristic, teenagers are very sensitive about criticism, and they see being critic as proof of being an adult. The problem in this the modern criticism is that it is continually popularized in social media making the culture a performance and a theatre which allows those people who callout to feel morally good and show their adherence to the vulnerable, diminishing the main reason why the trend topic is discussed on the social media and Internet (Placio et al., 2021). It could lead to cancel culture as "social murder" which is also inhumanity and youngsters can exaggerate the unethical behaviors which sometimes are not true. These misunderstandings harm society's moral values and lead to people behaving in suspended way to other cancelling even they are true and fair.

Cancel Culture and Social Media

Due to the description as a form of public shaming initiated on social media, cancel culture is directly related with social media and different digital environments (Bangun & Kumaralalita, 2022). By using social media, individuals who are trying to protect victims, aims of making public discourse more diffused and less monopolized by those in position of privilege. Moreover, cancel culture can have a positive role in social media, such as Twitter, that can play in social justice campaigns. There should be caution regarding how social media platforms, especially for today Twitter has a major role, are able to lead in such matters of social justice. With the complexity of social media, cancellation in the digital environments also empowers people to voice out and share their opinions, particularly to promote democratization and social justice. Even though the phenomenon instigates negative outcomes, generally it can be an effective tool to raise awareness in society, that is why further study of its potential for activism is important.

The use of broadcast-style social media platforms and digital environments such as Twitter, Youtube, Tiktok etc. allow marginalized groups to join and engaged in networked framing, a process by which collective experiences of an offending party's unjust and unfair behavior, action or sayings discussed, morally evaluated and prescribed a remedy or decide a solution such as being fired or choosing for resign, through the collective reasoning and justify of culturally aligned online crowds (Clark, 2020).

Platforms like Twitter, snap judgments can lead to cancelling to participants due to not allowing deeper explanations of taught. So, misunderstandings and cancelling wrong people or justifying unethical behaviors are also common. Especially "Reading" which "begat calling out" is an indigenous expressive form particular to the "other" (Johnson, 2011). When the users suddenly organize and cancel someone their cognitive rationalization becomes so visible and could be confused. Sometimes they can justify the perpetrators' unethical behaviors. This justification sometimes arises from impulsive reactions that are not thinking in depth. Placio et al (2021) argued that social media users bashed the individual engaged in news headlines without knowing what causes the Internet backlash. So, further investigation about cancel culture and finding the objective reason why individuals were cancelled in social media is important so that the concepts' main purpose is to educate, and enlightenment of wrongdoings can be attained. Roos (2017) underlined the importance of power in cancel culture. According to Roos (2017) if the bystanders had power and get organized, they can end their careers, mixed the activism into harassment, and restructured cancel culture as an excuse to censor anyone who questions, competes with, or critiques their idols.

In social media the cancel culture generally rises from social issues such as shaming, political stance, exercising privilege, toxic positivity and, racism (Placio et al., 2021). Due to the greater number of engagement of people and diverse contents in the virtual platform, the occurrence of criticisms inevitable which roots from the contradictory perceptions and opinions of people that center on arguments about an individual, cultural, racial, political class, and social issues (Shah, 2017).

The process of cancel culture generally raised from social media. Even the video or speech that subject to cancel culture could be said in public and real world, the clip or screenshot posted where account users then identify the person and attack the committed behavior. Eventually, individuals will find out their address, work, and the worst scenario is pressuring them to lose their employment. Posting perpetrators' personal social media holdings including photographs with their family, friends, and colleagues and often making memes to mock them are the common behavior of netizens when lining up others on trends list as officially cancelled. This also triggers other individuals to join the cancelling community (Placio et al., 2021).

Issues, Controversies and Problems

Cancel culture is sometimes beneficial and sometimes harmful form of social media activism. Moreover, the processes that shape cancel culture are sometimes misunderstood (Bangun & Kumaralalita, 2022). Now, it is time to turn these issues.

First of all, social media, behaviors of young people and social justice concepts should be examined in depth. The role and construction of social media is a vital part of cancel culture. While talking about the construction of social media, the first thing is any knowledge could easily spread. In addition, scandals and rumors also spread even faster. Any individual from South Africa can learn anything from South America. But that is not always a good thing. In terms of cancellation, it can be spreads wildfire on social media and it is virulently uncontrollable (Velasco, 2020). Moreover, media consumers who used to be passive sides can now become active in new media because the interaction between consumers and producers is increasingly possible with the new rules (Bangun & Kumaralalita, 2022).

There is a common and classical question raised via digital society. Who is the yardstick for acceptable behavior in todays' hypersocial reality? It is a real fact that there is not a clear-cut parameter that someone merits cancellation. With the ambiguous nature of cancel culture, an individual who undergoes this form of public shaming likewise has an extremely vague and unclear path to remediation and solution. Moreover, some people think cancelling culture as a manifestation of agency and cancelling someone is a form of cultural boycott (Velasco, 2020).

Due to some of the cases cancelling can lead to abusive behaviors, movements or simply it is a slander. As results people mostly see cancel culture as negative and exaggerated. According to Placio et al. (2021) cancel culture is still unclear if the goal is to correct wrong actions or to just simply perform condemnation and humiliation to the offenders out of satisfaction. Moreover, as freedom of speech is favored and always unlined in digital environments, cancelling somehow progresses into eliminating constructive discussion between citizens, encouraging lawlessness with foul and derogatory statements, and promoting public backlash.

Although there are many advantages to using and involving social media, Alperstein (2019) pointed out that cultural shifts that occurred in social media became more pervasive and visible. Moreover, based on the idea that thoughts and beliefs are merged on social media Alperstein underlined the importance of "virtual collective consciousness". Especially in digital environments when thoughts and beliefs are integrated and become identified, it becomes the collective consciousness of similarly minded individuals. Their mind is shaped as if manipulated and thinking in the same way. In addition to this, in social media individuals are mostly stuck in "echo chamber" where similarly minded individuals only hear what they wish to hear (Velasco, 2020). The main issue that is related with cancel culture about echo chamber is anything that might be contrary to similarly minded individuals' line of thinking and preference is deemed undesirable.

While trying to cancel someone the bystanders use a tactic to try to erase someone from public discourse- either through publicly shaming, deplatforming, or demanding that they be fired (Beiner, 2020). In order to achieve this "mission" bystanders used the power. In cancelling, power is the relational capacity that enables a social actor to influence asymmetrically the decisions of other social actor or actors in ways that favor the empowered actors' will, interests, and values.

There are so many consequences of cancel culture in terms of perpetrators and victims. According to the study results (Placio et al., 2021). In general framework the bashing, unsubscribing, and demands on job removal are the manner of netizens in cancelling the victims. Netizens type of cancellation in social media are criticizing, educating, and sympathizing with the victims. In terms of victims, they handle the cancellation by focusing on positive people, ignoring the bashers, social media detachment, and admitting accountability. On the cancelling's impact to their career and lives, victims stopped content creating, has ruined reputation, job removed, while some are motivated to work. Although it depends and changes from person to person, victims have undergone depression but gain enlightenment, and while one attains higher self-esteem.

Digital Citizenship Skills and Inclusive Education as A Protective Method for Cancel Culture

With the rise of the Internet and pervasive usage of technological devices, educators and policy makers are sensitive about protecting children and youths from harms and risks of Internet and digital devices (Walters et al., 2019; Mossberger et al., 2008). According to researchers (Yue et al., 2019) digital citizenship skills and competence enable and encourage children and youths to be aware of the risks of the cyber world, while benefiting it. Internet and technological devices change society in personal, educational, and professional domains. With this rapid change, digital citizenship is perceived as a coping and adaptation strategy at this fast-changing digital society's challenges and aggressive behaviors such as cancel culture. Generally, digital citizenship is defined with different components which are so vital not only for children and youths' online behaviors and provide a protection for cyber-harassment, fake news, and media manipulation (Whyte, 2020; Wojewidka, 2020; Vaccari & Chadwick, 2020; Hasan & Salah, 2019; Anderson, 2018). To improve children and youths' digital citizenship competences, we should define and portray digital citizenship skills in depth. Jones and Mitchell (2016) addressed digital citizenship in two parts: respectful behavior online and online civic engagement. Those skills are primarily defined as the ability to navigate, exist, and make sense on digital society which is accepted as a survive tool in digital society both for study and leisure time (Emejulu & McGregor, 2019; Gleason & Gillern, 2018; Kim & Choi, 2018; Vromen, 2017). Generally digital citizenship competencies focus on three main subjects. First, as most of the findings show digital citizenship competences provide a protection about cyberbullying and online trolling and cyberbullying; make pupils to show respectful behaviors in digital platforms; and teach how to protect privacy and intellectual property. Second, digital citizenship competences support pupils to become digitally informed and actively engage in digital communication and discussion with others. Lastly, students with high digital citizenship skills could have a chance to actively engage in political or government related issues which are also necessity for both offline and online citizenship (Flynn et al., 2017; Frenda et al., 2013).

Digital citizenship also takes attention of researchers in terms of education. Most of the researchers believe that in order to improve children and youths' digital citizenship skills education is one of the best tools. Internet safety education or computer education is beneficial for awareness about risks and harms of digital environments; but ideal education for children and youths' integration to digital world the education would be appropriate for characteristics of development and their behaviors (Jones & Mitchell, 2016; Ohler, 2011). Not only teaching children and youths about technology would not be enough. The main aim of education for the 21st century would aim to make children and youth participate in the digital world with higher digital citizenship competences. Moreover, with digital citizenship education pupils online civic engagements' have some outcomes for their offline civic engagement (Ghosn-Chelala, 2019; Jones & Mitchell, 2016). In the context of education, researchers (Choi et al., 2018) also consider teachers' digital citizenship competences in terms of individuals' thinking, skills, and behaviors relevant to Internet usage. Furthermore, not only researchers but also policy makers and educational community members believe that classroom teachers should be responsible, informed, and active digital citizens which are the main goal of education (Choi et al., 2018).

Born and grown up in digital age and with technological devices is not enough for digital competence which is needed for 21st century citizenship skills to effectively engage with digital world (Alvermann & Sanders, 2019). For engagement in digital environments, protect themselves from harms and risks of technology and benefit from it, we should teach them digital citizenship skills. As the subject of this chapter, phenomenon like cancelling culture, the pupils and students should be informed about manipulative effects of social media and consequences of those manipulations on individuals' lives. Now, we will discuss the relationship between deepfake technologies and digital citizenship.

Conclusions and Recommendations

The notion of cancel culture is narrowly applied by the practice of cancellation of withdrawing support for public and non-public figures and companies that committed objectionable or offensive remarks caught in the public's eye. As consumers of traditional media and digital media, scandals do not happen only in media environments, they appeal to the public also. Almost everyone worth knowing has been cancelled by someone. This common action is so dangerous and could be abused. Because those who were cancelled have breached the line of social acceptability, according to unmarked and entirely ambiguous norm of todays' social media climate (Velasco, 2020).

There are many cases as well that the public figures decided to quit the entertainment business and have an early retirement after being cancelled. Sometimes they only just vanished after giving some apology statements (Bangun & Kumaralalita, 2022). Public figures who unintentionally did or said something problematic, either in the present or past, netizens (social media people) immediately decide to stop supporting them and their work by completely cancelling them. It is a viral problem in the entertainment industry, even though they made mistakes years ago, people used it against them creating chaos in their present career until they are destroyed (Delgado, 2020). Except the vital or unforgivable crimes such as rape or murder it should not be forgotten that human can made mistakes and after an intense apologize, aware of the mistake the cancellation should be stopped. Because celebrities stand out and draw the public's attention, people tend to be less tolerant of any perceived moral or ethical misconduct. But although they are celebrities, they are human beings and do not have direct responsibilities to society. To apply an effective inclusive education programme for pupils and students who are cancelled, as mentioned above digital citizenship skills would be an option. With conscious social media usage, it could be possible to reduce cancelling toward any pupils or students.

Research based studies are very important to analyzing cancel culture in depth. Due to social media making the borders between countries and cultures invisible, different research based on different countries and cultures is very precious. Not only research but also policy practices in order to prevent and reduce cancel culture are also important. Maybe similar cultures can apply the policies to their countries. So, talking about the countries policies, application procedures and positive results about prevent cancel culture should be searched in different countries.

It is a fact that the culture of cancellation has become part and parcel of the vernacular of digital culture which is primarily targeted against public figures who break the loose norms of social acceptability (Velasco, 2020). Jonah Engel Bromwich who is a writer for the New York Times characterized the digital phenomenon of being cancelled as total disinvestment in something or anything (cited in Clark, 2020). In 21st century, people are seeking justice on social media. It could be understandable but if false cancellation practices are more visible it could damage the public conscience. Cancel culture victims should be searched in depth also. Their feelings, regrating, their life after cancellation should be analyzed. If the cancelling did not work, it means that there is a big mistake. So, due to the individuals' lives, careers even personal relationships are the subjects of cancellation, the public should be very careful.

References

Alperstein, N. M. (2019). *Celebrity and mediated social connections: Fans, friends and followers in the digital age.* Springer. https://doi.org/10.1007/-978-3-030-17902-1

Alvermann, D. E., & Sanders, R. K. (2019). Adolescent literacy in a digital world. *The International Encyclopedia of Media Literacy, 1–6.* https://doi.org/10.1002/9781118978238.ieml0005

Anderson, K. E. (2018). Getting acquainted with social networks and apps: Combating fake news on social media, *Library HiTech News, 35*(3), 1–6. https://doi.org/10.7282/T32J6GGK

Bangun, C. R., & Kumaralalita, N. (2022). Kim Seon Ho, you are cancelled: The collective understanding of cancel culture. *Jurnal Komunikatif, 11*(1), 1–10. https://doi.org/10.33508/jk.v11i1.3785

Beiner, A. (2020). *Sleeping woke: Cancel culture and simulated religion.* Medium. https://medium.com/rebel-wisdom/sleeping-woke-cancel-culture-and-simulated-religion-5f96af2cc107

Buckingham, D. (2008). Introducing identity: Youth, identity, and digital media. In D. Buckingham (Ed.), *Youth, identity, and digital media* (pp. 1–24). The MIT Press. https://doi.org/10.1162/dmal.9780262524834.001

Castells, M. (2005). The networked society: From knowledge to policy. In M. Castells & G. Cardoso (Eds.), *The network society: From knowledge to policy* (pp. 3–22). Center For Transatlantic Relations.

Choi, M., Cristol, D., & Gimbert, B. (2018). Teachers as digital citizens: The influence of individual backgrounds, internet use and psychological characteristics on teachers' levels of digital citizenship. *Computer & Education, 121*, 143–161. https://doi.org/10.1016/j.compedu.2018.03.005

Clark, D. M. (2020). DRAG THEM: A brief etymology of so-called "cancel culture". *Communication and the Public, 5*(3–4), 88–92. https://doi.org/10.1177/2057047320961562

Delgado, D. J. M., Oyedele, L., Beach, T., & Demian, P. (2020). Augmented and virtual reality in construction: drivers and limitations for industry adoption. *Journal of Construction Engineering and Management, 146*(7), 7 https://doi.org/10.1061/(ASCE)CO.1943-7862.0001844

Emejulu, A., & McGregor, C. (2019). Towards radical digital citizenship in digital education. *Critical Studies in Education, 60*(1), 131–147. https://doi.org/10.1080/17508487.2016.1234494

Flynn, D. J., Nyhan, B., & Reifler, J. (2017). The nature and origins of misperceptions: Understanding false and unsupported beliefs about politics. *Political Psychology, 38*(Suppl 1), 127–150. https://doi.org/10.1111/pops.12394

Frenda, S. J., Knowles, E. D., Saletan, W., & Loftus, E. F. (2013). False memories of fabricated political events. *Journal of Experimental Social Psychology, 49*(2), 280–286. https://doi.org/10.1016/j.jesp. 2012.10.013

Ghosn-Chelala, M. (2019). Exploring sustainable learning and practice of digital citizenship: Education and place-based challenges. *Education, Citizenship and Social Justice, 14*(1), 40–56. https://doi.org/10.1177/1746197918759155

Gleason, B., & von Gillern, S. (2018). Digital citizenship with social media: Participatory practices of teaching and learning in secondary education. *Journal of Educational Technology & Society, 21*(1), 200–212. http://www.jstor.org/stable/26273880

Hasan, H. R., & Salah, K. (2019). Combating deepfake videos using blockchain and smart contracts. *IEEE Access, 7*, 41596–41606. https://doi.org/10.1109/ACCESS.2019.2905689

Johnson, E. P. (2011). Queer epistemologies: Theorizing the self from a writerly place called home. *Biography, 34*(3), 429–446. http://www.jstor.org/stable/23541224

Jones, L. M., & Mitchell, K. J. (2016). Defining and measuring youth digital citizenship. *New Media & Society, 18*(9), 2063–2079. https://doi.org/10.1177/1461444815577797

Kato, B. (2021). *What is cancel culture? Everything to know about the toxic online trend.* The New York Post. https://nypost.com/article/what-is-cancel-culture-breaking-down-the-toxic-online-trend/

Kaufmann, E. (2022). The new culture wars: Why critical race theory matters more than cancel culture. *Social Science Quarterly, 103*(4), 773–788. https://doi.org/10.1111/ssqu.13156

Kim, M., & Choi, D. (2018). Development of youth digital citizenship scale and implication for educational setting. *Journal of Educational Technology & Society, 21*(1), 155–171. https://www.jstor.org/stable/26273877

Loh, R. S. M., & Lim, S. S. (2019). Youth digital culture. In R. Hobbs & P. Mihailidis (Ed. In Chief), G. Cappello, M. Ranieri, & B. Thevenin (Assoc. Ed.), *The International Encyclopedia of Media Literacy.* John Wiley & Sons.

Mossberger, K. (2008). Toward digital citizenship: Addressing inequality in the information age. In *Routledge handbook of Internet politics* (pp. 173-185). Routledge. Mossberger, K. (2008). Toward digital citizenship: Addressing inequality in the information age. In *Routledge handbook of Internet politics* (pp. 173-185). Routledge. https://doi.org/10.4324/9780203962541

Ng, E. (2020). No grand pronouncements here…: Reflections on cancel culture and digital media participation. *Television & new media, 21*(6), 621–627. https://doi.org/10.1177/1527476420918

Ohler, J. (2011). Digital citizenship means character education for the digital age. *Kappa Delta Pi Record, 47*(1), 25–27. https://doi.org/10.1080/00228958.2011.10516720

Özdemir, Z. (2015). Sosyal medyada kimlik inşasında yeni akım: Özçekim kullanımı. *Maltepe Üniversitesi İletişim Fakültesi Dergisi, 2*(1), 112–131.

Roos, A. S., & Rivers, D. J. (2017). Digital cultures of political participation: Internet memes and the discursive delegitimization of the 2016 US Presidential candidates. *Discourse, Context & Media, 16*, 1-11. https://doi.org/10.1016/j.dcm.2017.01.001

Sarıyar, H. (2019). *Dijital çağda kimliğin kavramsallaşması ve gerçeklik: Twitter parodi hesapları.* [Master's thesis, Marmara Üniversitesi Sosyal Bilimler Enstitüsü], İstanbul.

Shah, A. (2017). Ethnography? Participant observation, a potentially revolutionary praxis. HAU: *Journal of Ethnographic Theory, 7*(1), 45-59. http://dx.doi.org/10.14318/hau7.1.008

Subrahmanyam K., & Greenfield, P. (2008). Online communication and adolescent relationships: The Future of children. *Children and Electronic Media, 18*(1), 119-146. https://www.jstor.org/stable/20053122

Tandoc, E. C., Tan Hui Ru, B., Lee Huei, G., Min Qi Charlyn, N., Chua, R. A., & Goh, Z. H. (2024). #CancelCulture: Examining definitions and motivations. *New Media & Society, 26*(4), 1944–1962. https://doi.org/10.1177/14614448221077977

Vaccari, C., & Chadwick, A. (2020). Deepfakes and disinformation: Exploring the impact of synthetic political video on deception, uncertainty, and trust in news. *Social Media + Society, 6*(1). https://doi.org/10.1177/2056305120903408

Velasco, J. C. (2020). You are cancelled: Virtual collective consciousness and the emergence of cancel culture as ideological purging. *Rupkatha Journal on Interdisciplinary Studies in Humanities, 12*(5), 1–7. https://doi.org/10.21659/rupkatha.v12n5.rioc1s21n2

Vromen A. (2017). *Digital citizenship and political engagement. Interest groups, advocacy, and democracy series*. Palgrave Macmillan.

Walters, M. G., Gee, D., & Mohammed, S. (2019). A literature review: Digital citizenship and the elementary educator. *International Journal of Technology in Education (IJTE), 2*(1), 1–21. https://files.eric.ed.gov/fulltext/EJ1264251.pdf

Whyte, C. (2020). Deepfake news: AI-enabled disinformation as a multi-level public policy challenge. *Journal of Cyber Policy, 5*(2), 199–217. https://doi.org/10.1080/23738871.2020.1797135

Wojewidka, J. (2020). The deepfake threat to face biometrics. *Biometric Technology Today, 2020*(2), 5–7. https://doi.org/10.1016/S0969-4765(20)30023-0

Yue, A., Nekmat, E., & Beta, A. R. (2019). Digital literacy through digital citizenship: Online civic participation and public opinion evaluation of youth minorities in Southeast Asia. *Media and Communication, 7*(2), 100–114. https://doi.org/10.17645/mac.v7i2.1899

Dr. Bülent Sezgin

Chapter 6 Art-Game Based Learning in a Positive School Climate: A Discussion Framework

Abstract: For students and teachers, school is the most important socialization area where most of their lives are spent. Neo-liberal capitalism's excessive increase in the working hours of adults also causes the school hours of children and young people to increase excessively. Since autocratic school systems based on discipline and authority harm students and teachers, the concept of a positive school climate has begun to be discussed today.

In this book chapter, the sociological and pedagogical needs that develop the concept of a positive school climate will be examined and the pedagogical approaches of art and game-based learning will be discussed. Are art and games the reinforcing power of the dominant ideology or the transformative power of alternative education? How effective is the presence of art and play in the school environment? The effects of art and play on open-mindedness and critical thinking will be analyzed from a critical perspective.

Keywords: Art-based learning, game-based learning, positive school climate, neo-liberal education, critical pedagogy

In our world, which has evolved from the Anthropocene era to the digital surveillance society, we are in a time when the way of life of people is moving away from humanistic ideals and neo-liberal capitalism is having devastating effects on a global scale. As representatives of a generation marked by increasing pandemic outbreaks due to ecological disasters, we seek to understand the transformation in our lives. As an academician, artist, parent, and megacity citizen who is the author of this part of the book, I make post-humanist inquiries about my public and private life.

Most researchers advocating the critical paradigm in the field of social sciences write books, and articles and conduct numerous scientific studies to examine the effects of this transformation in different fields. When the negative socio-economic effects of neo-liberal policies are examined, it is seen that income inequality has increased worldwide and the polarization of economic power between countries has tended to become excessively rich and excessively impoverished. As the labor market and professions change due to migration population movements and ecological crises, and the professions evolve in the process of digitalization and artificial intelligence, there is data on both flexible working and precariatization in the post-pandemic world. The destructive effects of neo-liberal transformation are not only limited to institutions but also affect social relations, welfare levels and social relations (Harvey, 2007).

The effects of this transformation on education and learning communities; due to the increasing world population and income distribution inequalities; can be stated as the commercialization of education, increased school hours due to overwork of parents, inequalities in access to education, neglect of critical thinking and the spread of test-based exam-oriented systems. This change process also corresponds to the transformation of the Newtonian educational paradigm, the foundations of which were laid during the Industrial Revolution and nation-stabilization. To describe the new educational paradigms that emerged as a result of the transformations in the neo-liberal system after the 1990s, new concepts such as 21st-century skills, "homo economicus" human type (Cantekin, 2015) and quantum education (Garipağaoğlu, 2023) have emerged. It is noteworthy that there are many post-structuralist concepts in this style in literature.

In this part of the book, a critical review of art and play-based learning practices used in the fields of child, youth, and adult education as part of 21st century skills and positive school climate in the context of new educational debates will be made.

The Relationship Between 21st-Century Skills and Positive School Climate

Changes in the global economy after the 1970s caused nation-state systems to transform their education policies. The existence of transnational companies and global capital requires creative, flexible, and globally thinking individuals, and therefore the old Newtonian traditional education system is being questioned. The integration of national education systems, especially in the G-20 countries that constitute the ruling class, and the training of individuals who will defend the ideological needs of the neo-liberal economy have led to the transformation of old behavioral education paradigms.

One of the important concepts that we encounter in the field of neo-liberal education policies is the concept of 21st-century education skills and positive school climate. Equipping individuals with the capacity to compete in the global arena in line with the needs of the information society has become the subject of skills frameworks at different levels. The 21st century education skills framework is the sum of the skills that students need in both their education and professional lives, from pre-school to high school, accepted by the common consensus of companies and firms, educators, and politicians in the USA (Cansoy, 2018).

These skills have even begun to be included in educational curricula around the world, structured under headings such as life and career, learning and innovation, information and media, and technology.

The P21 skills set, developed for the changing needs of the economy, also emerged from the need to train people who can find solutions to the complex problems brought by globalization. 21st-century education skills are skills whose importance and necessity have been re-emphasized due to the new demands of knowledge-based economies in the current century (Levy & Murname, 2004; Rotherham & Willingham, 2009 cited in Çetin & Çetin, 2021). A framework for 21st century skills and competencies are related to life and career skills for students beyond academic career (Ball et al., 2016).

In this context, 21st-century competency skills are an important pedagogical framework that neo-liberal education policies need, especially in developed and developing countries. For these skills to be developed and effective, school culture must provide positive effects. In this context, the concept of positive school culture emerges within the educational management terminology.

The concept of positive school climate is a concept that describes the social, cultural, emotional, and academic atmosphere that affects all components of a school. This concept is not limited to physical and infrastructural needs but also includes common values and positive psychological effects of the community culture. It can be assumed that the development of a positive climate among teachers, students, administrators, parents, and school personnel at school will lead to the effective realization of 21st century competency skills.

To have a positive school culture, there must be a security and welfare environment, inclusive anti-discrimination practices, effective communication, participatory learning components, sustainability, and lifelong learning perspectives. Positive school culture consists of five main headings: safety, relationship, teaching and learning, institutional environment, and school improvement process (Thapa et al. 2013). Experts who research school climate draw attention to the relationship between positive school culture and socio-emotional learning. The National School Climate Council (2007) advocates that school climate is based on patterns of people's experiences of school life and reflects norms, goals, values, interpersonal relationships, teaching and learning practices, and organizational structures.

A sustainable, positive school climate fosters youth development and learning necessary for a productive, productive, and satisfying life in a democratic society. This includes climate norms, values, and expectations that support people feeling socially, emotionally, and physically safe. People are engaged and respected. Students, families, and educators work together to develop, live, and contribute to a shared school vision. Educators model and nurture an attitude that empha-sizes the benefits of, and satisfaction from, learning. Each person contributes to the operations of the school as well as the care of the physical environment (Thapa et al., 2013).

In conclusion, there is an important link between a positive school climate and 21st-century skills. The relationship between these two concepts is important in providing a more comprehensive learning experience by ensuring that students not only achieve academic success but also acquire skills such as strong com-munication, collaboration, critical thinking, and flexibility. However, it should not be forgotten that this dual correlation framework serves the new education policies needed by the neo-liberal economy. To have a positive school climate, there must be a democratic, egalitarian, and inclusive vision of education. For example, it is seen that developed Western countries attach more importance to a positive school climate in their schools, while simultaneously turning a blind eye to educational inequalities in underdeveloped countries. Even the fact that in some countries or in different schools within the borders of the same country, importance is given to anti-democratic and authoritarian education based on inequality shows us the class nature of the concept of a positive school climate. Therefore, it is essential not to overlook the socio-economic dimension of the concept of a positive school climate.

Art and Play-Based Learning Definition and Framework

Arts-based learning refers to a learning approach that includes elements of art and creativity, unlike traditional learning methods. This method uses various forms of art to provide students with knowledge and develop skills. Arts-based learning enables students to understand abstract concepts concretely and visu-ally through experiential learning. Arts-based learning, which includes the phi-losophy of learning by doing, generally includes dance, drama, music, visual arts, literature, and many art disciplines.

Transferring values through art and game-based learning has been a method used throughout history. In the ancient Greek period, after philosophers Aristotle and Plato analyzed the relationship between art and mimesis in their works called Poetics and State; It has been discussed whether art is a tool or an end. The fact that art is effective in teaching a concept, value or subject has been accepted in Ancient Greece, Rome, the Middle Ages, the Renaissance, and the modern periods. Plato's desire to use art in a utilitarian and formative manner for the sake of the survival of the state has caused discussions about art and free-dom throughout history.

Throughout history, state apparatuses have feared the liberating power of art and wanted to use art in a guided manner. It is known that education through art has been frequently used in the fields of language, religion, history, and values education throughout the world throughout history. For example, the church always used art as an educational method for religious propaganda in the Middle Ages, the Jesuit order for language education after the Renaissance period, and nation-states for history education during the early industrialization period of the 19th century.

The following issues regarding artistic production in the post-Renaissance period have been the most important discussion topics of researchers.

- Friedrich Schiller's (1954) defense of education through art against the alienation of modern people,
- After industrialization, John Dewey's (2008) idea of "Art as Experience "
- Peter De Bolla (2003) emphasizes that "art is a cognitive experience",
- Herbert Read's (1948) thesis that "art should be of primary importance in education"
- Gramsci's concept of "hegemony" (as cited in Martin, 1997)
- Louis Althusser's (1970/1971) claim that "art functions as one of the ideological devices of the state"
- Theses of the Frankfurt School (1923) on "art as a part of the culture industry" (as cited in Adorno, & Horkheimer, 1997).

Game-based learning is considered as an instinctive activity of humans and mammals (Rodriguez, 2006) and a cognitive activity of humans (Piaget, 1971). In the academic world, there are a wide range of studies from physical games to digital games, from games of chance to strategy games. Nowadays, game-based is used in every aspect of life. learning, play-based learning, and gamification applications are used.

Game-based learning refers to an approach that aims to promote learning by using game elements and game designs as an educational strategy. This method includes game dynamics, game design principles and game mechanics to provide students with knowledge and skills. Game-based learning aims to integrate game elements to make the learning process more effective, enjoyable, and participatory for students. It is seen that this concept, which has existed throughout history, is now defined as an educational strategy in the fields of child development and academic success. Game-based learning free-play in education systems and structured-controlled It is used within the scope of free time and curriculum activities within play patterns (Danniels & Payle, 2018).

Considering the discussions in this field; It seems that game-based learning is done mostly through controlled games today. It is known that children and young people's tendency to play games of their own free will has decreased, as free games have decreased worldwide due to the consumer society, the toy industry, and increasing digitalization. Neo-liberal education policies harm the free play areas of children and young people, and free play is negatively affected by unplanned urbanization, increasing population and migration movements, increasing school hours, and creating problems with school buildings.

In light of all this information, the effects of increasing controlled games and controlled game-based learning in terms of educational pedagogy also constitute topics of discussion. For example, when game-based learning is done in a controlled manner by adults such as teachers, academics, and educational leaders, what ideology will the possible learning gains serve? To what extent are the motivation, participation, and experientiality expected to be achieved through game-based learning possible in terms of controlled games? Can we ensure the liberation of children and young people through controlled play-based learning, without changing the banking education system based on the teacher and student hierarchy (Freire, 2020)? These and similar questions are important issues emphasized by those who criticize neo-liberal education.

P-21 and Positive Art and Game-based Learning in Terms of School Climate

When it comes to art and game-based learning, it can be said that the 21st-century competency skills framework has a direct attainment connection with the sub-headings of creativity, team spirit, cooperation, effective communication, risk-taking, cultural awareness, communication and problem-solving. Researchers, who emphasize the aspect of art in understanding the present and solving problems, emphasize that students are prepared for the future through art:

For students living in a rapidly changing world, the arts teach vital modes of seeing, imagining, inventing, and thinking. If our primary demand of students is that they recall facts, the children we educate today will find themselves ill-equipped to deal with problems like global warming, terrorism, and pandemics. "Those who have learned the lessons of the arts, however – how to see new patterns, how to learn from mistakes, and how to envision solutions – are the ones likely to come up with the novel answers needed most for the future" (Winner & Hetland, 2008).

The creativity acquisition required by the P 21 framework is parallel to the fact that art encourages students to think outside the box and discover new ideas. Critical thinking achievements are similar to the achievements of seeing the world from different perspectives and questioning the status quo in the artistic production process. The achievement of communication is equivalent to the achievement of establishing a dialogue with all segments of society through art.

Students' involvement in arts such as music, painting, drama, and dance produces positive results such as emotional relief, increased self-confidence, and sense of success, strengthening of attention and focus skills, and the ability to cope with difficulties and develop creative solutions.

When the International Baccalaureate program, which is valid all over the world, is examined, it can be easily seen that there are many similarities with 21st century skills. While the subjects in the arts allow a high degree of adaptability to different cultural contexts, the emphasis is on creativity in the context of disciplined, practical research into the relevant genres. In addition to this, each subject is designed to foster critical, reflective, and informed practice, help students understand the dynamic and changing nature of the arts, explore the diversity of arts across time, place and cultures and express themselves with confidence and competence. The aims of the DP arts subjects[1] (dance, film, music, theater, visual arts and literature and performance) are to enable students to:

➤ explore the diversity of the arts across time, cultures, and contexts.
➤ develop as imaginative and skilled creators and collaborators.
➤ express ideas creatively and with competence in forms appropriate to the artistic discipline.
➤ critical reflection on the process of creating and experiencing the arts.
➤ develop as informed, perceptive, and analytical practitioners.
➤ enjoy lifelong engagement with the arts[2].

The concepts of 21st-century education skills and a positive school climate should be coordinated with the ideas of the right to play and the game-oriented organization of free play times and breaks in schools. It is crystal clear that to have a positive school climate, "the right to play", which is one of the basic children's rights, must be protected. If children, young people, and adults have the right to play in school buildings throughout their education, it is possible to talk about a positive school climate. Games will help strengthen mutual communication

---

1 International Baccalaureate, accessed to 1 March 2024, https://www.ibo.org/program mes/diploma-programme/curriculum/the-arts/
2 International Baccalaureate, accessed to 2 March 2024, https://www.ibo.org/program mes/diploma-programme/curriculum/the-arts/theatre/

and sensory bonds between students, develop a sense of belonging, and increase teacher-student communication. It is known that students who relieve stress by releasing excess energy through games, relax psychologically, and establish social bonds with their friends will express themselves more easily. The development of winning and losing, competition, cooperation and teamwork in games will also increase the social commitment of students.

It is clear that fun learning, games and game-based learning should be used to support children to be creative, self-confident and motivated in a positive school climate. Researchers such as Caillous (2001) point out the importance of play in the formation of the creative individual type. Creative people often make incidental references to positive or playful moods and play with ideas when describing their work. Other scholars, such as Sternberg, O'Hara, and Lubart (1997), have also clearly emphasized that having fun is important for creativity. In previous discussions of creativity, many of the conditions that increase the generation of new ideas are precisely through play; conditions produced by playful play accompanied by a positive, joyful mood, especially those that foster divergent thinking and connecting previously unassociated thoughts. (Bateson & Martin, 2013)

Gray (2013), who has comprehensive analysis on games, emphasizes that encouraging playful activities increases creativity and problem-solving skills in children and makes it easier to solve logic problems. As a result, it has been emphasized in many publications and research that the positive effects of the game on the human body and soul contribute positively to the positive school climate (Gray, 2013).

Evaluation and Discussion

21st-century education skills, designed especially for developed countries in line with the needs of the neo-liberal economy, and the concept of positive school climate, which provides the infrastructure of this framework, are examined in detail in this section of the book. In the last section, a critical evaluation will be made of the two concepts examined in line with the data obtained from the literature reviews.

First of all, it should be emphasized that the 21st-century educational skills framework was created by the factors caused by globalization. This concept is not a humanistic and ideal pedagogy concept, on the contrary, it is quite pragmatic and arose as a result of the increasing need to cope with the ecological crisis, economic inequalities, crisis management, and uncertainties brought about by neo-liberal globalization. In a post-truth and post-modern world system, students need a flexible, adaptable, and enterprising individual type to cope with their future concerns, uncertainty, and despair. This type of individual should be an individual who lives a transitional life between countries with a transnational perspective, speaks more than one language and is integrated with technological infrastructure. Global citizenship and decentralization are also the basic perspectives of education. The rapid learning of digital competencies is also a result of changes in neo-liberal economics aimed at cost reduction, digital control and managing the ecological crisis. This situation has emerged again, especially in the world economy after the pandemic. It is known that individuals with 21st century education skills and knowledge of digital technology turned the crisis into an opportunity, while individuals stuck in the old education paradigm suffered serious economic and psychological damage. Especially in the field of art, it has once again been revealed how important adaptation skills are in experiencing widespread unemployment and psychological collapses after the pandemic.

The 21st century education skills framework provides very useful gains; it should also be questioned pedagogically because it ensures the reproduction of the dominant ideology. In this context, both the positive school climate environment and the purposes for which game and art-based learning should be used bring about an ethical debate for educators. In addition, factors such as practical application difficulties in terms of 21st century education skills, the existence of test-based measurement and evaluation systems, inequalities in access to technological resources and the resistance of teachers from traditional education are also a subject of criticism.

It is very important to question the "innovative" gains that are likely to be achieved through art and game-based learning within the ideological framework of 21st century educational skills. In order to facilitate this discussion, the following research questions were prepared by me.

➢ Can the educational gains that seem beneficial to be acquired through art and game-based learning in theoretical sources have an egalitarian pedagogical effect during practices?

➢ Artistic production based on free and democratic thought and the neo – liberal system based on inequality and discrimination?

➢ Will art and game-based learning practices, which seem rhetorically "innovative and egalitarian", be able to be democratic in the relationship between teacher and student hierarchy?

➢ While 21st century education skills and positive school climate are given great importance in developed countries of the world, why are these practices not given enough importance in underdeveloped countries?

➢ What kind of discussions are held about the pedagogical and political perspectives of education in universities, k-12 educational institutions, vocational courses, and non-governmental organizations where art and game-based learning training is provided?

In the light of these questions, I think that art and game-based learning is not a technical education but will be beneficial for humanity when done with perspective and philosophy. I have put forward a critical discussion framework based on the views put forward in this book chapter. I hope that field researchers who read this section will enrich the discussion with concrete data in the future and continue to touch the lives of students with art and games.

References

Adorno, T. W., & Horkheimer, M. (1997). The culture industry: Enlightenment as mass deception. In G. S. Nörr (Ed.), *Dialectic of enlightenment* (pp. 120–167). Verso.

Althusser, L. (1970). *Ideology and ideological state apparatuses (Notes towards an investigation)*. Monthly Review Press.

Ball, A., Joyce, H. D., & Anderson-Butcher, D. (2016). Exploring 21st century skills and learning environments for middle school youth. *International Journal of School Social Work, 1*(1), 1–15. https://doi.org/10.4148/2161-4148.1012

Bateson, P. G., & Martin, P. (2013). *Play, playfulness, creativity, and innovation.* Cambridge University Press.

Caillous, R. (2001). *Man, play and games.* University of Illinois Press

Cansoy, R. (2018). 21st century skills and their acquisition in the education system according to international frameworks. *Journal of Human and Social Sciences Research, 7*(4), 3112–3134.

Cantekin, D. F. (2015). Globalization and education: The transformation of the "Homo Economicus" view of education. *Academical Elegance, 2*(4), 43–72.

Çetin, M., & Çetin, G. (2021). A critical look at the MEB pre-school education program in terms of 21st century skills. *Education for Life, 35*(1), 235–255.

Danniels, E., & Pyle, A. (2018). Defining play-based learning. *Encyclopedia on Early Childhood Development* https://www.child-encyclopedia.com/play-based-learning/according-experts/defining-play-based-learning

De Bolla, P. (2003). *Art matters.* Harvard University Press.

Dewey, J. (2008). Art as experience. In H. Cannatella (Ed.), *The richness of art education* (pp. 33–48). Brill. https://doi.org/10.1163/9789087906092_003

Freire, P. (2020). Pedagogy of the oppressed. In *Toward a sociology of education* (pp. 374–386). Routledge.

Garipağaoğlu, B. Ç. (2023). Leading by becoming a learning organization in the age of quantum. In S. Dulay (Ed.), *Empowering educational leaders: How to thrive in a volatile, uncertain, complex, and ambiguous world* (pp. 115–134). Peter Lang.

Gray, P. (2013). *Free to learn: Why unleashing the instinct to play will make our children happier, more self-reliant, and better students for life.* Basic Books.

Harvey, D. (2007). *A brief history of neoliberalism.* Oxford University Press.

Levy, F., & Murnane, R. J. (2004). Education and the changing job market. *Educational leadership, 62*(2), 80. https://www.michiganassessmentcon sortium.org/wp-content/uploads/Mod1-Article-Education-and-the-Chang ing-Job-Market.pdf

Martin, J. (1997). Hegemony and the crisis of legitimacy in Gramsci. *History of the Human Sciences, 10*(1), 37–56. https://doi.org/10.1177/09526951970 1000103

National School Climate Council. (2007). The school climate challenge: Narrowing the gap between school climate research and school climate policy, practice guidelines and teacher education policy. Retrieved on https://schoolclimate. org/climate/advocacy.php

Piaget, J. (1976). Cognitive development in children: Piaget development and learning. *Journal of Research in Science Teaching, 2*, 176–186. https://doi.org/ 10.1002/tea.3660020306

Read, H. (1948). *Education through art.* Pantheon.

Rodríguez, H. (2006). The playful and the serious: An approximation to Huizinga's Homo Ludens. *Game Studies, 6*(1), 1604–7982. https://api.sema nticscholar.org/CorpusID:35755442

Schiller, F. (1954). *On the aesthetic education of man: In a series of letters* (E. M. Wilkinson & L. A. Willoughby, Trans., & Ed.). Oxford University Press.

Sternberg, R. J., O'Hara, L. A., & Lubart, T. I. (1997). Creativity as investment. *California Management Review, 40*(1), 8–21. https://doi.org/10.2307/ 41165919

Thapa, A., Cohen, J., Guffey, S., & Higgins-D'Alessandro, A. (2013). A review of school climate research. *Review of Educational Research, 83*(3), 357–385. https://doi.org/10.3102/0034654313483907

Winner, E., & Hetland, L. (2008). Art for our sake school arts classes matter more than ever-but not for the reasons you think. *Arts Education Policy Review, 109*(5), 29–32. https://doi.org/10.3200/AEPR.109.5.29-32

Dr. Burcu Erdemir

Chapter 7 A New Mindset in Teacher Education: A Case Study from Turkey

Abstract: Casting a comprehensive look at the transformative effects of the 21st century, the world has witnessed fast changing developments in technology that affected the way work being done in different sectors including educational systems. With these changing features, new roles and skills are being defined for students and educators. In this sense, teacher education programs have a serious responsibility in deciding what skills, knowledge and competencies teachers need to be endowed in their present era. Based on this understanding, this study aims to map out the kinds of skills and competences pre-service teachers in Turkey need to develop to prepare themselves and their future students to the challenges of the 21st century through document analysis method. The main findings were that, in the area of learning and innovation skills, the capacity of pre-service teachers range from competent to adequate; in terms of ICT skills, pre-service teachers use them in their life sufficiently though this is limited to the amount of time spent using them and the intention to use them; preservice teachers' competency is higher in life and career skills compared with others, and pre-service teachers have average interest and performance in any of the pillars of P21 21st century skills. Finally, teachers need to raise their awareness more about the efficient use of these skills, and more financial and academic support need to be given to preservice teachers so that they can practice especially technology related skills more.

Keywords: 21st century skills, technology, teacher education, pre-service teachers

Casting a comprehensive look at the transformative effects of the 21st century, the world has witnessed fast changing developments in technology that affected the way work is being done in different sectors including educational systems. With these changing features, new roles and skills have been defined for students and educators in different areas that will support their development and ease their compatibility with the transforming world. As the period from pre-school to higher education plays a great part in students' developmental process, teachers getting quality teacher education is highly important. In this sense, teacher education programs have a serious responsibility in determining what skills, knowledge and competencies teachers need to be endowed with in the present era.

As a list of 21st century skills have been announced globally through different organizations, the curricula of teacher training institutions have started to be updated to equip teachers with creative and critical thinking skills that include collaborative communication, digital literacy, and social mastery. Redmond (2016) suggests that knowledge, skills, and proficiency that individuals possess should be sufficient to enable their integration into the digital and globalized world. Tang and Chaw (2016) elaborated on the sufficiency of digital literacy as the mastery of not only knowing "*how to find information from the web*" but also "*the ability to understand and assemble information from different print or digital sources.*" (p. 56). In other words, 21st century skills are about applying the knowledge into different contexts and using it rather than keeping it in the memory (Silva, 2009; Valtonen et al., 2021) To be able to adapt to the swift changes ranging from socio-economic to political developments and necessities stemming from the globalized world, teachers of the 21st century need to prepare themselves against any kind of challenges.

Examining researchers' studies alongside government reports in Turkey, one can observe that since the beginning years of the Republic, teacher training has been one of the most important problems of the education system. The issue of training teachers for primary schools has especially been emphasized in every period. The idea of teacher training witnessed its best examples in the Turkish history with Village Institutes from 1940 to 1954. The main source of teacher training for secondary schools was the Three-Year Education Institutes and these schools existed under the name of Higher Teacher Training School between 1978 and 1982 (Öztürk, 2014). Teacher training for high schools was executed through Higher Teacher Training Schools and universities. Until 1982, although the task of training teachers was entirely given to the Ministry of National Education (MoNE), universities have been a significant source in teacher training. As of 1982, the duty of training teachers has been handled by education faculties of universities, with the establishment of the Council of Higher Education (CoHE).

One of the developments in teacher training has been the decision taken by the CoHE in 2010 where non-thesis master's programs were abolished and replaced with pedagogical formation education. Graduates attended paid pedagogical formation courses opened by universities and permitted by the CoHE. At present, with the February 20, 2014 decision of the MoNE Board of Education and Discipline, pedagogical formation education as well as non-thesis teacher training master's programs can be offered by universities (CoHE, 2023). Although teacher training has been an issue discussed throughout the years, some questions remain to be answered like; how candidate teachers will be selected for programs, what kind of a pre-service training will be given to candidates, how occupational and field education will be blended, what kind of an internship system needs to be created so that candidate teachers can get experience in real-life situations and how the quality and principles of in-service training should be

(Akdemir, 2013). As teachers are cornerstones in improving the quality of education, so teacher education needs to be given in a standard that competes with the one in the international arena and catch the developments of the 21st century. This is imperative to raise well-educated students of the future and a country with a powerful stance. Therefore, both faculties of education, professors and teacher trainers shoulder a great responsibility in the quality-training of pre-service teachers. The competencies of academics who provide teacher education are also of great importance.

There are both national and international reports and research on teacher competencies and teacher education. It is thought that examining these documents will be useful for teacher education, which constitutes an important area in the Turkish education system. Based on this understanding, this study aims to map out the kinds of skills and competences pre-service teachers in Turkey need to develop to prepare themselves and their future students for the challenges of the 21st century. The research questions that guided the study are as follows: "*What aspects of the present teacher education in Turkey remains to be inadequate in meeting the 21st century skills and competencies?*" and "*what kind of input and planning for teacher education in Turkey can help cope with the necessities of the 21st century?*"

Revisiting Teacher Education Based on the 21st Century Skills and Competencies

After the Covid-19 pandemic, globally, citizens had to deal with a long-lasting emergency period that brought uncertainties on many fronts including how different sectors would continue their lives, and if their economies and human resources capacities could survive out of this crisis or not. All these developments have made the goal of attaining a quality teacher education even more vital and necessitated restructuring the skills and competences of the 21st century based on changing needs of the evolving era. This era has also brought some unexpected circumstances like pandemics, earthquakes, or other natural disasters. Hence, there has arisen the need to view and plan the 21st century teacher education from a comprehensive perspective.

Various organizations have made their own categorizations to define 21st century skills by using different terminologies (Table 1). To start with, Partnership for 21st Century Learning (P21) is a platform founded in the United States of America in 2002 by gathering think tanks from the business world, educational leaders, and policy makers. It was formed around the idea of preparing students of the 21st century through a common vision that includes certain skills, abilities, knowledge, and competencies and helps students be successful in their work and everyday lives. The framework, Assessment and Teaching of 21st Century Skills (Griffin & Care, 2015), by bringing together researchers from more than 250 countries, aims to form skill-based class and curricula. Formed by The Metiri Group and The Learning Point Associates, EnGauge (2003) cooperates with North Central Regional Educational Laboratory (NCREL) and educational stakeholders to search new ways for the youth to learn better through web-based educational technology. Another foundation, International Society for Technology in Education (ISTE)'s standards form a guide for educators and leaders who believe in the power of technology in the transformation of education and teaching so that students can actualize themselves in work and life. They defined standards for both students and educators and these standards have been implemented by all the states in the United States of America and other countries all around the world (ISTE, n.d.). The National Assessment of Educational Progress (NAEP) prepared an assessment framework made up of 5 categories (Ruiz-Primo, 2009) to provide an independent, fair, cross-jurisdictional assessment of learning outcomes that also follow measurement trends over time (Shepard et al. 2020). American Association of School Librarians (AASL) decided on standards for students and learners in general, school librarians, and school libraries that offer an integrated framework (Inquire, Include, Collaborate, Curate, Explore, and Engage) combined with four domains and competencies (think, create share, grow) as well as application and assessment of 81 standards (AASL, 2018). The European Union (EU) and *Organization for Economic Co-operation and Development* (OECD) have also had some initiations to clarify 21st century skills and goals for learners (Kotluk & Kocakaya, 2015).

Table 1. 21st century Skills as Envisioned by Different Organizations.

P21	ATC21S	EnGauge	ISTE	NAEP	AASL	EU	OECD
Learning and innovation -Creativity, critical thinking, problem solving, communication and collaboration	**Ways of thinking** -Creativity and innovation -Critical thinking, problem solving, decision making -Leadership for learning, metacognition, communication and cooperation **Ways of working** -Communication -Cooperation (teamwork)	**Inventive thinking** -Adaptability, managing complexity and self-direction, -Curiosity, creativity and risk-taking -Higher-order thinking and sound reasoning **Effective communication** -Teaming, collaboration and interpersonal skills -Personal, social, and civic responsibility -Interactive communication	**Empowered learner** -Using technology to be competent in learning goals. **Knowledge constructor** -Critical analysis of resources via digital tools to form meaningful learning experiences **Innovative designer** -Using various technologies in a design process and finding new and useful solutions to problems. **This develops in parallel with the **Computational Thinker** as students develop strategies to solve problems and test solutions.	**Adaptability** -Dealing with unpredictable work situations -Learning work tasks, technologies, and procedures -Demonstrating interpersonal, cultural, physically oriented adaptability -Handling emergency situations and work stress **Non-routine problem solving** -Recognizing meaningful patterns -Diagnosing problems -Organizing information -Monitoring problem solving activities -Information gathering -Creating innovative and new solutions	**Inquire** Build new knowledge through inquiry, critical thinking, problem identification, and strategy development for problem solving. **Collaborate** Work effectively with others to broaden perspectives and work toward common goals. **Curate** Make meaning by collecting, organizing, and sharing resources of personal relevance.	Learning to learn, communication (in mother tongue), communication through a foreign language.	**Interaction with heterogeneous groups** -Building good relationships with others -Cooperation, working in teams -Conflict management and resolution

(continued on next page)

Table 1. Continued

P21	ATC21S	EnGauge	ISTE	NAEP	AASL	EU	OECD
Life-career skills -Flexibility and ability of adaptability, -Entrepreneurship and self-leadership, -Social and cross-cultural skills, -Productivity and accountability -Leadership and responsibility	**Life on Earth** -Global and local citizenship, -Life and career -Personal and social responsibility (cultural awareness and competence)	**High Productivity** - Prioritizing, planning, and managing for results -Effective use of real-world tools -Ability to produce relevant high-quality products	**Creative communicator** -Communicating clearly and creatively using different platforms, tools, formats, and digital media aligned with their goals. **Global communicator** - Using digital tools, enriching learning by collaborating and teamwork.	**Complex communication/ social skills** - Displaying custom communication -(Non)verbal information processing -Distilling, filling, in information **Self-management/ development** - Working autonomously - Being self-motivated and monitoring -Willingness in acquiring work-related skills and information	**Include** Demonstrate an understanding of and commitment to inclusiveness and respect for diversity in the learning community. **Explore** Discover and innovate in a growth mindset developed through experience and reflection.		**Behaving autonomously** -Moving in the bigger picture, -Forming life plans and personal projects and leading them -Defending and asserting rights
Information, media, and technology - Information, media and technology literacy	**Tools for working** -Information literacy -Information and communication technology literacy	**Digital Age Literacy** -Basic, scientific, economic, and technological literacies -Visual and information literacies -Multicultural literacy and global awareness	**Digital citizen** -Recognizing rights, responsibilities, opportunities in a digital world and learning safe, legal and ethical digital citizenship.	**Systems thinking** -Understanding the way systems work -Judging and decision-making -System analysis and evaluation	**Engage** Demonstrate safe, legal, and ethical creating and sharing of knowledge products, use of information technologies while engaging in a community of practice and in an interconnected world.	-Digital skills -Cultural awareness and expression -Social and citizenship competency -Entrepreneurship and initiative taking	**Interactive Use of Tools** -Interactive use of the language, symbols, and the text - Interactive use of knowledge ad information - Interactive use of technology

P21	ATC21S	EnGauge	ISTE	NAEP	AASL	EU	OECD
Core Subjects							
-English, reading or language arts							
-World language(s)							
-Arts							
-Mathematics							
-Economics							
-Science							
-Geography							
-History							
-Government /civics							
Interdisciplinary Themes							
-Global awareness							
- Financial, economic, business, and entrepreneurial literacy							
-Civic, health and environmental literacy							
-Learning and innovation skills							

Source: Adapted from AASL, 2018; Griffin & Care, 2015; EnGauge, 2003; ISTE, n.d.; Kotluk & Kocakaya, 2015; P21, 2019; Ruiz-Primo, 2009; Shepard et al., 2020 by the researcher

When the above suggested skills by various organizations are examined (Table 1), four common skills that come out are creativity, communication, cooperation, and knowledge and information technologies. Due to its multilateral examination of the 21st century skills and widespread use throughout the world, Partnership for 21st Century Learning (P21) system (P21, 2019) has been taken as the base to analyze teacher education system in Turkey. It is believed that some of these perspectives may be helpful to strengthen the Teacher Strategy of Turkey.

P21 aims to realize the necessary skills of the present era for every student from early learning to beyond school across the world. Although the movement started in the United States of America, Ohio, and has been applied in 21 states and supported by 33 institutions, it has been taken as an example by other countries and educational systems too. As teachers are the guides for students, first, practitioner teachers need to be equipped with the 21st century skills to help develop their students' related skills for the present century.

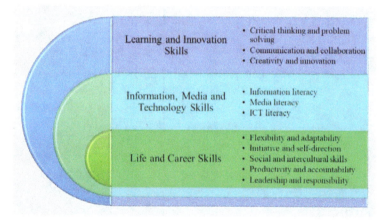

Figure 1. *21st Century Skill Components*
(Source: P21, 2019)

P21 grouped the skills under the three main pillars that represent learning outcomes (Figure 1) as well as support systems made up of "learning environments, classes and curricula, raising professionals and assessment and evaluation". The first pillar is "learning and innovation" that includes many sub skills like creativity and innovation, critical thinking and problem solving, and communication and collaboration. Each component in the model works in cooperation with each other during the learning and teaching processes. These are the basics to help make students get ready for the future. They aim to differentiate students who try to get prepared for the complicated 21st century work and life environments. The second pillar of P21 refers to "information, media and technology" that are about information, communications, and technology (ICT) literacy. In a world where there are many opportunities to access information, technological tools are rapidly changing and there is an increasing tendency to collaborate and contribute. Citizens and workers need to be able to create, evaluate, and effectively use information, media, and technology to be effective. The third pillar of P21 covers "life and career skills" that include flexibility and adaptability, initiative and self-direction, social and intercultural skills, productivity and accountability, leadership and responsibility. In the 21st century, students need to develop thinking skills, content knowledge and social-emotional competencies to exist in complex living and working environments.

P21, different than other organizations, also defined the main themes and core subjects that individuals need to adopt in the 21st century. While the key subjects are English, reading, or language arts, world languages, arts, mathematics, economics, science, geography, history, and government and civics, the 21st century interdisciplinary themes are; global awareness, financial, economic, business, and entrepreneurial literacy, civic literacy, health literacy, environmental literacy, learning and innovation skills. Curricula at universities should be revised based on this input and aim to help individuals exceed their main competencies.

Turkey's Teacher Strategy (2017–23), although it does not directly aim to cover the 21st century skills, still relates to those skills in the overall sense. The Strategy pointed out some core objectives as *building a group of well-trained and professionally qualified teachers; ensuring ongoing personal and professional development*; and *improving societal perceptions and status of the profession* (The MoNE, 2017), which were also integrated into the 2023 Turkey's Education Vision (MoNE, 2018). While OECD also encouraged these objectives, it additionally suggested that these competencies be adapted in curricula, and all parts of the teaching profession (Kitchen et al., 2019). Due to its membership to the United Nations (UN), Turkey's also has to fulfill its responsibility about inclusivity and equity-related educational goals (SDG 4 and 10) that have been set in the 2030 Agenda (*The United Nations Educational, Scientific and Cultural Organization*-UNESCO, 2017). Although it is not only teachers' responsibility, one of the most effective and successful ways to implement these SDGs is to provide a quality teacher training that includes the related goals.

Gelen (2017) refers to the initiation of the MoNE in 2017–18 academic year to integrate the 21st century skills to curricula in the lower levels of education. However, he criticizes this initiative as when compared with the P21, in the renewed education program, the pattern for the basic skills, common values, content, and assessment and evaluation dimensions were not formed adequately, lacked integrity and certainty in explanations, and were not fully associated with the learning outcomes. Although the attempt of this integration seems not so successful, this can be thought as an initial step and the deficiencies can be corrected by further planning. A similar action should be taken by faculty members by juxtaposing their curricula with the 21st century skills framework for better adaptation of students to the present digital and fast-changing age.

To conclude, education of skillful and competent teachers is pivotal to cope with the realities of the 21st century and possible emergencies. This starts from a meticulous selection process of talented and ambitious teachers and training them to gain relevant qualifications. It can best be done by following both national and international standards and ensuring that they are being implemented.

Methods

In order to find the extent to which present teacher education programs make use of 21st century skills in Turkey, systematic review was followed. Towards this aim, review of the grey literature made up of reports, circulars and strategy papers of the national state organizations and international non-governmental organizations, as well as articles from peer-reviewed journals and related organizational websites were made use of. This review article has been subjected to the processes of data collection, deciding about exclusion and inclusion criteria, and data analysis (Çınar, 2021). "A systematic review attempts to bring together all available evidence on a specific, clearly defined topic" (Charrois, 2015). The reliability of the study was ensured with the steps followed below.

Initially, the main research problem was decided as the issues in teacher education programs in Turkey and the extent to which they have been adapted to the 21st century skills. Accordingly, two research questions were formed. The first research sought answers to the main research problem and the second research question focused on the resolutions developed for the main problem.

Based on the inclusion criteria, national state documents, reports, peer reviewed journals and international reports of non-governmental organizations and articles that examine issues in teacher education programs and adoption of 21st century skills in those programs. The sources were sought with the key words of "21st century skills and competences", "pre-service teachers" and "teacher education programs" in Turkey. To map out the present issues in teacher education programs in Turkey, last five-year's documents were taken as the main sources of reference but some older sources with necessary information were also included in fewer numbers.

The data were evaluated through document analysis method, which is defined as a technique to gather data with the aim of searching, reading, and taking notes on documents, and finally evaluating them (Karasar, 2016). To check reliability, Ravitch and Carl (2019)'s suggested steps have been followed. First "credibility" was obtained by gathering data from multiple resources like books, state documents, articles published in peer-reviewed journals, and reliable online sources. Second, to ensure "transferability", sufficient contextual information was provided for other researchers to be able to relate to the topic, and lastly, to achieve "confirmability" objective analyses were tried to be made out of the cited sources, to enable other researchers to derive similar outcomes.

Results

The aim of this study is to examine the kinds of skills and competences pre-service teachers in Turkey need to possess to equip themselves and their future students against the challenges of the 21st century. Regarding this aim, the study was guided by the following research questions: "*what aspects of the present teacher education in Turkey remains to be inadequate in meeting the 21st century skills and competencies?*" and "*what kind of input and planning for teacher education in Turkey can help it cope with the necessities of the 21st century?*" Below can be found the findings under two titles in parallel with the two research questions. The findings were structured based on the three-pillars of the P21 21st century framework that have already been explained in the literature review section.

Present Situation of Teacher Education in Turkey Regarding the Implementation of the 21st Century Skills

Referring to the "first research question", taking the 21st century skills and competencies as a reference point, while Turkish pre-service teachers possess certain skills, they still need to improve some others. The first pillar is made up of "learning and innovation skills" (e.g. creativity and innovation, critical thinking and problem solving, communication, collaboration). Pertaining to this category, in Karakoyun and Lindberg (2020)'s study, pre-service teachers perceived the second most necessary 21st century skills as problem-solving and critical thinking. Aktaş (2022), based on mathematics and science pre-service education teachers' views, concluded that pre-service teachers had an average skill level on "learning" and what he calls "entrepreneurship". Erten (2019), on the other hand, in her study with 243 pre-service teachers from different departments concluded that students had enough level of learning and innovation skills, which presents a similar result with that of Aydın and Şişman (2021)'s study where students felt competent especially in the technology literacy skill. Kozikoğlu and Altunova (2018) found that pre-service teachers in Education Faculty who had a tendency for life-long learning were also the ones who wanted to have a graduate education. This also proves the desire of tomorrow's teachers to improve their learning skills in a continuous fashion. Saavedra and Opfer (2012) suggested that the use of different ways of technology integrated into teaching will also help improve students' problem solving and critical thinking skills, referring to the sub-skills in this first pillar. Göktalay and Özeke (2015)'s study findings reflect that learning and innovation skills were covered in teacher education programs from the 1st to the 4th grades through the courses of entrepreneurship, project development and management, youth projects development, computer literacy, and creative drama. In brief, as the level of practicing learning and innovation skills among pre-service teachers seems to range from average to good, based on the literature that was accessed, this area can be given more attention by providing more opportunities for learners to improve themselves, as can be seen in the latter example above. The interesting finding among all competencies was that "collaborative" skills did not cover an important space among the skill set of Turkish pre-service teachers unlike the findings stated in international literature such as the one about Finnish teachers, where it was an important part of the teacher education process (Valtonen et al., 2021).

For the second pillar, ICT (e.g. information, technology and media literacy), Aktaş (2022), based on mathematics and science pre-service education teachers' views, concluded that pre-service teachers have a high level of ICT skills. Erten (2019) found that pre-service teachers, 42 % of whom were not coming from information and technology-related fields, believed they had satisfactory level of ICT skills. Demirli (2013) compared pre-service teachers' level of ICT usage in Turkey and Bosnia and Herzegovina and stated that while the increase in knowledge, attitude and the duration of internet use went in parallel with the ICT integration in learning and teaching, cultural difference was also a factor to determine the use of ICT. For both countries, the researcher indicated positive attitude towards ICT usage. Kozikoğlu and Altunova (2018), on the other hand, indicated a low-level relationship between life-long learning tendencies of pre-service teachers, and information, media and technological skills. Dinçer (2018) stated about primary, middle and high school teachers, and Akayoğlu et al. (2020) about pre-service English Language teachers that they were competent enough to use many digital tools both for their personal and professional needs. These included, for the latter, using their creativity, critical thinking skills and collaborative abilities. Akayoğlu et al. also noted that if professors, with the role model image they constitute make use of digital tools in their classes, this can contribute to the improvement of students' digital literacy levels. Similarly, Ataberk and Mirici (2022), who examined ELT courses at some universities in Turkey found through student comments that while some courses such as "material development using technology"; "critical thinking", "oral communication", "critical reading and writing" were adapted to the 21st century skills of learning and innovation, life and career, and media and technology, other courses such as "reading and listening, skills and literature" that were dominantly executed as lectures were not adapted to the related skills. This, the writers suggested, caused students to master only certain skills and remain weak in others. In Göktalay and Özeke (2015)'s study, ICT courses presented to pre-service teachers were computer literacy, teaching science and technology, instructional technologies and material design, computer programming languages, and graphics and animation in education. These findings suggest that although students and teachers were not bad at adapting ICT skills into their learning processes, the fostering effect of the intention to use them, the level of knowledge and the attitude of faculty in using ICT themselves in classes and adapting their courses to the 21st century skills were also effective in students' development. Thus, this should be taken into consideration both by students to be autonomous learners and faculty to appeal to students' needs.

Finally, the third pillar, "life and career skills" (e.g. flexibility and adaptability, initiative and self-direction, social and cross-cultural skills, accountability, leadership). Kozikoğlu and Altunova (2018) stated that there existed an average-level significantly positive relationship between pre-service teachers' learning and innovation skills, and life and career skills, which suggests that they made use of the skills in this pillar in their (non)academic lives. Aydın and Şişman (2021), who conducted their study on pre-service teachers explained that students felt most competent in respecting different views and beliefs under cross-cultural skills component, in being entrepreneurs categorized under career skills, and in using the time efficiently examined under life skills component. Aktaş (2022), based on mathematics and science pre-service education teachers' views, briefed that pre-service teachers had a very high level of competency on the third pillar as career skills. In one of the state universities, the courses that were related to life and career skills in teacher education programs were composed of courses such as community service, project development and management, youth projects development and entrepreneurship, and were offered to 2nd–4th year students (Göktalay & Özeke, 2015). In general, it seems that pre-service teachers, with the help of the courses they were provided with, have become more competent in skills mentioned in this pillar compared to the other two.

Overall, for the first pillar of learning and innovation skills, students either intended to do better or had average level of success. For the second pillar of ICT, the skill level ranged from adequate to high, and students' intention, duration of internet use and knowledge levels were important factors to influence learning and teaching, as well as instructors' setting an example in the implementation of ICT skills in their courses. As for the third pillar of life and career skills, pre-service teachers displayed a much more satisfactory performance. Hence, it can be concluded that it is not enough and fair to expect students to do something to improve their 21st century skills, as professors too need to take action like integrating those, professors too must integrate those skills into their curricula. Namely, Aydın and Şişman (2021) put forth that, student teachers in their study believed 21st century skills could be seen respectively more in their field education courses (40 % of students), occupational knowledge courses (20 % of students) and cultural courses (10 % of students). These low levels of percentages indicate the insufficient importance given to the integration of all courses into 21st century skills. This is a pity because using 21st century skills in classes by instructors will not only ease students' understanding of the coverage of those skills but also help students learn how to integrate them into any topic they study.

Suggestions to Integrate 21st Century Skills and Competencies into Teacher Education Programs in Turkey

As an answer to the "second research question", some implications are presented below that are aligned with the 21st century learning goals fitted into the three main pillars of the P21 framework.

For "learning and innovation skills" that include many sub skills like creativity, critical thinking, problem solving and communication, considering the changing and developing countries, Arslan and Eraslan (2003) pointed out the importance of raising a teacher model that has good communication skills, that learns how to learn and knows how to access information, internalize it and produce new knowledge and share it. Akdemir (2013) suggested that to improve teachers' occupational skills and abilities, both national and international experience opportunities should be provided. In Karakoyun and Lindberg (2020)'s study, the fact that pre-service teachers put using problem-solving and critical thinking skills in the second most important place may be associated with the prevalent traditional way of teaching in classes in Turkey, or as Sağlam and Büyükuysal (2013) stated, with teaching and curricula based on memorization. Referring to the development of problem-solving skills, it was suggested that pre-service teachers are taught how to deal with migration-related diversity (Bischoff et al., 2016). This can be specifically important in the Turkish context as Turkey has been hosting an influx of forced migrants since 2011, especially Syrians, and most teachers have been experiencing difficulties handling issues that come up in classrooms ranging from academic to language problems (Erdemir, 2022).

For the second pillar of "ICT skills" that is about information, media and ICT literacy, Akayoğlu et al. (2020) pointed out an inevitable need for pre-service teachers to be digitally literate, a part from knowing how to use present technological tools; they need to develop a critical eye in using those tools safely, efficiently and wisely. They also suggested pre-service teachers develop the ability to adapt the existing digital input to suit their own context, which will help them throughout their future careers. Additionally, researchers believed the importance of integrating social media platforms into the curricula as this may benefit learners further in their professional development. Akdemir (2013) clarified that supervision and encouragement should be provided to address teacher candidates' reluctance to use new technologies during their pre-service and in-service education, and opportunities about technology and project design should be presented that can enhance their vision with the support of cooperative contributions of universities and the MoNE.

Finally, about "life and career skills", Tutkun and Aksoyalp (2010), based on a multicultural 21st century environment, suggested that teacher training programs should not educate students as robots that implement imposed plans and programs. It is because only teachers with professional autonomy can teach learners how to be self-confident and autonomous learners and have a direct contribution to the society and shape it. They added that raising the professional status of teachers in society in which they will provide education will allow them to have a respectable status, and that teachers should also be prepared for development, change and possible risks they may come across in the new era. The other important suggestion is about the cultural development of teachers, which is not a new issue. Wiggins and Follo (1999) and Darling-Hammond (1996), even in the previous century, stressed the necessity for teachers to practice teaching in environments that include students from diverse cultural backgrounds and get support from other teachers that are already experienced teaching in multicultural settings. Similarly, Kostner (2016), emphasized the importance for candidate teachers to practice necessary skills that will enable them to welcome diversity and know how to treat students with considerable diversity.

Discussion

This review study explored the aspects of the present teacher education in Turkey that remain to be inadequate in meeting the 21ˢᵗ century skills and competencies. It also sought suitable kinds of input and planning to overcome inadequacies of students and help them cope with the challenges of the 21ˢᵗ century. Overall, pre-service teachers in Turkey in different departments displayed a good level of success in understanding and implementing 21ˢᵗ century skills.

More specifically, for the first research question, while some Turkish pre-service teachers felt competent in "learning and innovation skills" such as creativity, critical thinking and problem solving, collaboration and communication, some others remained at average level. Yılmaz (2020), in his mixed method study with pre-service teachers found that teachers' gradual exposure to technology enabled them to improve their critical and creative thinking skills as well as academic achievements. A part from this, the fact that collaborative skills do not take place much in the present literature for Turkish pre-service teachers, can be related to the education system in Turkey that does not prioritize collaboration. This can also be associated with the cultural structure of the country that in academia, some faculty prefer to study individually although this is not appreciated by other colleagues (Erdemir, 2023). This is different in the international literature, where Finnish teacher education puts great emphasis on collaborative work (Valtonen et al., 2021).

For the second pillar of "ICT skills", there exists comparably more research as teachers from different nations perceive the most important skill of the 21ˢᵗ century to be ICT skills. Although pre-service teachers in Turkey presented a satisfactory profile in terms of using ICT skills, as the second pillar of P21 framework, there is still the necessity to spare more time using them to become more competent, and learn more about new technologies more. This finding in Turkey has been mentioned in the international literature as well that teachers lack competence and have prominent beliefs that prevent them from integrating technology into their classes (O'Neal et al., 2017; Wachira & Keengwe, 2011). This can be related to the inadequate physical infrastructure at universities as well as the low socio-economic status of students.

As revealed in this study, adaptation of courses into 21ˢᵗ century skills by faculty has not been done fully, which puts students in disadvantaged positions. This finding is in parallel with the one in Aydın and Şişman (2021)'s study. Since students can learn better in technology-integrated environments, the use of ICT in classrooms is of vital importance (Ghavifekr & Wan Athirah, 2015). Therefore, pre-service teachers need to be presented with more opportunities to use new technology in classes and guided more about ICT skills. Evaluation of those digital literacy skills should also be based on a framework. This suggests responsibility for HEIs (Tondeur et al., 2017) and teacher training programs at universities (Kirschner et al., 2009) to guide students in getting equipped with the necessary skills, as especially the latter can help raise students' self-perception about their capabilities (Gudmundsdottir & Hatlevik, 2018). Professors at universities also need to possess a certain digital literacy level and be able to use them with pedagogical knowledge (Valtonen et al., 2017).

Compared with the other two pillars, "life and career skills" such as adaptability, accountability, social and cross-cultural skills, and productivity that form the third pillar constitute a more favorable place among Turkish pre-service teachers. This can be explained with cultural factors as Turkey is known to host many cultures that enable its citizens to develop their skill of empathizing with people from different cultures and developing a welcoming attitude towards them. Besides, due to their occupational predisposition, i.e. the need to get to know different students frequently and building good relationships with them can also help teachers to be competent in this area. Similarly, in a study conducted with Asian teachers, from the perspectives of teachers, their supervisors and students, teachers both teachers', their supervisors' and students', teachers were "very competent" (i.e. highly successful in performing instructional and other duties in teaching) in facilitating learners' life and career skills, as one of the highest competencies among others (Real, 2022). On the accountability dimension, it is important to underline that since the 21st century skills have not been adopted fully in neither of the education levels, the future steps should take their roots from "research-based standards" and "validated measures" to ensure quality, as suggested by Mayer (2013).

Implications

Examining the 21st century skills and competencies literature, specifically based on the P21 skills set, the overall analysis would be that, the performance of Turkish pre-service teachers in any of the three pillars is not distinctively better than the others, except slight differences. Therefore, a thorough planning needs to be done if visible changes in the performances of students towards new skills adoption are wanted to be observed. To serve this aim, some implications for decision makers and faculty are suggested below.

Firstly, a more specific picture of the human model that is targeted than the one drawn in Turkey's Teacher Strategy (2017–13) should be explained by the MoNE. The one given in the Strategy expressed with the following words seems vague and subjective: "...*well-trained and professionally qualified teachers*" (what is meant by well-trained and qualified exactly?), "...*ongoing personal and professional development*" (what kind of development is expected and with what kinds of input or support these are planned to be improved?); and "*improving societal perceptions and status of the profession*" (what is the societal perception, what can be done to improve that and towards which direction exactly; what kind of a status is envisioned for the profession and how can it be achieved?).

Secondly, HE level seems to be a bit late for certain skills to be adopted; hence, investments need to be made starting from the lower levels of education for certain behavior patterns and mindset in students to be internalized and become habitual. For this, the structure of the education system as a whole, including curricula, learning environments, specific student and teacher model needs to be reorganized to decide the kinds and extent of changes wanted to be achieved at each level of education. To do that, as a start, international models in other countries can be examined and adapted to the specificities of the Turkish education system and cultural dynamics.

Thirdly, at the HE level, different than other departments and fields, in choosing candidate teachers, tests to determine skills and abilities can be given to detect more suitable candidates to raise the students of the future. Once students are in the teacher education system, in order to improve their problem-solving skills, students should be exposed to real-life classroom issues apart from their teaching practices. In addition, pre-service teacher education needs to be supported financially by the CoHE in terms of making them familiarized with the new digital technology. As mentioned before, research indicated that not all students have the interest in using and integrating digital tools into their learning. However, disintegration may not only stem from the lack of interest but also low socio-economic background of students. Therefore, new technology should be provided at last for the common use of students at universities, if not for their individual/private use.

Fourthly, faculty themselves should be familiar with the new technology and integrate them into their classes as much as possible, not only to make the learning process richer and enable students practice new technologies but also to set as role models to students in terms of how and where to integrate them into the lessons.

Conclusion

Developments, technological inventions, and innovations in the world and in our country require many elements of life to be reviewed. In this respect, it is necessary to determine various standards or competencies in order for trained teachers to have the desired and appropriate characteristics for our age. Along this line, this study, through review method examined the grey literature as well as articles published in peer-reviewed journals with the aim of detecting the kinds of skills and competences preservice teachers in Turkey need to possess to face the challenges of the 21st century.

The findings indicated that in the area of "learning and innovation skills" the capacity of pre-service teachers ranged from competent to adequate. In terms of "ICT skills", pre-service teachers used them in their life sufficiently though this was limited to the amount of time spent using them and the intention to use them. Preservice teachers were more competent in "life and career skills" compared with the other two skills. Overall, literature indicated that pre-service teachers were not very good or very bad in performance teachers indicated an average performance and interest related to the P21 pillars of the 21st century skills. Hence, more awareness needs to be raised on the part of teachers about the efficient use of these skills and more financial and academic support need to be given to preservice teachers so that they can practice especially technology related skills more.

Researchers who would like to study this topic in the future may further may want to explore further the specific actions to take in teacher training programs to improve students' 21st century skills and competencies. Additionally, experimental research can be conducted to find out the extent to which pre-service teachers are ready to overcome the challenges of the new era for all competencies. Researchers may also want to collect data from the seven regions of Turkey and conduct in-depth interviews with pre-service teachers and faculty to explore their ideas, willingness, and capacities in incorporating 21st century framework into their learning and teaching processes. A mixed method approach can put forth a more precise picture of the remaining input that is to be presented to students and necessary planning to be done by teacher education programs with the support of decision makers such as the CoHE. This will enable a stronger and a more sustainable base to be formed for the economic, political, and scientific future of the country and support its presence in the international arena as well.

References

Akayoglu, S., Satar, H. M., Dikilitas, K., Cirit, N. C., & Korkmazgil, S. (2020). Digital literacy practices of Turkish pre-service EFL teachers. *Australasian Journal of Educational Technology*, 36(1), 85–97. https://doi.org/10.14742/ajet.4711

Akdemir, A. S. (2013). Türkiye'de öğretmen yetiştirme programlarının tarihçesi ve sorunları. *Turkish Studies, 8*(12), 15–28. http://dx.doi.org/10.7827/Turkish Studies.5706

Aktaş, İ. (2022). Examination of 21st-century skills of pre-service teachers in terms of various variables. *Journal of Interdisciplinary Educational Research, 6*(12), 187–203.

AASL. (2018). *AASL standards framework for learners.* American Library Association. https://standards.aasl.org/wp-content/uploads/2017/11/AASL-Standards-Framework-for-Learners-pamphlet.pdf

Arslan, M. M., & Eraslan, L. (2003). *Yeni eğitim paradigması ve Türk eğitim sisteminde dönüşüm gerekliliği. Milli Eğitim Dergisi, 160.* https://dhgm.meb.gov.tr/yayimlar/dergiler/milli_egitim_dergisi/160/arslan-eraslan.htm

Ataberk, B., & Mirici, İ. H. (2022). An investigation of the 21st century skills in English language teaching programs in Turkey. *International Online Journal of Education and Teaching, 9*(4), 1513–1544.

Griffin, P., Care, E. (2015). The ATC21S Method. In: Griffin, P., Care, E. (eds) Assessment and Teaching of 21st Century Skills. Educational Assessment in an Information Age. Springer, Dordrecht. https://doi.org/10.1007/-978-94-017-9395-7_1

Aydın, A., & Şişman, G. T. (2021). 21st century skills in pre-service English teacher education. *The Journal of Turkish Educational Sciences, 19*(2), 1223–1251. https://doi.org/10.37217/tebd.975533

Bischoff, S., Edelmann, D., & Beck, M. (2016). Students with a migration background in teacher education: A potential or a challenge? Insights into the DIVAL research project at the University of Teacher Education St. Gallen. In B. Kürsteiner, L. Bleichenbacher; R. Frehner, A. M. Kolde (Eds.) *Teacher education in the 21ˢᵗ century: A focus on convergence* (pp. 66–88). https://phrepo.phbern.ch/id/eprint/951

Charrois, T. L. (2015). Systematic reviews: What do you need to know to get started? *The Canadian Journal of Hospital Pharmacy, 68*(2), 144–148. https://doi.org/10.4212/cjhp.v68i2.1440

Çınar, N. (2021). İyi bir sistematik derleme nasıl yazılmalı? [How should a good systematic review be written?] *Online Turkish Journal of Health Sciences, 6*(2), 310–314. https://doi.org/10.26453/otjhs.888569

Darling-Hammond, L. (1996). What matters most: A competent teacher for every child. *Phi Delta Kappan, 78* (3), 193–200. https://www.proquest.com/scholarly-journals/what-matters-most-competent-teacher-every-child/docview/218472535/se-2

Demirli, C. (2013). ICT usage of pre-service teachers: Cultural comparison for Turkey and Bosnia and Herzegovina. *Educational Sciences: Theory and Practice, 13*(2), 1095–1105.

Dinçer, S. (2018). Are preservice teachers really literate enough to integrate technology in their classroom practice? Determining the technology literacy level of preservice teachers. *Education and Information Technologies, 23*(6), 2699–2718. https://doi.org/10.1007/s10639-018-9737-z

EnGauge (2003). *EnGauge 21ˢᵗ century skills: Literacy in the digital age.* NCREL and Metiri Group. www.ncrel.org/engauge

Erdemir, B. (2022). Higher education policies for the Syrian refugees in Turkey: Opportunities and challenges. In A. W. Wiseman (Ed.), *2021 Annual review of comparative and international education* (*International Perspectives on Education and Society*) (pp. 185–205). Emerald Publishing. https://doi.org/10.1108/S1479-36792022000042A015

Erdemir, B. (2023). Sustainability of higher education in emergencies: The case of Turkey. *Opus Journal of Society Research, 20* (Special Issue-Human Behavior and Social Institutions), 751–769. https://doi.org/110.26466//opusjsr.1344652

Erten, P. (2019). Öğretmen adaylarının 21. yüzyıl becerileri yeterlilik algıları ve bu becerilerin kazandırılmasına yönelik görüşleri. *Milli Eğitim, 49*(227), 33–64. https://dergipark.org.tr/tr/pub/milliegitim/issue/56322/778233#article_cite

Gelen, İ. (2017). P21-program ve öğretimde 21. yüzyıl beceri çerçeveleri (ABD uygulamaları) *Disiplinlerarası Eğtim Araştırmaları Dergisi, 1*(2), 15–29. https://dergipark.org.tr/tr/download/article-file/386403

Ghavifekr, S., & Wan Athirah, W. R. (2015). Teaching and learning with technology: Effectiveness of ICT integration in schools. *International Journal of Research in Education and Science, 1*(2), 175–191. https://files.eric.ed.gov/fulltext/EJ1105224.pdf

Göktalay, Ş. B., & Özeke, S. (2015). Essential skills for 21ˢᵗ century teachers in Turkey: Uludag University example. *E-Pedagogium, 15*(2), 100–110. https://doi.org/10.5507/epd.2015.020

Gudmundsdottir, G. B., & Hatlevik, O. E. (2018). Newly qualified teachers' professional digital competence: Implications for teacher education. *European Journal of Teacher Education, 41*(2), 214–231. https://doi.org/10.1080/02619768.2017.1416085

ISTE. (n.d.). *Standards.* https://iste.org/standards

Karakoyun, F., & Lindberg, O. J. (2020). Preservice teachers' views about the twenty-first century skills: A qualitative survey study in Turkey and Sweden.

Education and Information Technologies, 25, 2353–2369. https://doi.org/10.1007/s10639-020-10148-w

Karasar, N. (2016). *Bilimsel irade algı çerçevesi ile bilimsel araştırma yöntemi: Kavramlar, ilkeler, teknikler [Scientific research method with scientific perception framework: Concepts, principles, techniques]* (31st ed.). Nobel

Kirschner, P., Wubbels, T., & Brekelmans, M. (2009). Benchmarks for teacher education programs in the pedagogical use of ICT. In J. Voogt & G. Knezek (Eds.), *International handbook of information technology in primary and secondary education* (pp. 435–447). Springer.

Kitchen, H., Bethell, G., Fordham, E., Henderson, K., & Li, R. R. (2019). *OECD Reviews of evaluation and assessment in education: Student assessment in Turkey.* OECD. https://doi.org/10.1787/5edc0abe-en

Kotluk, N., & Kocakaya, S. (2015). Digital storytelling for developing 21st century skills: From high school students' point of view. *Journal of Research in Education and Teaching, 4*(2), 354–363.

Kostner, S. (2016). Teaching and learning diversity: Making (higher) education more accessible and equitable. In B. Kürsteiner, L. Bleichenbacher, R. Frehner, A. M. Kolde (Eds.), *Teacher education in the 21ˢᵗ century: A focus on convergence.* (pp. 40–65). https://phrepo.phbern.ch/id/eprint/951

Kozikoğlu, İ., & Altunova N., (2018). Öğretmen adaylarının 21. yüzyıl becerilerine ilişkin öz-yeterlik algılarının yaşam boyu öğrenme eğilimlerini yordama gücü. *Yükseköğretim ve Bilim Dergisi/Journal of Higher Education and Science, 8*(3), 522–531. https://doi.org/10.5961/jhes.2018.293

Mayer, D. (2013). Policy driven reforms and the role of teacher educators in reframing teacher education in the 21ˢᵗ century. *Waikato Journal of Education, 18*(1), 7–19. https://doi.org/10.15663/wje.v18i1.133

O'Neal, L. J., Gibson, P., & Cotten, S. R. (2017). Elementary school teachers' beliefs about the role of technology in 21st-century teaching and learning. *Computers in the Schools, 34*(3), 192–206. https://doi.org/10.1080/07380569.2017.1347443

Öztürk, C. (2014). Türkiye Cumhuriyeti'nde eğitim. In M. Şişman (Ed.). *Eğitim tarihi.* Anadolu Üniversitesi Yayınları.

P21. (2019). *Framework for 21st century learning.* https://www.battelleforkids.org

Ravitch, S. M., & Carl, N. M. (2019). *Qualitative research: Bridging the conceptual, theoretical, and methodological.* Sage Publications.

Real, J. A. B. (2022). 21st century competencies of teachers in teacher education institutions: Basis for designing faculty development program. *International Research Journal of Science, Technology, Education, and Management, 2*(2), 153–164. https://doi.org/10.5281/zenodo.6951452

Redmond, T. A. (2016). Learning to teach the media: Pre-service teachers articulate the value of media literacy education. In *Pre-Service and In-Service Teacher Education: Concepts, Methodologies, Tools, and Applications* (pp. 993–1015). https://www.igi-global.com/gateway/chapter/215617

Ruiz-Primo, M. A. (2009). *Towards a framework for assessing 21st century science skills*. National Academies. https://citeseerx.ist.psu.edu/document?repid=rep1&type=pdf&doi=fa97051b64d2f5845c225d885048e718b28a8317

Saavedra, A. R., & Opfer, V. D., (2012). Learning 21st century skills require 21st century teaching. *Phi Delta Kappan, 94*(2), 8–13. https://journals.sagepub.com/-doi/10.1177/003172171209400203

Sağlam, A. Ç., & Büyükuysal, E. (2013). Eğitim fakültesi son sınıf öğrencilerinin eleştirel düşünme düzeyleri ve buna yönelik engellere ilişkin görüşleri. *International Journal of Human Sciences, 10*(1), 258–278.

Shepard, L. A., Kitmitto, S., Daro, P., Hughes, G. B., Webb, D. C., Stancavage, F, & Tucker-Bradway, N. (2020). *Validity of the national assessment of educational progress to evaluate cutting-edge curricula*. NAEP Validity Studies Panel American Institutes for Research. https://www.air.org/sites/default/files/2022-04/Validity-of-NAEP-to-Evaluate-Cutting-Edge-Curricula-2020.pdf

Silva, E. (2009). Measuring skills for 21st-century learning. *Phi Delta Kappan, 90*(9), 630–634. https://www.jstor.org/stable/27652741

Tang, C. M., & Chaw, L. Y. (2016). Digital literacy: A prerequisite for effective learning in a blended learning environment? *The Electronic Journal of e-Learning, 14*(1), 54–65. https://academic-publishing.org/index.php/-ejel/article/view/1743/1706

Tondeur, J., Van Braak, J., Ertmer, P. A., & Ottenbreit-Leftwich, A. (2017). Understanding the relationship between teachers' pedagogical beliefs and technology use in education: A systematic review of qualitative evidence. *Educational Technology Research and Development, 65*(3), 555–575. https://doi.org/10.1007/s11423-016-9481-2

The CoHE. (2023). *Details regarding pedagogical formation education have been determined*. https://www.yok.gov.tr/Sayfalar/Haberler/2023/pedagojik-formasyon-egitimine-iliskin-detaylar-belirlendi.aspx

The MoNE. (2017). *Teacher strategy paper 2017–23*. MoNE. https://oygm.meb.gov.-tr/meb_iys_dosyalar/2018_05/25170118_Teacher_Strategy_Paper_2017-2023.pdf..

The MoNE. (2018). *Turkey's education vision 2023*. https://planipolis.iiep.unesco.org/sites/default/files/ressources/turkey_education_vision_2023.pdf

Tutkun, Ö. F., & Aksoyalp, Y. (2010). 21. yüzyılda öğretmen yetiştirme eğitim programının boyutları. *Selçuk Üniversitesi Sosyal Bilimler Enstitüsü Dergisi*, *24*, 361–370.

UNESCO. (2017). *UNESCO moving forward the 2030 agenda for sustainable development*. https://unesdoc.unesco.org/ark:/48223/pf0000247785

Valtonen, T., Sointu, E. T., Kukkonen, J., Häkkinen, P., Järvelä, S., Ahonen, A., et al. (2017). Insights into Finnish first-year pre-service teachers' perceptions of their 21st century skills. *Education and Information Technologies, 22*(5), 2055–2069. https://doi.org/10.1007/s10639-016-9529-2

Valtonen, T., Hoang, N., Sointu, E., Näykki, P., Virtanen, A., et al. (2021). How pre-service teachers perceive their 21st-century skills and dispositions: A longitudinal perspective. *Computers in Human Behavior, 116*, 106643. https://doi.org/10.1016/j.chb.2020.106643

Yılmaz, A. (2020). The effect of technology integration in education on prospective teachers' critical and creative thinking, multidimensional 21st century skills and academic achievements. *Participatory Educational Research, 8*(2), 163–199. http://dx.doi.org/10.17275/per.21.35.8.2

Wachira, P., & Keengwe, J. (2011). Technology integration barriers: Urban school mathematics teachers' perspectives. *Journal of Science Education and Technology, 20*, 17–25. https://doi.org/10.1007/s10956-010-9230-y

Wiggins, R. A., & Follo, E. J. (1999). Development of knowledge, attitudes, and commitment to teach diverse student populations. *Journal of Teacher Education, 50*, 94–105. https://journals.sagepub.com/doi/epdf/10.1177/002248719905000203

Duygu Öztekin

Dr. Yelkin Diker Coşkun

Chapter 8 New Realities of Adult Education: A Futuristic View

Abstract: Adult education can be uttered as more educated human power, and it has a role for attainment of life fulfillment in that it can stand for a second chance, remedy, or self-actualizing. It can be formal, technical, higher, or complementary for those who desire an intellectual or vocational development besides basic knowledge. It is somewhat an intervention for change, competency, and empowerment (Seyoum & Basha, 2017). Adult education plays a significant role in adults' personal life, in contemporary societies and in the world because it provides adults with chances of personal development, professional development, social skills, ability to adapt into new situations, quality of life and so on by formal or informal ways. As a result, adult education aspires to create an adult mindset that challenges the former ideas, beliefs, habits, well-established traditions, and all sorts of life constraints thereby creating an increased sense of mindfulness, self-satisfaction and self-value in adults that will eventually help them adapt to post-industrialized lifestyle and welfare by supporting the recovery of mind and body together. In this chapter, new realities of adult education at present and future of it will be analyzed around these various aspects: lifelong learning; the novice patterns of "third age", "andragogy", "gerontology"; and new curriculum design models (e.g. "adult learner model", "COI" or "ASIE", "CIDS").

Keywords: Adult education, lifelong learning, new adult learner models

Adult education – as most famously said "lifelong learning – is unique in that adults have a certain level of maturity, consciousness, stability, values, goals, and it tries to build on all these levels by renewing, completing, extending mentally and culturally, giving proficiency in a contemporary society. Also, learning about society means a desirable, enlightened form of society (Hubackova & Semradova, 2014). Furthermore, adult education doesn't have to center upon only informational, educational or proficiency approach, adults have also a chance to develop a wider world view, a critical approach to life, an aesthetical way of life, more complex view of mind, ability to deal with an uncertain, changing world (Kokkos, 2014). In the light of these explanations adult education has no way but to have powerful associations with the popular theme lifelong learning. Lifelong learning is setting forward the industrialization of education, a way of ensuring education in an accelerated economy, offering a flexible citizenry and workforce

besides pursuing interests to empower themselves also it is related to post industrialization era which includes social mobility and offers lifelong learning as a
route (Murphy, 2000). It has a mission to enhance adult life, it provides continuous information on the current world, knowledge, and skills and it is an effort
to refine the thoughts of adults and sustain control of their life within a changing
society (Kamp, 2011). One of the most prominent advantages of adult education
is that it is a personal choice, and it is for adults realizing their untapped potential
and ready to use this potential in a comfortable class atmosphere for community
and social wellbeing (Forrest & Peterson, 2006).

The Novice Patterns of "Third Age", "Andragogy", "Gerontology"

The concept of "third age" learners and the increasing number of third age learners are involved in the subject of new realities of adult education. Third age refers
to the period of active retirement in life, the welfare of retired adults, well of
aging, it is somewhat related to the economic and social well-being of adults. The
social and cultural transformation of this century of the world give way to the
concept of "third age" because adults of this century are the first to experience
aging consciously, healthily, meaningfully and trying to shape it productively; its
significance is so much that it gives way to a new science called "gerontology"
which means the scientific study of old age (Gilleard & Higgs, 2002). Changing
demographics i.e. severe decline in the mortality and fertility rates as opposed to
drastic increase in the life expectancy rates in all age groups since 1950 raised the
subject of lifelong learning and education for third age people (Fent, 2008). This
similar trend is expected to go on in future until 2050. The concept of andragogy
comes into attention by the increase of population. Andragogy means teaching
and learning principles specially tailored for older people. The focus here is taking the enjoyment in learning, being contented with the learning process, having
the sense of belonging within a community as well as the feeling of achievement, the sense of cognitive development, responsibility, and control (Devaele
& MacIntyre, 2014).

Lifelong learning and adult education provide healthy aging period, make
them productive and have social, physical, and cognitive benefits for the world
in need of healthy population. Mental activity recovers cognitive reserve which
is the source for dealing with age caused brain harm by using cognitive networks
effectively (Stern, 2002). Tan et al. (2017), put forward the cognitive and physical
interventions such as cognitive tasks can make the older people more independent in their life. Education in late adulthood is not designed specifically for job

performance; individuals in late adulthood have mostly inner motivations and different educational needs such as life satisfaction, development or conservation of mental and physical competence, social responsibilities, engagements in societies, being able to confront with the new challenges of the world such as digital age (Maderer & Skiba, 2006). The ways of learning, late adulthood preferences also differ with age due to their biographical experiences, their present life conditions, socioeconomic situations, and interests etc. Computer literacy and digital media affect this diversity one step further as there are some opportunities like online learning, distance education, flipped courses, organized courses via informal methods. Old adults may create intrinsic interest as they make education easy to achieve. Specifically, the changes in information and communication technology make adult education the focus of studies. The educational gerontology focuses on the program development models for the old adults and to transport these programs to these people. Pihlainen et al. (2022) tried to shed light on reasons to learn digital skills among late adulthood by making research in Finland, Austria, and Germany. In their research they found out that the desire to be active, independent, having external pressures to have hobbies and to learn digital skills were the reasons that can be generalized to other educational goals in late adulthood.

New Curriculum Design Models Like "Adult Learner Model", "COI" or "ASIE", "CIDS" in Adult Education

Adult learner model: Ongoing change is an integral aspect of our daily life and as our world changes ongoing learning also becomes an integral aspect of our lives. To take pace with the evolving needs of life and needs of our profession people need a high adaptability. Technology has a big role here and individuals must adapt to its changing speed. These individuals are mostly made up of adults. The economy also has a big role in making lifelong learning and adult education essential as well-paid jobs require advanced education and skilled workforce which is a key factor for growth and popularity. Adults are actively seeking education and training opportunities more than ever. Adults endeavor to develop new fundamental skills which are demanded by societies, employers, and their peers. Critical thinking, communication skills, technological literacy, analytical abilities, language skills, time managements skills and even new hobbies such as taking up a new sport are only a few of these skills (Dan-Messier, 2011). All these are the reasons why there is greater focus on the studies of adult education, and the concept of "whole learner". The concept of "whole learner" stands here because adults bring a lot of life issues with them from the sleep, they get on every day to working environments, from their community and family to their job opportunities, from their age to their complex experiences, from their habits to their adaptation paces. As a result of this, adults vary in terms of their cognitive abilities, social and emotional well beings, and unique backgrounds. The adult learner model arises here to acquire new skills better. To enlighten "whole learner" concept in adult learner model, it can be said that whole learner is at the center of the learning and teaching process with all his or her own growing knowledge, abilities, values, motivations, beliefs, behaviors, emotions, physical wellbeing, and characteristics. Accordingly, "whole learning environments" with instruments, technologies, community reserves, informal educational places like art galleries and museums, and formal educational backups such as assessments, professional support, new educational policies are the new elements of the new classrooms for the individually different learners (ASCD, 2007).

Adult learner model is designed by cognitive psychology, sociology, basic and higher education, adult literacy, workforce training, digital literacy, and English language acquisition. Social support, community resources, motivation, social awareness, emotion, adverse childhood experiences, housing insecurity, traumas all are the factors that affect adults. The goal of adult learner model is to represent the whole learner in its strategies and factors, to provide details for how factors create their personal backgrounds and by this way to provide useful strategies which support these factors into learning environments: classrooms, online, and self-directed study (Tare et al., 2020). The literacies, cognition, social-emotional, and learner background create the framework. Digital literacy levels, working memory, motivation, and adverse experiences of adult learners are defined and well-designed personalized learning experiences are created by instructional design strategies to provide active learning, collaboration, and metacognitive stakes. The Adult learner model includes three main themes, one of which is that adults need a variety of 21st century foundational skills to survive and thrive. That means adults need 21st century skills such as digital literacy and oral communication skills, problem solving skills, peer feedback and some multimedia projects. Another theme is that adults must see the benefits of learning tasks to be included. It means that they have a variety of motivations to learn something. For this reason, the framework must create authentic learning environments because adults want to use the knowledge or experience in their daily life building upon their mindset. The last theme is engaging in lifelong learning activities to add into general well-being which means physical health, healthy cognition and emotions contribute learning and vice versa learning contributes both physical and psychological health. Physical activities contribute to mindfulness, job satisfaction, cognitive and metacognitive competencies, and self-esteem (Tare et al., 2020).

Community of Inquiry "COI": The need for adult education puts training and degree programs and other educational opportunities for adults on the rise. In this contemporary world, learning does not only occur in formal settings, but it can also take place in non-formal or informal learning environments as adults are busy people and they have many responsibilities both at home and at work. These are the reasons why online learning environments are gaining popularity. Adult educators pay attention to designing these environments to meet their needs and to maximize their potential. COI is one of these design studies (Selwyn, 2006).

COI, which stands for Community of Inquiry, can be another 21st century instructional model. This model is a kind of formal education which is implemented with the potential of computer-based instruction by creating a constant community of inquiry (Garrison et al., 2010). The main elements of COI are social presence, cognitive presence, teaching presence and these all a system of an online educational experience. Social presence means emotional sense of belonging and the priority for most students in a formal educational context is shared social identity, not a personal identity meaning participants communicating purposefully in a trusting environment and developing interpersonal relationships (Garrison, 2009). Cognitive presence means reflective thinking by exploration, integration, resolution to construct meaning (Garrison et al., 2001). Teaching presence is designing the COI, facilitating, and directing the learning process across populations of students (Garrison et al., 2010).

There are some studies that show adult learners have positive attitudes towards COI. COI serves as a well-organized blueprint for creating successful online learning communities for adults as COI involves meaningful integration of teaching, social interaction, and cognitive engagement. If contextual factors like class size and time limitations of adults are considered COI framework and its approach to build effective online environments are highly effective for adult learners (Akyol & Garrison, 2010).

Some new instructional design models "ASIE", "CIDS": The journey of instructional design models goes from the acronym ADDIE to ASIE. The ASIE model is another new kind of model for the 21st century instructional environments in that it integrates 21st century needs, skills, tools, potentials. Also, ASIE is flexible with an online version which makes sharing easy, encourages to think while doing. "A" stands for analyzing learner's profiles and instructional media profiles; "S" stands for strategize and means integrating instructional media, applying tools, 21st century skills, formulating questions; "I" stands for implementing; "E" stands for evaluating which means responding, revising, reviewing (Zain et al., 2016).

Skills such as innovation, critical thinking, communication, interaction, collaboration, are very important in today's current world. Accordingly, the collaborative instructional design system (CIDS) is another 21st century instruction method. It arises from the fact that 21st century's learning should prepare learners to cope with future work and life challenges. The key factors of CIDS are creativity, innovation, competition to be successful. Life and career skills, innovation skills, information, media, and technology skills are the key skills to adopt around the core subject (Zain, 2017). Zain (2017) puts forward that at the core of instruction; the 21st century learner must have creativity, critical thinking, communication and collaboration skills, the learner must behave with curiosity, mindfulness, courage, leadership, ethics, and the learner must know tradition, modern and interdisciplinarity. The learners' metacognition and growth mindset are important too.

The 21st century is also made up of multiculturalism. Multiple cultures instructional model for e-learning has come out from the view that e-learners and e-teachers belong different cultural, pedagogical, academic, government backgrounds but as the design aims these e- learners and teachers are in partnership to learn in the same global context. E-learning is at the center and around it there are dominant culture, global culture, current culture, and ethnic minorities culture full of interplay among global academia, global training (Henderson, 2007).

Online Education and Its Related Developments and Self-skills

Information technologies in educational area have undergone great changes since emergence however the Covid 19 pandemic in 2020 is the peak point as it forced governments, higher education institutions, schools, and business areas to turn into digital services in an accelerated way and accordingly adults have developed their digital literacy skills (Webb et al., 2021). The contemporary world witnesses two highly remarkable trends which are never experienced before. One of these trends is widespread digitization of society and the other one is the increasing aging of population (Ziyun & Feng, 2022). These trends can be used for the benefit of each other to create healthier societies that means information technology and related developments can back up adult people to take education on almost everything and they can age healthier by having education on their interest. Having the chance to take education in many subjects causes the birth of an education industry, market demand and customers for a special type of education. This education industry enables educators from around the world to offer online guidance to students via various means called MOOC (Massive Open Online Courses) such as Coursera, Khan academy, Udemy, Cambly etc… These platforms consist of live video instructions, recorded video broadcasts, discussion forums, chat rooms and like these places. These platforms are network teaching systems in which adult learners can conveniently access whatever subject they want to study, adapt the subject to their learning style in a flexible environment creating a personal quality education (Duan, 2020). In fact, open, online and distance learning platforms such as Open Educational Resources (OER), Open Course Ware (OCW) and Global Knowledge Networks are a breakthrough in adult education and a rebellion against barriers to access into university level education sometimes with the help of a fee but mostly free. Learning in these kinds of educational platforms involves making sense of knowledge by having connections, reinterpreting, sharing with other people, discoveries, synthesis, learning in a collaborative way but creating their individual learning paths as they get their past experiences with themselves. Also consuming, connecting, creating, and contributing around a collective knowledge are four phases of behaviors in these networks (Siemens & Downes, 2013). To learn effectively in these environments, self-regulation skills of adults gain a high importance: they should self-regulate their goals, self-monitor themselves, do self-reflection; a typical model of this social cognitive learning is Self-regulated learning (SRL) model (Zimmermann & Kitsantas, 2005).

Self-regulation refers to the capacity of control which students have over their own cognition, behavior, emotions, and motivation by using individual strategies to attain their desired objectives (Panadero & Tapia, 2014). Self-regulated learning theory states that learning is governed by a variety of interacting cognitive, meta-cognitive, and motivational components (Butler & Winne, 1995; Zimmerman, 2000). Self-directed learning which means the adult learner has his or her own locus of control in learning to initiate and progress stands among the learning theories in andragogy especially if it takes place on open, distance and online platforms. Characteristics of self-directed learners can be listed: self-directed learners have independence, confidence, discipline, organization skills, they are volunteer to learn, and they take up the learning responsibility, enjoy and persist in learning during hard times (Cercone, 2008). In fact, all these self-skills are crucial, and they are the new reality of adult education in the 21st century.

The Introduction of Information Technologies and Artificial Intelligence into the Adult Education

Artificial intelligence is the most striking reality in the educational world in our era; in fact, AI which is the acronym for artificial intelligence is a reason of excitement and can be a breaking point in education. AI can create a revolution for adult education and for lifelong learning due to its application system, learner centered and flexible mode. Artificial intelligence can be defined as programming a computer or a device to perform like a human, to think like a human, to act as if it has human intelligence. Besides this, artificial intelligence bears much more complexity which is the key word in this definition as it can come through more complex jobs (Brett, 2017). AI in education means application of its techniques to the existing learning approaches, automating educational practices, digging up new teaching and learning possibilities however at the same time challenging the existing pedagogy (Holmes et al., 2023). In AI enhanced education, learners have the advantage of limitless access to available knowledge that is; the knowledge is ready, but the learners need necessary skills to navigate through all this knowledge and navigating through all this huge knowledge necessitates a critical assessment and right judgement. Collaborating mnemonics to accumulate knowledge is achieved by the assistance of machine in the form of cognitive aids such as looking up, taking notes, creating models, diagrams, reference sources, calculating. To sum up; the process of learning turns into a task of structuring mental frameworks, constructing models, searching for evidence, validating (Cope et al., 2021).

Artificial intelligence has matured to a great degree in the last ten years. However, it has millstones to settle in educational environments and classrooms as existing educational systems still insist on sticking in their traditional forms. It is beyond dispute that AI will find its place in education and here is an analysis and a sample of AI in adult education. As a sample China can be on target because it has a rapidly aging society, and it has policies for adults around the AI. China offered the development of AI systematically at the national strategic level in 2017 and this means a macro policy to promote vocational education for adults and China government also includes innovations in education methods for older adults that requires all the older adult education based on artificial intelligence. To achieve this national goal, it strengthens the 5G network, its data centers and provides utilizations of information technologies. Strengthening includes in depth services such as allowing the data to communicate its findings, feedback, reworking on the data, arranging the education to the aptitude of the adult and older adult learners, appealing to their individuality. AI fulfils their lifelong learning desires by making learning possible for everyone at their pleasure at any time, any place and by designing a curriculum content focusing on the learner not the raw knowledge. Furthermore, traditional methods and even e-learning have drawbacks for older adults as they have eye diseases or hearing disorders, but AI has audible, playable or readable applications as a solution.

Increasing number of WeChat platform on the mobile phones of adults is an example of AI in older adult education in China (Ziyun & Feng, 2022).

Artificial intelligence is an individualized learning companion for everyone, but the word "companion" is more meaningful when adults are the matter. AI is a lifelong learning companion for adults serving the roles of a learning partner, sometimes a guide for discovering learning resources, an instructor, it also keeps learners' interests and progress, secures all of these. To give an instance for this kind of companion; Siri, Cortana, Alexa can be mentioned but we can see more of them in a world of education enhanced by AI. When the learner decides what to learn, this learning companion can offer instructional activities, track the learner's progress, act as a reminder, give feedback, work at a strategic level by helping to decide what to learn, where and how to learn, the learning companion can draw pathways, it can connect the learner through these pathways, encourage and reflect on during the learning journey, create opportunities to meet people with the same interests, it can give way to team work and create intercultural connections (Holmes et al., 2023).

An AI model of assessment can be a better choice for adult learners due to its structure. Assessments in an education system enhanced by artificial intelligence turn into a continuous system, a constantly monitoring system to understand the progression of a learner instead of standardized stop and test examinations which do not reflect an adult learner's understanding. These traditional assessment systems cause anxiety, rivalry and negative emotions that can lead to giving up as adult education isn't compulsory mostly and furthermore interrupting the learning phase. AI assessment system takes place in the background by following the learners' mastery level and making deductions about their understanding at the same time, by giving feedback, by authenticating the learners' identity as a whole learner instead of focusing on questioning (Holmes et al., 2023). For instance, in a foreign language learning process, AI assessment systems give us knowledge about the learners' motivation or confidence in addition to their progress and knowledge. All these developments can be summed up like Hill & Barber (2014) wrote "a renaissance in assessment."

The Cognitive Aspect of Adult Education

Adult education, besides its benefits in the field of subject, has advantages for the cognitive structure, cognitive skills, and functions of the brain. There are a lot of studies showing these relations. Kremen et al. (2019) display the links between education, occupational complexity, and cognitive intellectual activities by giving evidence about positive effects on cognitive functions in later life and reduced risk of mild cognitive impairment. This evidence means the more the accessibility and quality of education for adults during the earlier years of adulthood increase, the less the cognitive decline and risk of dementia in later years. As individuals age, a decline starts in cognitive abilities in fact findings show that when individuals leave behind the first four decades in their life cognitive skills give up improving and start declining from then on (Clark et al., 2006). Furthermore, if that individual has less or limited education in his or her life, this causes a risk for dementia (Ball et al., 2007). However good news is on the stage too giving evidence about the strength of education in adulthood or older ages to prevent cognitive decline and dementia. Stern (2012) and Amieva et al. (2014) state that the cognitive reserve in individuals who have more education and by this way more intellectual protects them against cognitive decline and impairment. Cognitive functions especially attention and memory have a tendency to decline by age as evidenced by neuropsychological tests on the other hand more educational experience and chances of formal learning opportunities even later in life cause better performances on these tests (Matallana et al., 2011). Education affects cognitive skills and cognitive functions in different rates such as the most affected ones are attention, calculating, reading, writing, and drawing skills however even less education still has effects on memory and memory related skills, repetition skills (Laks et al., 2010).

There are also studies analyzing the cognitive processes of brain from a more biological aspect and the results of these researchers can be a support for not abandoning having education in adult ages. Boldrini et al. (2018), found out that healthy older individuals without a specific impairment have preserved producing new neuron and this sustains cognitive functioning throughout life and if possible, declines occur, it may be due to compromised cognitive-emotional resilience. This finding says that the cognitive functions are here to perform throughout your life so there is no reason to give up. There are a lot of reasons to go on as Dweck (2015) has growth mindset theory which means people can train their brain, intelligence can be developed, effort gets you to mastery, learn from failure and embrace challenges and it is better to step out of comfort zone and believe in yourself and this is valid for adult education. Education creates social interaction, surrounds individuals with different kinds of relations, it includes adults into the social life in heterogeneous environments (Kil et al., 2013). Being active in social life helps having a better cognition so strong that research offers if you have better social relations, your risk of dementia is 60 % less (Fratiglioni et al., 2000).

The Fact of Heavy Migration the Contemporary World Faces Today and Its Compulsory Relations with Adult Education

One of the new realities of adult education is the subject of "migration". For decades people have experienced migration, but the quantity and the speed of migration have not been that much in 21st century and especially nowadays in 2020s. According to the results of IOM (2017), nearly 244 million people are in the situation of being migrants in the world and that means nearly 3,3 of world population. Findings also show the common characteristics of migrants they are from Asia, China or India to West, high income countries which are totally different educational backgrounds revealing a big educational gap. The reason can be voluntary or a force such as economy, war, disasters but the reason is not important here, education is important. The migrants need to be educated to integrate into the culture, to learn the foreign language of the country, to be skilled workers, to be included in society and to contribute to the society they live in. Adult education has a key role and importance in migration subjects such that it is among the highest rate in the policies and practices of governments and related social institutions (Kukovetz & Sprung, 2014). Adult education at this point has more than personal satisfaction or life-long learning, adult education here is a human right, it is a globalization matter. Adult education here has a lot to do about economic matters, political matters, demographic issues, competitiveness, social inclusion, all humankind matters; shortly to sustain the healthy future of nations and communities according to UNESCO who declares this fact as member states can no longer afford to be without adult education (UNESCO, 2009). To give an instance; Germany has been witnessing a huge rate of migration since years and they have "Volkshochschulen" which is the name of state supported public adult education centers and the world is facing an increasing need for these kinds of nation building integration courses. The adult education content such as language, culture and employment are not enough, a larger extent of adult education is needed for a long term settled population calling for new techniques, new strategies, new learning communities both formal and informal. Classrooms to integrate and include migrants are contact zones but mobile learning technologies and information technologies of this century are also a big assistance (Morrice et al., 2017). Information technologies are found out to be highly effective and a big contribution to learn languages, support their peers, integrate into the culture, participate in local activities, create confidence and social justice and not only in public places but also in the private spaces of migrants

(Pearson, 2011; Ruge, 2012). Besides formal education, adult immigrants can also undergo an informal education process spontaneously which is outside the usual classroom atmosphere and outside any other school-based systems in their daily life or at work. Furthermore, non-formal way of education gains popularity among individuals because it is characterized by flexibility, which is very important for adults, diversity according to their needs, embracing all forms professions, compensating the lack of formal education, non-formal way of education also gives way for individualization as adults desire it more, giving satisfaction for their cognitive needs, narrowing the knowledge gap (Ogienko & Terenko, 2018).

A Sample from the World: The Case of Adult Education in Britain

What about the case in Britain for the future of adult education? "The adult education 100" campaign is published for adult education and lifelong learning for 21st century Britain. Its vision is attention capturing as it claims that adult education must not be privileged for a few selected people, it must be an integral part of being a citizen and it must last lifelong and defines adult education as a fundamental and enduring national requirement. To promote adult education, there are 18 recommendations which can stand for other nations all over the world and these recommendations are listed by Holford (2019) to show the seriousness of the case "Adult Education". This can be listed as: creating a national ambition is recommended for democratic life to reduce the gap between the most and the least educationally active person, for economic prosperity and individual wellbeing. The minister responsible for adult education is an item in recommendations. Universities and colleges are invited to be partnerships. A stable and long-term government funding is a necessity defending that investments in lifelong learning and adult education will pay off in every aspect and fundings should also be made on innovations to spread informal adult education. National campaigns should use the media to engage people in lifelong learning. Powerful information technologies and artificial intelligence should get on the stage and take the field. Apprenticeship, which means attending to work and being on the area should be encouraged. Employers are advised to pay for off-work if the person is off for learning and they are also advised to create learning spaces in the usual workplaces besides it must be compulsory to report about their spending on employee education every year.

One of the Most Common Subjects of Adult Education in Global World: Foreign Language Learning

Foreign language learning is one of the ways to promote capacity building and sustain this capacity for adults as it has social, cognitive, and neurobiological aspects. Foreign language education can be a part of educational policies related to lifelong learning to support healthy cognitive functions in adults. The aging process and afterwards retirement is because of cognitive decline which is related to the frontal regions responsible for the memory and loss of neural synaptic connections (Greenwood, 2007). Foreign language learning is a solution for this decline as it develops cognitive plasticity by including neural networks in the job and making them active and stimulating some cognitive concepts such as working memory, executive functions, reasoning, task switching, memory practices, rule learning (Ware et al., 2017). Besides cognitive benefits, learning a language also has a lot to do with the lifestyle of adults during retirement by the experiences they encounter stimulating their intellectual development (Stern & Munn, 2010). Remaining active is a prestige, and a satisfaction for retired population and all of these create a reliable and sustainable framework to include foreign language learning into the educational policies. The foreign language education process makes lifelong learning sustainable and provides motivation for future as it helps finding the goal of their life during retirement by engaging in a meaningful activity (Pikhart & Klimova, 2020). Including such a learning process into the government educational policies contributes to the whole wellbeing during retirement giving way to healthy aging.

Conclusion

The OECD learning framework for 2030 has some explanations and vision for the future of education which sums up new realities of education for learners. On one side the first thing they acknowledge is the rapidly changing world such as the unprecedented advancements in science, technology, artificial intelligence, the advent of big data and the uncertainty of the world such as the migration, urbanization, increasing rate of social and cultural diversity, population growth, wars, pandemic. On the other side stands the individual and collective well-being of learners as it is vital for their growth and "whole learner" who is the learner with cognitive, social, emotional, creative, and motor skills deeply integrated. Navigating through the world of education is among the most crucial things for learners in the era of digital transformation and OECD 2030 stakeholders suggest "a learning compass" to navigate. OECD learning framework describes the future ready learners with these broad set of skills: They are equipped with disciplinary knowledge which is raw; epistemic knowledge which gives way to think like a mathematician or a scientist; procedural knowledge to understand the series and steps by problem solving, system and design thinking. However, this is not enough as they present the world in a framework of transition and uncertainty, the future learners need cognitive and metacognitive skills (critical and creative thinking, self-regulation), social and emotional skills (empathy, self-skills like self-efficacy), practical and physical skills (ability to use new information technologies). In addition to these skills the future learner has values like motivation, trust, respect for diversity and transition. Three further competencies can be added to the future learner under the title of transformative competencies: ability to create new values to be innovative and creative involving curiosity, adaptability, and open-mindedness; ability to mediate tension and dilemmas, to secure their own wellbeing to be aware and system thinker in a world of inequities full of diversities and ability to take responsibility to be responsible which requires moral and intellectual maturity (OECD, 2019).

References

Akyol, Z., & Garrison, D. R. (2010). Community of inquiry in adult online learning: Collaborative-constructivist approaches. In *Web-based education: Concepts, methodologies, tools, and applications* (pp. 474–489). IGI Global.

Amieva, H., Mokri, H., Le Goff, M., Meillon, C., Jacqmin-Gadda, H., Foubert-Samier, A., … & Dartigues, J. F. (2014). Compensatory mechanisms in higher-educated subjects with Alzheimer's disease: A study of 20 years of cognitive decline. *Brain, 137*(4), 1167–1175. http://doi.org/10.1093/brain/awu035

ASCD. (2007). The learning compact redefined: A call to action, a report of the Commission on the Whole Child. Alexandria, VA: ASCD. http://www.ascd.org/ASCD/pdf/Whole%20Child/WCC%20Learning%20Compact.pdf

Ball, K., Edwards, J. D., & Ross, L. A. (2007). The impact of speed of processing training on cognitive and everyday functions. *The Journals of Gerontology. Series B, Psychological Sciences and Social Sciences, 62 (Spec No 1)*, 19–31. https://doi.org/10.1093/geronb/62.special_issue_1.19

Becker, B. A. (2017). Artificial intelligence in education: What is it, where is it now, where is it going? In B. Mooney (Ed.), *Ireland's Yearbook of Education 2017–2018* (pp. 42–46). Education Matters. https://educationmatters.ie/artificial-intelligence-in-education/

Boldrini, M., Fulmore, C. A., Tartt, A. N., Simeon, L. R., Pavlova, I., Poposka, V., ... & Mann, J. J. (2018). Human hippocampal neurogenesis persists throughout aging. *Cell Stem Cell, 22*(4), 589–599. https://doi.org/10.1016/j.stem.2018.03.015

Butler, D. L., & Winne, P. H. (1995). Feedback and self-regulated learning: A theoretical synthesis. *Review of educational research, 65*(3), 245–281. https://doi.org/10.3102/00346543065003245

Cercone, K. (2008). Characteristics of adult learners with implications for online learning design. *AACE review (formerly AACE Journal), 16*(2), 137–159. https://eric.ed.gov/?id=EJ805727

Clark, C. R., Paul, R. H., Williams, L. M., Arns, M., Fallahpour, K., Handmer, C., & Gordon, E. (2006). Standardized assessment of cognitive functioning during development and aging using an automated touchscreen battery. *Archives of Clinical Neuropsychology, 21*(5), 449–467. https://doi.org/10.1016/j.acn.2006.06.005

Cope, B., Kalantzis, M., & Searsmith, D. (2021). Artificial intelligence for education: Knowledge and its assessment in AI-enabled learning ecologies. *Educational Philosophy and Theory, 53*(12), 1229–1245. https://doi.org/10.1080/00131857.2020.1728732

Dann-Messier, B. (2011). This is our time: Renewing adult education for the 21st century. *PAACE Journal of Lifelong Learning, 20*(1), 1–20. https://www.iup.edu/pse/files/programs/graduate_programs_r/instructional_design_and_te chnology_ma/paace_journal_of_lifelong_learning/volume_20,_2011/dann-messier.pdf

Dewaele, J. M., & MacIntyre, P. D. (2014). The two faces of Janus? Anxiety and enjoyment in the foreign language classroom. *Studies in second language learning and teaching, 4*(2), 237–274. https://doi.org/10.14746/SSLLT.2014.4.2.5

Duan, Y. (2020). Research on joint cultivation mechanism of adult education under collaborative innovation environment in China. *Creative Education, 11*(5), 797–805. https://doi.org/10.4236/ce.2020.115057

Dweck, C. (2015). Carol Dweck revisits the growth mindset. *Education Week, 35*(5), 20–24.

Fent, T. (2008). Department of economic and social affairs, population division, United Nations expert group meeting on social and economic implications of changing population age structures. *European Journal of Population, 24*(4), 451–452. http://doi.org/10.1007/s10680-008-9165-7

Forrest III, S. P., & Peterson, T. O. (2006). It's called andragogy. *Academy of Management Learning & Education, 5*(1), 113–122. https://www.jstor.org/stable/40212539

Fratiglioni, L., Wang, H. X., Ericsson, K., Maytan, M., & Winblad, B. (2000). Influence of social network on occurrence of dementia: A community-based longitudinal study. *The Lancet, 355*(9212), 1315–1319. https://doi.org/10.1016/S0140-6736(00)02113-9

Garrison, D. R., Anderson, T., & Archer, W. (2010). The first decade of the community of inquiry framework: A retrospective. *The Internet and Higher Education, 13*(1–2), 5–9. http://doi.org/10.1016/J.IHEDUC.2009.10.003

Garrison, D. R., Anderson, T., & Archer, W. (2001). Critical thinking, cognitive presence, and computer conferencing in distance education. *American Journal of Distance Education, 15*(1), 7–23. https://doi.org/10.1080/08923640109527071

Garrison, D. R. (2009). Communities of inquiry in online learning. In P. Rogers, G. Berg, J. Boettcher, C. Howard, L. Justice, & K. Schenk (Eds.), *Encyclopedia of Distance Learning, Second Edition* (pp. 352–355). IGI Global. https://doi.org/10.4018/978-1-60566-198-8.ch052

Gilleard, C., & Higgs, P. (2002). The third age: Class, cohort, or generation? *Ageing & Society, 22*(3), 369–382. https://doi.org/10.1017/S0144686X0200870X

Greenwood, P. M. (2007). Functional plasticity in cognitive aging: Review and hypothesis. *Neuropsychology, 21*(6), 657–673. https://doi.org/10.1037/0894-4105.21.6.657

Henderson, L. (2007). Theorizing a multiple cultures instructional design model for e-learning and e-teaching. In *Globalized e-learning cultural challenges* (pp. 130–154). IGI Global.

Hill, P. W., & Barber, M. (2014). *Preparing for a renaissance in assessment*. Pearson.

Holford, J. (2019). *"A Permanent National Necessity…" Adult Education and Lifelong Learning for 21st Century Britain*. University of Nottingham School of Education. http://doi.org/10.17639/nott.7027

Holmes, W., Bialik, M., & Fadel, C. (2023). *Artificial intelligence in education*. Globethics Publications.

Hubackova, S., & Semradova, I. (2014). Research study on motivation in adult education. *Procedia-Social and Behavioral Sciences, 159*, 396–400. https://doi.org/10.1016/j.sbspro.2014.12.395

IOM, 2017. *Migration and migrants: A global overview*. World Migration Report.

Pihlainen, K., Ehlers, A., Rohner, R., Cerna, K., Kärnä, E., Hess, M., … Müller, C. (2023). Older adults' reasons to participate in digital skills learning: An interdisciplinary, multiple case study from Austria, Finland, and Germany. *Studies in the Education of Adults, 55*(1), 101–119. https://doi.org/10.1080/02660830.2022.2133268

Kamp, M. (2011). *Facilitation skills and methods of adult education. A guide for civic education at grassroots level.* Konrad-Adenauer-Stiftung.

Kil, M., Motschilnig, R., & Thöne-Geyer, B. (2013). *What can adult education accomplish. The benefits of adult learning – The approach, measurement, and prospects.* https://www.die-bonn.de/doks/2013-benefits-en-01.pdf

Kokkos, A. (2015). The challenges of adult education in the modern world. *Procedia-Social and Behavioral Sciences, 180,* 19–24. https://doi.org/10.1016/j.sbspro.2015.02.079

Kremen, W. S., Beck, A., Elman, J. A., Gustavson, D. E., Reynolds, C. A., Tu, X. M., ... & Franz, C. E. (2019). Influence of young adult cognitive ability and additional education on later-life cognition. *Proceedings of the National Academy of Sciences, 116*(6), 2021–2026. https://doi.org/10.1073/pnas.1811537116

Kukovetz, B., & Sprung, A. (2014). Is adult education a "white" business? Professionals with migrant backgrounds in Austrian adult education. *European Journal for Research on the Education and Learning of Adults (Adults), 5*(2), 161–175. https://doi.org/10.3384/rela.2000-7426.rela9051

Laks, J., Coutinho, E. S. F., Junger, W., Silveira, H., Mouta, R., Baptista, E. M. R., ... & Engelhardt, E. (2010). Education does not equally influence all the Mini Mental State Examination subscales and items: Inferences from a Brazilian community sample. *Brazilian Journal of Psychiatry, 32,* 223–230. https://doi.org/10.1590/S1516-44462010005000009

Luckin, R., Holmes, W., Griffiths, M., & Forcier, L. B. (2016). *Intelligence unleashed: An argument for AI in education.* Pearson. https://static.googleusercontent.com/media/edu.google.com/en//pdfs/Intelligence-Unleashed-Publication.pdf

Maderer, P., & Skiba, A. (2006). Integrative geragogy: Part 1: Theory and practice of a basic model. *Educational Gerontology, 32*(2), 125–145. https://doi.org/10.1080/03601270500388158

Matallana, D., De Santacruz, C., Cano, C., Reyes, P., Samper-Ternent, R., Markides, K. S., ... & Reyes-Ortiz, C. A. (2011). The relationship between education level and mini-mental state examination domains among older Mexican Americans. *Journal of Geriatric Psychiatry and Neurology, 24*(1), 9–18. https://doi.org/10.1177/0891988710373597

Morrice, L., Shan, H., & Sprung, A. (2017). Migration, adult education, and learning. *Studies in the Education of Adults, 49*(2), 129–135. https://doi.org/10.1080/02660830.2018.1470280

Murphy, M. (2000). Adult education, lifelong learning, and the end of political economy. *Studies in the Education of Adults, 32*(2), 166–180. https://doi.org/10.1080/02660830.2000.11661428

OECD. (2019). *An OECD Learning Framework 2030* (pp. 23–35). Springer.

Ogienko, O., & Terenko, O. (2018). Non-formal adult education: Challenges and prospects of the 21st century. *Edukacja-Technika-Informatyka, 9*(2), 169–174. https://doi.org/10.15584/eti.2018.2.22

Panadero, E., & Alonso-Tapia, J. (2014). How do students self-regulate? Review of Zimmerman's cyclical model of self-regulated learning. *Anales de psicologia, 30*(2), 450–462.

Pearson, L. (2011). Exploring the effectiveness of mobile phones to support English language learning for migrant groups. *Journal of the Research Centre of Educational Technology, 7*(1), 90–105. https://rcetj.org/index.php/rcetj/arti cle/view/154/239

Pikhart, M., & Klimova, B. (2020). Maintaining and supporting seniors' wellbeing through foreign language learning: Psycholinguistics of second language acquisition in older age. *International journal of environmental research and public health, 17*(21), 8038. https://doi.org/10.3390/ijerph17218038

Ziyun, Q., & Feng, L. (2022). Analysis of an older adults' education service model driven by big data. *International Journal of Multidisciplinary Research and Publications (IJMRAP), 4*(12), 87–93. https://ijmrap.com/wp-content/uplo ads/2022/06/IJMRAP-V4N12P94Y22.pdf

Ruge, B., (2012). Learning Greenlandic by SMS: The potentials of text messages support for second language learners in Greenland. In J. Dıaz-Vera (Ed.), *Left to my own devices: Learner autonomy and mobile assisted language learning innovation and leadership in English language teaching* (pp. 197–212). Emerald Group.

Selwyn, N. (2006). ICT in adult education: Defining the territory. In D. A. Wagner & R. Sweet (Eds.), *ICT and learning: Supporting out-of-school youth and adults* (pp. 13–42). OECD. https://doi.org/10.1787/9789264012288-en

Seyoum, Y., & Basha, G. (2017). Andragogical methods to sustain quality adult education in Ethiopia. *International Journal of Instruction, 10*(3), 47–62. https://doi.org/10.12973/iji.2017.1034a

Siemens, G., & Downes, S. (2013). *What is a MOOC.* CEMCA EdTech Notes. https://www.cemca.org/ckfinder/userfiles/files/EdTech%20Notes%202_Lit tlejohn_final_1June2013.pdf

Stern, C., & Munn, Z. (2010). Cognitive leisure activities and their role in preventing dementia: A systematic review. *International Journal of Evidence-Based Healthcare, 8*(1), 2–17. https://doi.org/10.11124/01938924-200907 290-00001

Stern, Y. (2002). What is cognitive reserve? Theory and research application of the reserve concept. *Journal of the international neuropsychological society, 8*(3), 448–460. https://doi.org/10.1017/S1355617702813248

Stern, Y. (2012). Cognitive reserve in ageing and Alzheimer's disease. *The Lancet Neurology, 11*(11), 1006–1012. https://doi.org/10.1016/S1474-4422(12)70191-6

Tan, Z. S., Spartano, N. L., Beiser, A. S., DeCarli, C., Auerbach, S. H., Vasan, R. S., & Seshadri, S. (2017). Physical activity, brain volume, and dementia risk: The Framingham study. *The journals of gerontology. Series A, Biological Sciences and Medical Sciences, 72*(6), 789–795. https://doi.org/10.1093/gerona/glw130

Tare, M., Cacicio, S., & Shell, A. R. (2020). *The science of adult learning: Understanding the whole learner*. Digital Promise.

UNESCO. (2009). *Harnessing the power and potential of adult learning and education for a viable future – Be'le'm Framework for Action*. UNESCO Institute for Lifelong Learning.

Ware, C., Damnee, S., Djabelkhir, L., Cristancho, V., Wu, Y. H., Benovici, J., … & Rigaud, A. S. (2017). Maintaining cognitive functioning in healthy seniors with a technology-based foreign language program: A pilot feasibility study. *Frontiers in aging Neuroscience, 9*(42), 1–10. https://doi.org/10.3389/fnagi.2017.00042

Webb, A., McQuaid, R. W., & Webster, C. W. R. (2021). Moving learning online and the COVID-19 pandemic: A university response. *World Journal of Science, Technology and Sustainable Development, 18*(1), 1–19. https://doi.org/10.1108/WJSTSD-11-2020-0090

Zain, I. M. (2017). The collaborative instructional design system (CIDS): Visualizing the 21st century learning. *Universal Journal of Educational Research, 5*(12), 2259–2266. https://doi.org/10.13189/ujer.2017.051216

Zain, I. M., Muniandy, B., & Hashim, W. (2016). An integral ASIE ID Model: The 21st century instructional design model for teachers. *Universal Journal of Educational Research, 4*(3), 547–554. https://doi.org/10.13189/ujer.2016.040311

Zimmerman, B. J. (2000). Attaining self-regulation: A social cognitive perspective. In M. Boekaerts, P. R. Pintrich, & M. Zeidner (Eds.), *Handbook of self-regulation* (pp. 13–39). Academic Press. http://dx.doi.org/10.1016/B978-012109890-2/50031-7

Zimmerman, B. J., & Kitsantas, A. (2005). The Hidden dimension of personal competence: Self-regulated learning and practice. In A. J. Elliot & C. S. Dweck (Eds.), *Handbook of competence and motivation* (pp. 509–526). Guilford Publications.

Dr. Burcu Erdemir

Chapter 9 Accountability-Based Performance in Education (A Case from Turkey)

Abstract: While accountability in education is an indispensable indicator of democracy, it aims to give responsibility to educational stakeholders to develop quality individuals and effective instructional practices. Considering that we live in an information age surrounded by digital technologies that are improving incredibly fast, performance of educational institutions needs to keep up with this pace and global standards, and functional policies need to be devised. Based on this discourse, this paper aims to examine the extent to which the Turkish education system exhibits legal, administrative, professional, and result-oriented accountability and the resulting performance quality. In this study, where non-systematic literature review method with a critical style to identify central issues was used, implications were also presented to enable a more functional educational system that catches up with the time. The key findings were that; about *legal accountability*, there are flaws in the frequency and duration of course inspections done by school principals; in terms of *administrative accountability*, the number of observations within the whole Turkish education system is lacking, causing some teachers without being observed at all, and inspections not catching up with the 21st century needs to guide teachers and increase their and system's performance; as for *professional accountability*, more care needs to be given by principals to inform the teacher to be observed prior to the observation about the time of observation, also to check the appropriateness of their manners and words during this process towards the teacher during this process, and to maintain transparency in giving feedback. Finally, for *result-oriented accountability*, as effort put through principal observations to increase professional development of teachers and student success is insufficient, more planned and target-oriented observations need to be.

Keywords: Accountability in education, Turkish education system, Performance indicators in education

While accountability in education is an indispensable indicator of democracy, it aims to give responsibility to educational stakeholders to develop quality individuals and effective instructional practices. These practices range from examination of student knowledge, skills, and behaviors to the evaluation of educational institutions and their personnel about whether they have reached the goals of the national education system or not. In other words, it is the performance indicator of the system. The performance in the 21st century is measured in terms of the degree to which educational professionals, students, administrators, and institutions are preparing themselves to cope with the necessities of the information age and technologies as well as a set of skills in various areas. These skills, P21 define under four main groups as, "learning and innovation" based on creativity, critical thinking, problem solving, communication and collaboration; "information, media and technology literacy", and "life-career skills" that include accountability (Erdemir, 2024). Enabling the implementation and improvement of these skills will not only make it possible to perform at global standards but also promise the country to prosper through its well-equipped youth. To this end, along with personal efforts of students, and educational and administrative personnel in educational institutions, governmental support is of at most importance in terms of devising functional policies that aim the development of the performance of all educational institutions and their personnel, as well as ensuring their accountability.

The Turkish Ministry of National Education (MoNE) is composed of 92.902 schools (including pre-education, basic and secondary education levels), 19,155.571 students and 1,183.702 teachers as of 2021–22 (the most recent data present for all categories) academic year (MoNE, 2022a). For 2023, 14.6 % of the Central Government's Budget was spared to education (MoNE, 2022b). The MoNE, with its 23 general directorates and presidencies, forms a huge, multi-divisional organization. Both due to its size and centralized governing structure, one can wonder if and to what extent the MoNE executes its role of both managing the Turkish education system (TES) and implementing multi-level accountability efficaciously and transparently enough to fulfill the level of performance desired by citizens and the main societal stakeholders. In this sense, the more well-structured inspections can be realized, the better TES can adapt itself to the new situations that are planned and/or unexpected. For this to happen, more importance should be given to accountability and transparency in educational inspection.

The MoNE has faced prolonged criticisms due to inherent regulatory and operative shortcomings such as being multi-branched and divisionalised, and having a heavy and centralized structure, and thus, being far away from efficiency. Another point of concern was the inadequate transparency and accountability observed in the MoNE's major policies, decisions, and implementations (Fretwell, 2001; Özdemir, 2021). In addition, the fact that educational policies and the way things are being done in the TES have been exposed to too many changes also adds to the complexity and the lack of clarity in the system. What is more, since inspection reports are not shared with the public and major stakeholders, possible amelioration is being prevented. Therefore, both performance and accountability of the TES need to be revised revised based on the necessities the necessities of the 21st century.

In recent years, according to the requirements of the 21st century in education in Turkey, there is no comprehensive study on accountability in performance improvement. Based on this discourse, this paper aims to examine the extent to which the TES exhibits legal, administrative, professional, and result-oriented accountability and the resulting performance quality. Non-systematic literature review method was chosen in this study where relevant information were collected through articles published in refereed journals, books, governmental and non-governmental reports, theses and reliable organizational websites on education. Based on Creswell (2018)'s specifications of the literature review, this paper's style is closer to a "critical" style to "identify central issues". The specific questions of the study to which answers were sought are: *"How effective and efficient are the practices and services of TES in terms of their performance and accountability?" "What kind of strategies can improve the performance and accountability in the 21st century TES?"*

The paper first explains what educational inspection and accountability means. Then, legal, administrative, professional, and result-oriented accountability are explained regarding their qualities in the TES. Following that part, the effectiveness, and efficiency of these systems in MoNE are discussed regarding performance and accountability in the TES, and strategies are presented to improve performance and accountability in the TES. After making a comparison with the international and some national sources, concluding remarks are shared by making suggestions for practitioners and researchers.

Educational Inspection

An effective inspection is necessary for the formation, continuity, strengthening and continuous control of the efficiency of the organizational structure (Aydın, 2014). To Taymaz (2011), inspection is the process of comparing the plan and applications prepared in accordance with the objectives on site, finding errors and problems, identifying the causes, eliminating them and helping to ensure success. If we are to give a comprehensive definition of educational inspection, it can be stated as; systematic and democratic controls carried out in order to reveal the extent to which educational and organizational activities of everyone in the education, training, curriculum and system are carried out in educational organizations where the human element predominates to increase the quality of education and the effectiveness of teachers (Demirkasımoğlu, 2011; Janssens & Van Amelsvoort, 2008; Memduhoğlu et al., 2014). To put it briefly, educational inspection is the process of understanding whether the actions in educational organizations go in parallel with the principles and rules determined by the accepted objectives. Inspection is one of the most effective tools in the management approach, especially in the creation of a participatory, transparent, accountable, human rights and freedom-based public administration.

According to Article 42 of the Constitution of the Republic of Turkey (1982), educational inspections in Turkey are carried out under the supervision and control of the state in accordance with the principles and reforms of Atatürk, based on the principles of modern science and education. According to Article 56 of the National Education Basic Law No. 1739 published in the Official Gazette dated 24.06.1973 and numbered 14574, MoNE is responsible for the execution, observation and inspection of the education and training service on behalf of the state, relying on the provisions of this Law (Resmi Gazete, 1973). Types of supervision in education are divided into two as the supervision of administration and the supervision of teaching.

The supervision of the administration is the control of the institution whereas the supervision of the teaching corresponds to the inspection of the course (Balcı, 2024). We can define the inspection of the institution as making a judgment about the general functioning of the institution by examining the procedures related to the education and management processes of the school (Taymaz, 2015). Institutional inspections in schools are carried out by Education Inspectors in accordance the Regulation of the Inspection Board of the MoNE, which was published in the Official Gazette dated 20.08.2017 and numbered 30160 (Resmi Gazete, 2017). Institutional inspections are carried out periodically every three years in order to determine the status of the educational activities and management activities of institutions in terms of suitability and efficiency within the framework of the legal texts in force, to train the personnel on the job, to determine the level of achievement of the training goals and objectives and to increase their compliance with the task (MoNE, 2015a). Institutional inspections can also be defined as an audit of the management of the school. In the inspection of the institution, whether the school has completed the deficiencies seen in the previous inspection is observed, what needs to be done in the next one is decided, and the past, present and future of the institution are determined.

Course inspection, in general, is the observation and evaluation of the teacher in terms of their dominance in their field based on the objectives stipulated in the Basic Law of National Education, and of studies that are carried out to contribute to the academic success of students (Taymaz, 2015). Course inspection can also be defined as an audit process for teachers. Until 2014, course inspections in schools were mainly carried out by inspectors and rarely by school principals, but after 2014, it was left to school principals to carry out course inspections regularly (MoNE, 2014).

Other job descriptions of school principals regarding course inspections in pre-school (p. 63), primary education (p. 67) and secondary education (p. 71) institutions in the Tebliğler Dergisi (Journal of Communiques) No. 2508 of the MoNE can be summarized as follows based on the Articles 3, 10, 13, 18, 49 (MoNE, 2000): In addition to the preparing the principles and objectives of the National Education system, implementing and supervising the work plans in order to achieve the special objectives of the school; ensuring that education and training at school are carried out in a disciplined manner; guiding teachers in the preparation of plans according to educational programs and other work, supervising the work of teachers; receiving an annual plan from teachers at the beginning of the school year, approving the plans, supervising their implementation; encouraging teachers to train in areas related to their profession; closely monitoring the classes and other activities of teachers; observing and evaluating the performance of the personnel, investigating the reasons for low productivity, providing employment according to the abilities of the personnel, ensuring their training; monitoring teachers' use of social facilities such as laboratories and libraries. These articles constitute the legal basis for school principals to conduct course inspections. Accordingly, school principals are required to conduct course inspections twice a year, at least once a semester (MoNE, 2011).

Accountability in Education

Leithwood (2005), who explains the root of the word *account* to refer to "a report on, furnishing a justifying analysis or explanation, providing a statement of explanation of one's conduct, offering a statement or exposition of reasons, causes, grounds, or motives, or simply providing a statement of facts or events" (2005), suggests that the system of accountability necessitates answering five points: "the level of accountability", "whom the count will be given by?", "to whom the account will be given?", "what is to be accounted for?", and "the consequences of giving an account". Accountability in educational organizations is the written or verbal disclosure to an internal or external authority of the activities of the educational services that are carried out according to the determined purposes and standards, the performance results and the responsibility for the resources used while carrying out the activities (Cendon, 2000). The phenomenon of accountability also allows organizations to create a sense of trust about their functions at the social level (Balcı, 2013). For this reason, accountability is a hierarchical order in which the responsible manager explains the bureaucratic structure within their duty or responsibility (World Bank, 2004).

Accountability in education has been a phrase frequently used in the United States of America since the 1970s, after which in the 1980s, it began to develop as a standards-based accountability movement. It was followed by the Improving America's Schools Act (IASA) in 1994, which initiated a discussion of the accountability system at the state level, and in 2001, the No Child Left Behind Act provided a more established accountability system allowing for a specific framework for states to develop their own accountability systems (Hamilton et al., 2012; Perie et al., 2007). When it comes to the more recent past, talking about the 21st century educational standards, many organizations set out certain criteria for schools to meet and one of those criteria is "accountability". For instance, Partnership for 21st Century Learning (P21, 2019), which aims to prepare competent, skillful, knowledgeable, and successful students who can cope with the demands of the present age both in their everyday and work lives, included accountability as one of the important components of the 21st century life and career skills that students need to adopt. As not all educational institutions in Turkey have aligned themselves with the 21st century criteria yet, as Mayer (2013) suggested, educational policies created to this end should aim at "research-based standards" and "validated measures" that prioritize quality.

In Turkey, the requirement of accountability for employees in state institutions has been legally stated in the law. For instance, in Article 8 of the Public Financial Management and Control Law No. 5018, which entered into force in 2003 (Republic of Turkey Ministry of Finance Strategy Development Unit, 2013), in Article 1 of the Law No. 5176 on Establishing Council of Ethics for Public Service and Amending Some Laws issued in 2004 and Article 5 of the Regulation on the Principles of Ethical Conduct for Public Officials and Application Procedures and Principles, which entered into force in 2005 (Resmi Gazete, 2004). Likewise, in course inspections, school principals are required to exhibit transparent, impartial, and ethical behaviors and carry out their inspection in accordance with the laws and rules. There is no need to say that all these processes of inspection are executed by those at all levels of education systems, i.e. teachers, schools, school administrations, ministries of education and governments, to maximize students' learning environments and increase teacher performances.

Accountability Practices in the Turkish Educational System and the Resulting Performance

This section answers the first research question as *"How effective and efficient are the practices and services of TES in terms of their performance and accountability?"*.

Adams and Kirst (1999) put forth six types of educational accountability as "bureaucratic accountability, legal accountability, professional accountability, political accountability, moral accountability, and market- or choice-based accountability". In this section, legal, administrative (bureaucratic), professional and result-oriented accountability systems are explained and their effectiveness and efficiency are discussed.

Legal Accountability

The definition of legal accountability is the capacity to attest to one's actions (Joubert & Prinsloo, 2009). To Balcı (2013), it is proving adherence to legal requirements in terms of the efficiency of the tasks and transactions proposed, and it serves as an explanation for why the authority holders' acts are conducted fairly. Legal accountability is actually a necessary condition for the realization of its superiority of the rule of law.

In Uzun (2019)'s study, It has been reported that most school principals don't carry out the quantity and frequency of course inspection tasks outlined in the legislation, nor do they work with teachers in advance of inspections, and even when they do, they typically take the form of demands for documents and files; when doing a course inspection, school principals don't go into the classroom with the teacher; instead, they arrive one to ten minutes late, spend an hour in the classroom, and only a small percentage of them stay longer. While Fırıncıoğulları Bige (2014) claimed that varied amounts of time are allotted by school principals to course audits, Yılmaz (2018) similarly indicated that school principals' audit periods vary greatly from standard and are dependent on the supervisor. According to Yeşil and Kış (2015), the principals often conduct course audits once a year. Tonbul and Baysülen (2017) stated that the school principals were not trained in course supervision, that they had not conducted course audits frequently since 2014, and that the teachers had found the course audits to be ineffective. Demirtaş and Akarsu (2016) claimed that the principals of the schools who conducted the teacher inspections took sides, were deficient in course supervision, and had an entirely critical attitude toward the teachers. Overall, these findings underscore the importance of legal accountability in education and reveal significant shortcomings of school principals' carrying out their supervisory responsibilities. Better performance outcomes necessitate a need for improved training, standardized practices, and a more collaborative approach between school leaders and teachers so that effective course supervision and accountability in schools can be realized.

Administrative Accountability

Administrative accountability can be explained as the authority given by senior managers to their subordinates and the supervision of the level of realization of the orders or commands given for the fulfillment of the tasks in line with the determined goals and objectives. There are often two components to administrative responsibility: vertical and horizontal. While administrative accountability connects lower-level administrative jobs with higher-level political or administrative positions in the vertical dimension, in the horizontal dimension, citizens, as prospective or actual users of public services, exist in addition to various external oversight and control mechanisms including inspection bodies, audit organs, and ombudsmen for administrative accountability (Cendon, 2000).

In TES, supervision is being executed through two routes. One, through the Supervisory Board (Central) Authority, which oversees higher education establishments, and the other through Primary Education Supervisory (Provincial), which manages individuals and procedures, public early childhood education facilities, primary schools, and special education facilities, in addition to private educational establishments and supplementary classes and courses at primary and secondary educational level (Özdemir et al., 2010). Supervisors primarily oversee, evaluate, investigate, and analyze schools. They also take the appropriate action to address any inadequacies or flaws found during inspections (Eurydice, 2007).

In light of their duties and obligations, there are not enough inspectors (Turkish Education Association [TED], 2007). The inspectors at the Ministry are about 750 in number (450 inspector, 50 chief inspector and 250 assistant superintendent) (Hürriyet Gazetesi, 2017) and for the 2021–22 academic year, they inspected 384 high schools (state and private) out of 12.804, 24 pre-schools (state) out of 29.099; 80 primary schools (state) out of 22.480 (state); 52 secondary schools out of 16.651 (MoNE 2022a; MoNE, 2022c). Based on these figures, one may argue that while some high school instructors depart without facing significant inspections, many high schools enjoy extended periods without stress of inspection. Moreover, even if many schools are using new abilities and skills for the twenty-first century, those inspectors are still using outdated methods for evaluating educators and school administrators. Maybe this is the reason why the supervision and inspection units in the Turkish education system are considered the most archaic and traditional (Bursalıoğlu, 2002, 130).

The quality of the inspections that inspectors perform and the training they get are the other inspection-related issues. Following a written exam and an interview process, teachers with eight to ten years of experience are typically selected to be inspectors, or graduates of faculties of law, political sciences, economics and administrative sciences, economics and business administration that provide at least four years of undergraduate education or from higher education institutions in Turkey and abroad whose equivalence is accepted by the CoHE can be inspectors too (Resmi Gazete, 2022). This means that to be an inspector, one does not have to have a university degree or a certification specifically on inspection. Only in-service training by the MoNE is regarded as sufficient once they get their supervision position. It was reported that teachers believed inspectors did not adhere to the inspection-related rules and procedures strictly and were highly concerned with rigorous control and formal investigation but not much with advice and development (Akbaba, 1997). While the latter finding was supported by a report of the TED (2007), the same report concluded that teachers (71 %) believed that the assessment system was not being used appropriately and that it should be set up to serve as a guiding tool (pp. 70–71). Even though in accountability sideways, organizations are thought to be extremely attentive to the needs and desires of their members and report to them (Mahony, 2000), in the TES, it is not customary to take into account the opinions of some of the key players regarding the performance and success of schools, such as parents, teachers, and students.

The fact that school inspection results are kept private and not made public makes transparency another barrier to performance improvement and openness. However, since we live in a technological age, doing so ought to be practical. Accountability in the public and private sectors is greatly improved by openness and transparency (Organization for Economic Cooperation and Development [OECD], 2003). Openness allows the administration to be examined from the outside while transparency means allowing others to view the truth if they so want, or have the resources, time, and ability to do so (Yüksel, 2005). Nonetheless, even though most educational organizations and schools in Turkey have their own technology services and websites, the financial resources and spending of the national and provincial education authorities and schools are not accessible and transparent enough. Using democratic assessment methods that involve the communities in which they perform and exist, schools ought to exercise accountability democratically (Ryan, 2004). Major stakeholders and school staff should get together to establish a group to assess the success of the present policies and guidelines.

Major arrangements regarding the budget and financial management of public sector institutions are set by the Internal Audit Coordination Board, a supervisory mechanism that has been used successfully for years in many European countries. The Board was established in 2003 in the TES and it binds the MoNE (Eurydice, 2007). However, internal auditing is not functioning well, and the duties and authorities of MoNE internal auditors are not apparent. As Yaman's study (2008) indicated, MoNE managers and internal auditors reported a medium level of adaptation to the internal audit model's application criteria, suggesting that additional time and work will be required to fully apply the necessary elements. These results suggest opportunities for improvement to promote efficient monitoring, transparency, and equity in educational procedures while shedding light on the intricacies and difficulties of administrative responsibility within the Turkish educational system.

Professional Accountability

Professional accountability covers the evaluation of expertise, appreciation and special areas of work (Romzek, 2000). It necessitates a system of standards and procedures with both technical and ethical components, such as guidelines to control members of the profession's attitudes, actions, and output. These standards are incorporated into public administration's natural framework. As a result, professionals adhere to the normative framework that is ingrained in public administration. Nonetheless, their performance and behavior, which stem from their professionalism, serve as the main standards for their professional accountability (Cendon, 2000).

Educational accountability in Turkey at the central, provincial, and school level are generally employed in a traditional context which is very linear, unidirectional and upwards. The implementation of accountability in that way reflects on educational staff's understanding, attitudes, and behavior. The findings of the research on English and Turkish teachers' conceptions of their professional responsibility revealed that in Turkey, teachers feel responsible to students, parents, and teacher colleagues for more limited and more classroom-focused actions and teaching than their English counterparts (Karakaya, 2004). The reason for this difference could be rooted in the tradition of central control in Turkey and the fact that Turkish teachers' duties are strictly defined by the Ministry of Education. The research also showed that Turkish teachers generally feel accountable to their superiors, while their English colleagues feel accountable more to their students, colleagues, parents and the school.

There are studies that say that some school principals inform the teacher the day before, usually verbally and in daily communication language, that they will inspect the teacher before the class inspections, as well as studies that say that "most of them" do not (Yeşil & Kış, 2015) and "some" do not (Duykuluoğlu, 2016). In Uzun's study (2019), it was indicated that school principals do not fully abide by their duties about filling out evaluation forms fully during course inspections, about knocking on the door when entering the classroom, explaining the evaluation reports to the relevant teachers in detail after the inspections by by stating the rationales, and not allowing bilateral relations (e.g., political views and union differences or similarities) affect the evaluation process.

There are also studies indicating the existence of unethical behaviors and a lack of professional accountability resulting in some unjust actions. While in Uzun (2019)'s study, minority of teachers thought principals practiced positive discrimination towards teachers who adopted a similar political viewpoint with them, in some other studies, observations were stated to be done unethically due to political views and union differences between teachers and principals (Demirtaş & Akarsu, 2016; Şanlı et al., 2015). Sabancı and Yücel (2014) revealed that the supervisors exhibited moderate unethical behavior in the dimensions of teacher supervision and post-audit evaluation. Other studies on the TES revealing students' views indicated that 50 % of Turkish students thought that injustices were done to their peers (Akengin, 2008). In another study (Aydogan, 2009), a great deal of inequity was observed in schools where students felt that teachers favored students whose parents were better off financially or were either friends or family of the teachers, and shared similar political beliefs with them. These study results highlight the significance of professional accountability in education, particularly within the Turkish context, and emphasize the need for ethical standards and transparent practices to address perceived injustices and promote equity within the educational system.

Result-Oriented Accountability

According to the MoNE Course Supervision Guide in Turkey (MoNE, 2011), the aim of class observations is to enable an improvement in teacher performance that is about improving "results of inspection". After the course inspections, the majority of school principals did not put required effort to increase the professional development of teachers, and school principals thought that their course inspections had an effect on increasing the academic success of students whereas teachers did not agree with this (Uzun, 2019).

According to discussions in the literature, it is stated that standardization cannot be achieved before, during and after the course inspection of all types and levels in Turkey; in other words, each school principal carries out a different inspection practice by not fulfilling the laws and rules (Yeşil & Kış, 2015; Tonbul & Baysülen, 2017). It is expressed by the teachers that objectivity, openness, and transparency are ignored in the inspections, and that the bilateral relations between school principals and teachers are reflected in the process (Demirtaş & Akarsu, 2016; Ergen & Eşiyok, 2017; Konan et al., 2016; Şanlı et al., 2015). It was stated that the feedback after the principal evaluation were either limited or the teachers could not see the results of the evaluation at all; the guidance and on-the-job training activities that contributed to the development of the teachers during and after the audit process were almost never carried out and these limited studies did not contribute to the development of the teachers (Fırıncıoğulları Bige, 2014; Duykuluoğlu, 2016). As a result, in terms of preventing the abuse of the process, it is considered important for school principals' management and supervision practices to show characteristics in accordance with the principles of accountability beyond the traditional understanding. These results point to serious problems with the TES's accountability and course inspection procedures. To guarantee equity, openness, and efficacy in teacher evaluations and professional development programs, these problems must be resolved.

Suggestions to Improve Performance and Accountability in the Turkish Education System

This section is prepared in reply to the second research question *"What kind of strategies can improve the accountability and performance of educational institutions in the 21st century TES?"*. Although it is thought that the development of e-Government practices and the increasing use of information systems in the recent years will improve the decision-making process and ease accessibility of information, which will contribute to accountability, still, some recommendations that can further improve based on the 21st century needs and make the accountability process more transparent are presented below.

- *Policy building*: Erdağ and Karadağ (2017) stated that school principals and teachers thought that strong policies are needed that emphasize teachers' occupational competency and professional development. Accordingly, models that increase teacher autonomy and correct use of accountability can be put into practice.
- *Teacher occupational support alternatives*: Teachers can be encouraged to pursue graduate education for the continuity of their professional development (Kocak et al., 2012).
  - The positive aspects of the teachers can be reflected along with their deficiencies, specifying exemplary studies, motivating teachers, trying to eliminate the deficiencies of teachers and subjecting them to in-service training (Ergen & Eşiyok, 2017); inspections can be used as more than spotting a

negative situation but as mediums for betterment of teacher performance and the education system (Demirkasımoğlu, 2011).

• *Trust-based cooperation among stakeholders*: An environment of trust should be created in the school climate and closer cooperation between stakeholders should be ensured (Kocak et al., 2012).

• *Setting goals in strategic plans of schools*: In the annual implementation plans of the strategic plans prepared in the schools, targets should be determined in line with the deficiencies and disruptions seen in schools, and the achievement of the targets determined in the plan should be documented at the end of each term (Özen, 2011).

• *Transparency of accountability*: A web-based management information system should be established at the school and country level, and the system should enable all developments related to education in the school and in the country to be monitored by the public and the stakeholders of the educational institutions (Özen, 2011).

• *School principals inspecting teachers*: To increase school principals' competency in teacher inspection, they should go through in-service-training, classes should be supervised with the same frequency no matter what the experience of the teacher be, the inclusion of teachers in decision-making during course inspections should be legally guaranteed, and the course inspection of principals in secondary schools should be standardized through legal regulations. (Duykuluoğlu, 2016).

• *Objectivity of inspections*: As Şanlı et al. (2015) thought school principals inspecting teachers in the same school was not ethical since they knew them personally, and this could violate objectivity of observations. Therefore, it was suggested that inspections be done by independent observers outside the school. In other studies, due to the same concern, and also as inspectors are experts in their field, inspectors doing the inspections was considered more suitable (Demir & Tok, 2016).

Discussion

This study investigated the extent to which the TES exhibits legal, administrative, professional and results-oriented accountability and the resulting performance quality. Based on this aim, two research questions were formed that explored "the effectiveness and efficiency of the practices and services of TES in terms of their performance and accountability" and "strategies to improve the performance and accountability of the TES" through non-systematic literature review method. With this aim, four types of accountabilities were examined as legal, administrative, professional, and result-oriented accountability. Finally, some suggestions for policy were introduced. Below can be found the findings in the literature review compared and contrasted with existing studies in the national and international literature.

Regarding *legal accountability*, although teachers have to be inspected by their school principals at least once during an academic year in Turkey, there happened to be cases where teachers had not been inspected at all, and this is a common issue in both Turkish and international studies (Ünal & Şentürk, 2011; Makindi et al., 2017). The reason why school principals did not fulfill their duties of inspection can be them not being educated for being managers (Yılmaz, 2009). In international literature, there stated to be principals who knew what to do within the scope of inspection such as giving feedback, sharing information, observing and revising activities to be done all the time (Ayeni, 2012). This suggests that individuals who wish to shoulder the responsibility of inspection need to be subjected to stricter controls by the MoNE regarding the fulfillment of their duties.

Related to administrative *accountability*, the methods of inspection in the TES need to go through a renewal considering the necessities of the 21st century and the skills that students need to develop. The inadequate number of inspectors leaves most of the system uninspected. Another problem is about inspectors not getting a specific degree in college to document their expertise in inspection and using outdated methods for inspection. This caused dissatisfaction on the part of teachers as their expectations of receiving development-oriented feedback was missing and was replaced by control-based method. Demirkasımoğlu (2011) also criticized this issue of Turkish inspectors focusing more on the investigation function of their roles (the only country stated to be so in her study, compared with England, France, Germany, the United States of America, Japan, Iran, Russia, and the Republic of South Africa) rather than occupational guidance and advice, which overshadows their roles of ameliorating and developing the system.

In terms of *professional accountability*, there occur issues originating from employing traditional style of accountability for the central, provincial, and school level inspections. The implementation of accountability in that way reflects on educational staff's understanding, attitudes, and behavior. Regarding Turkish inspectors' inconsistency in in whether to make an explanation about coming to the class for inspection, the international literature suggests that due to occupational ethics, not only teachers but also school principals need to be accountable (Kantos, 2010). Similar to the findings in Turkey, Makindi et al. (2017) stated that school principals rarely used a professional document during teacher inspections. However, Range et al. (2011) explained that school principals used follow-up instructions for inspection. Similar to Turkish teachers' statements that school principals do not explain their post-observation reports to them with their rationales, Makindi et al. (2017) agreed that principals did not share their feedback with teachers. Regarding this issue, Taymaz (2015) mentioned the necessity for principals to get into contact with teachers in a democratic environment upon finishing class observations to explain the strengths of the class, discuss the reasons for weaknesses, and suggest ways for improvement. There are other researchers' views in support of this suggestion that principals need to come together with the teacher to spot the problems in the class and solve them, after which a second observation should take place (Ergen & Eşiyok, 2017). As for unethicality of doing observations within the responsibility of professional accountability, it is explained in many (non)governmental documents that during education inspection, school principals need to maintain equality and meritocracy among teachers, which involves not discriminating or favoring teachers based on factors such as political and/or differences or similarities in religion, language, ethnicity, gender, social class, disability and so on (MoNE, 2015b; OECD, 2009).

About *result-oriented accountability*, few teachers agreed on principals' views that the latter worked on teachers' improvement through guidance and exchange of ideas. Other studies reported similar results that principal observations did not serve the purpose of teacher improvement but just a formality picturing an inspection-heavy role (Demir & Tok, 2016; Reinhorn & Johnson, 2015) based on bureaucratic control, and thus, are not effective practices (Koç, 2018; Ünal & Şentürk, 2011; Tonbul & Baysülen, 2017). In relation to this, Bouchamma and Basque (2012), emphasizing the role of the inspector, drew attention to the importance of guiding the teacher in the initial and subsequent training.

Pertaining to the second research question about suggestions for more accountable and better performance in the 21st century TES, international literature also presents some examples that worked toward this aim, some of which can be adapted to the TES. The most comprehensive measure that can be taken will be about powerful policy building that aim for teachers' occupational development. According to the Eurydice Report (Eurydice, 2018), most schools in Europe are expected to develop continuous development plans for all personnel, and in less than one third of countries, teachers need to have continuous occupational development plans. This is important for occupational improvement and increase in salaries in countries like Spain, Bulgaria, Lithuania, Portugal, Romania Slovenia, and Slovakia. An example of these processes is explained to be the candidacy process, which is seen as a structured support program for beginning teachers that lasts for a year on average. It asks new teachers to perform all or many of the tasks that are the responsibility of experienced teachers, and they get paid for their hard work. Induction programs include regular meetings with the advisor, help with lesson planning and other pedagogical advice, opportunities for follow-up work, and training modules provided by instructors. For instance, in France, Italy, Luxembourg, Malta, Portugal and the United Kingdom, candidacy is seen as a trial period, and in some cases, allows for a transition to a permanent contract. Whereas in Turkey, teachers do not go through a mandatory education period under the supervision of an experienced teacher. If a formal guidance is provided by experienced teachers, and this is inspected by schools or inspectors of the MoNE, and if both parties are get paid for it, this kind of a formal buddy system can also work in Turkey.

About principals' competency in teacher evaluations, issues were stated in the Turkish literature. Similarly, in Mosoge and Pilane (2014)'s study, it was also criticized that due to "a lack of knowledge and expertise" on performance management, "mentoring, coaching and monitoring" activities were dimming the enthusiasm for putting performance management into practice. Therefore, teachers' important role in contributing to the development of the educational policies and transforming the educational system together with the inspection mechanism was pointed out.

Conclusion

In this study, the issue of accountability in the TES was discussed considering the requirements of the 21st century and the resulting performance of schools, students and teachers. In this context, the effectiveness and efficiency of the performance of the TES have been put under spotlight using non-systematic literature review. The studies, reports, and various documents about the topic were presented within the framework of legal, professional, administrative, and result-oriented accountability.

Within the framework of "legal accountability", it was put forth in the study that although course supervision, which is among the main duties of school principals, should be carried out twice a a year and at least at least once a semester, according to the laws and standards specified in the regulations, inspectors do not do this often. In addition, it was noted that while school principals have to follow at least one class "in full", only some showed this care, while others stayed in the classroom for less time or preferred to do observations for different periods of time. All these suggest that legal accountability principles are not fully followed in the TES.

For "administrative accountability", the major concern was found to be the insufficient number of observations done by inspectors that left many teachers uninspected in the TES. Plus, the outdated methods of inspection that feel short of relating to the needs of the 21st century was also indicated. It was underlined the need for inspectors to get a degree on inspection to increase their competence. This would also contribute to the performance improvement of teachers and students.

In terms of "professional accountability", it has been observed that school principals should schedule their visit with their teachers prior to course audits. However, However, not only few of them follow this protocol, but also there is no standard for when to visit the classrooms, whether to knock on doors whether they knock on doors, or what mannerisms and sentence construction to use. Additionally, there is a lack of compliance with the inspection guidelines. Furthermore, it has come to light that although principals shoulder the duty of course supervision, they are not entirely fulfilling their obligation to use teacher assessment forms for notetaking when they they visit classrooms in order to maintain neutrality and openness. In addition, after the inspections, school principals failed to provide their instructors with a thorough feedback and explanation of the teacher evaluation reports along with their justifications, and the feedback they did provide was insufficient. Bilateral contacts were only partly appropriate for conducting the inspections due to differences or similarities in unions and political ideas. All of these indicate a lack of complete adherence to the professional responsibility principles.

About "result-oriented accountability", it has been revealed that most of the work has not been done to increase the professional development of teachers after the course inspections of school principals' thinking that their course inspections contributed to the enhancement of the academic success of students despite teachers' disagreement with the idea. These outcomes pointed out the fact that the principles of result-oriented accountability are not fully adhered to.

Numerous administrative, political, and organizational issues plague the Turkish educational system. It does not work well enough to live up to public expectations. In tests, students typically fall short of the rigorous national and international norms. MoNE's laborious, centralist, and ineffective organizational structure is the root of these issues. Furthermore, the Ministry lacks the authority to enact the rules and guidelines required to establish effective accountability standards and high-performance requirements. An up-to-date, efficient accountability mechanism in Turkey's educational system cannot be substituted for the ineffective, inefficient, and highly traditional supervision and evaluation that is now in place. However, there is no need for despair in the age of information, technology, and space, as these will compel legislators to establish an efficient, democratic, and responsible TES.

Suggestions for Practitioners

For course inspections to achieve their objectives in schools in Turkey, inspections carried out by principals can be rearranged within the frames of legal accountability, administrative accountability, professional accountability, and result-oriented accountability, and necessary studies on the accountability of teachers and principals can be initiated by the MoNE. Teacher inspections can be carried out in a multifaceted and planned manner, with a process-oriented approach, according to the issues specified in the laws and rules. The inspection legislation regarding the objective, transparent and ethical behavior of school principals in the course audit process can be updated and a new teacher inspection guide for the use of school principals can be published. Course inspections can be carried out in the form of developing the teacher and guiding the teacher beyond formality and document investigation, and all school principals can be required to have a master's degree in the field of educational management and supervision for course inspections to contribute more to the professional development of teachers.

Suggestions for Researchers

Within the framework of accountability in education, a new course inspection model can be created by making use of examples from around the world. The opinions of education inspectors and academicians working in educational sciences can be consulted on the subject too.

References

Adams, J. E., & Kirst, M. (1999). New demands for educational accountability: Striving for results in an era of excellence. In J. Murphy & K. S. Louis (Eds.), *Handbook of research in educational administration* (2nd ed., pp. 463–489). Jossey-Bass.

Akbaba, S. (1997, August 12–16). *Teachers and the role of the inspectors in centralized Turkish primary schools* [Paper presentation]. The 51st Annual Conference of the National Council of Professors of Educational Administration, Vail, Colorado.

Akengin, H. (2008). A comparative study on children's perceptions of the child rights in the Turkish community of Turkey and Northern Cyprus. *Preview Education, 129*(2), 224–238.

Aydın, İ. (2014). *Öğretimde denetim*. Pegem Akademi Yayıncılık.

Aydoğan, İ. (2009). Favoritism in the classroom: A study on Turkish schools. *Journal of Instructional Psychology, 35*(2), 159–168. https://eric.ed.gov/?id= EJ813319

Ayeni, A. J. (2012). Assessment of principals' supervisory roles for quality assurance in secondary schools in Ondo state, Nigeria. *World Journal of Education, 2*(1), 62–69. http://dx.doi.org/10.5430/wje.v2n1p62

Balcı, A. (2024). *Açıklamalı eğitim yönetimi terimleri sözlüğü* (9th ed.). Pegem Akademi Yayıncılık.

Balcı, A. (2013). Kamu yönetiminde hesap verebilirlik anlayışı. In A. Balcı, A. Nohutçu, N. K. Öztürk, & B. Coşkun (Eds.), *Kamu yönetiminde çağdaş yaklaşımlar* (pp. 155–180). Seçkin Yayıncılık.

Bouchamma, Y., & Basque, M. (2012). Supervision practices of school principals: Reflection in action. *US-China Education Review, 7,* 627–637. https:// files.eric.ed.gov/fulltext/ED535512.pdf

Bursalıoğlu, Z. (2002). *Okul yönetiminde yeni yapı ve davranışlar.* Pegem Akademi Yayıncılık.

Cendon, A. B. (2000). Accountability and public administration: Concepts, dimensions, developments. In M. Kelle (Ed.), *Openness and transparency in governance: Challenges and opportunities* (pp. 22–61). Network of Institutes and Schools of Public Administration in Central and Eastern Europe.

Creswell, J. W., & Creswell, J. D. (2018). *Research design: Qualitative, quantitative, and mixed methods approach* (5th ed.). Sage Publishing.

Demir, M., & Tok, T. N. (2016). Lisansüstü öğrenci görüşlerine göre eğitim denetimi. *Trakya Üniversitesi Eğitim Fakültesi Dergisi, 6*(2), 102–125.

Demirkasımoğlu, N. (2011). Türk eğitim sisteminde bir alt sistem olan denetim sisteminin seçilmiş bazı ülkelerin denetim sistemleri ile karşılaştırılması. *Abant İzzet Baysal Üniversitesi Sosyal Bilimler Enstitüsü Sosyal Bilimler Enstitüsü Dergisi, 2*(23), 23–48. https://dergipark.org.tr/tr/pub/basbed/- issue/43916/174761

Demirtaş, H., & Akarsu, M. (2016). Öğretmen teftişini müfettiş yerine okul müdürünün yapmasına ilişkin öğretmen görüşleri. *İnönü Üniversitesi Eğitim Fakültesi Dergisi, 17*(2), 69–93. https://dergipark.org.tr/tr/pub/inuefd/issue/- 26708/280939

Duykuluoğlu, A. (2016). *Lise müdürlerinin ders denetim görevine ilişkin öğretmen görüşleri* [Unpublished master's thesis, Ankara University]. Council of Higher Education Thesis Center.

Erdağ, C., & Karadağ, E. (2017). Öğretmenler ve okul müdürleri perspektifinden okul hesap verebilirliği politikaları. *Uluslararası Toplum Araştırmaları Dergisi, 7*(13), 459–496. http://dx.doi.org/10.26466/opus.292614

Erdemir, B. (2024). A new mindset in teacher education. In B. Ç. Garipağaoğlu (Ed.), *Need for a new paradigm in education*. Peter Lang. (In publication process)

Ergen, E., & Eşiyok, İ. (2017). Okul müdürlerinin ders denetimi yapmasına ilişkin öğretmen görüşleri. *Çağdaş Yönetim Bilimleri Dergisi, 3*(1), 1–18.

Eurydice. (2007). *Türk eğitim sisteminin örgütlenmesi*. www.eurydice.org

Eurydice. (2018). *Key data on teachers and school leaders in Europe:* 2013 Edition. [Eurydice Report]. Luxembourg: Publications Office of the European Union. Retrieved April 1, 2024, from https://eurydice.meb.gov.tr/meb_iys_dosyalar/2023_1

Fırıncıoğulları Bige, E. (2014). *İlkokul müdürlerinin ders denetimleri ile ilgili öğretmen görüşleri* [Unpublished master's thesis, Adnan Menderes University]. Council of Higher Education Thesis Center.

Fretwell, D. H. (2001). *Turkey secondary education and training*. Secondary education series. World Bank, Human Development Network, Education Group. https://documents1.worldbank.org/curated/zh/774481468779124355/pdf/multi0page.pdf

Hamilton, L. S., Stecher, B., & Yuan, K. (2012). Standards-based accountability in the United States: Lessons learned and future directions. *Education Inquiry, 3*(2), 149–170. http://dx.doi.org/10.3402/edui.v3i2.22025

Hürriyet Gazetesi. (2017, August 21). MEB'in müfettiş sayısı 750'ye çıktı. https://www.hurriyet.com.tr/egitim/mebin-mufettis-sayisi-750ye-cikti-40557231

Janssens, F. J. G., & van Amelsvoort, G. H. W. C. H. (2008). School self-evaluations and school inspections in Europe: An exploratory study. *Studies in Educational Evaluation, 34*(1), 15–23. http://dx.doi.org/10.1016/j.stueduc.2008.01.002

Joubert, R., & Prinsloo, S. (2009). *The law of education in South Africa*. Van Schaik.

Kantos, Z. E. (2010). *İlköğretim okulu yönetici ve öğretmenlerinin görüşlerine göre kamu ve özel ilköğretim okulları için bir hesap verebilirlik modeli* [Unpublished doctoral dissertation, Ankara University]. Council of Higher Education Thesis Center.

Karakaya, Ş. (2004). A comparative study: English and Turkish teachers' conceptions of their professional responsibility. *Educational Studies, 30*(3), 200–205. http://dx.doi.org/10.1080/0305569042000224170

Koç, M. H. (2018). Okul müdürleri tarafından yapılan öğretmen denetimlerine ilişkin ilkokul müdürlerinin görüşleri. *Marmara Üniversitesi Atatürk Eğitim Fakültesi Eğitim Bilimleri Dergisi, 48*(48). https://doi.org/10.15285/marua ebd.349727

Koçak, E., Turan, S., & Aydoğdu, E. (2012). Öğretmenlerin yetki devri, otonomi ve hesap verebilirliklerine ilişkin görüşlerinin incelenmesi. *Eğitim ve İnsani Bilimler Dergisi, 3*(5), 117–148.

Konan, N., Aslan, M., Bozanoğlu, B., & Çetin, R. B. (2016). *Ders denetimi görevinin okul müdürlerine verilmesine ilişkin okul müdürü ve öğretmen görüşleri* [Paper presentation] 8th International Education Inspection Congress, Antalya.

Leithwood, K. (2005). *Educational accountability: Issues and alternatives* [Research Report]. Saskatchewan School Boards Association.

Mahony, P. (2000). *Reconstructing teaching: Standards, performance and accountability*. Routledge.

Makindi, F. M., Adhiambo, J., & Gikuhi, M. (2017). Supervisory roles of principals during classroom instruction and effective implementation of life skills education in public secondary schools in Nairobi County, Kenya. *International Journal of Innovative Research and Advanced Studies, 4*(11), 229–236. http://www.ijiras.com/2017/Vol_4-Issue_11/paper_38.pdf

Mayer, D. (2013). Policy driven reforms and the role of teacher educators in reframing teacher education in the 21st century. *Waikato Journal of Education, 18*(1), 7–19. http://dx.doi.org/10.15663/wje.v18i1.133

Memduhoğlu, H. B., Mazlum, M. M., & Acar, M. (2014). Eğitim denetmenlerinin iletişim becerilerine ilişkin öğretmen algıları. *Kastamonu Eğitim Dergisi, 23*(4), 1535–1552.

MoNE. (2000). Okul müdürünün görev, yetki ve sorumluluğu. *Milli Eğitim Bakanlığı Tebliğler Dergisi, 63*(2508). https://dhgm.meb.gov.tr/tebligler-dergisi/-2000/2508-ocak-2000.pdf

MoNE. (2011). *Öğretmen denetim rehberi*. Ankara: Milli Eğitim Bakanlığı Rehberlik ve Denetim Başkanlığı Yayını.

MoNE. (2014). Millî Eğitim Bakanlığı Rehberlik ve Denetim Başkanlığı ile Maarif Müfettişleri Başkanlıkları Yönetmeliği. https://www.resmigazete.gov.tr/eskiler/2014/05/20140524-18.htm

MoNE. (2015a). *Maarif müfettişleri görev standartları*. Rehberlik ve Denetim Başkanlığı. https://www.memurlar.-net/common/news/documents/497810/-maarfmfettlergrevstandartlari.pdf

MoNE. (2015b). *Circular on professional ethical principles for educators*. https://mevzuat.meb.gov.tr/dosyalar/1997.pdf

MoNE. (2022a). *Örgün eğitim istatistikleri*. Retrieved March 28, 2024, from https://istatistik.meb.gov.tr/

MoNE. (2022b). *Bakan Özer, TBMM Plan ve Bütçe Komisyonu'nda 2023 yılı eğitim bütçesine ilişkin sunum yaptı.* https://www.meb.gov.tr/bakan-ozer-tbmm-plan-ve-butce-komisyonunda-2023-yili-egitim-butcesine-iliskin-sunum-yapti/haber/28055/tr

MoNE. (2022c). *2021 Administration activity report.* https://sgb.meb.gov.tr/meb_iys_dosyalar/2022_03/01003833_MEB_2021_YYlY_Ydare_Faaliyet_Raporu.pdf

Mosoge, M. J., & Pilane, M. W. (2014). Performance management: The neglected imperative of accountability systems in education. *South African Journal of Education, 34*(1), 1–18.

OECD. (2003). *Public sector transparency and the international investor.* https://www.oecd.org/investment/investment-policy/18546790.pdf

OECD. (2009). *Teacher evaluation. A conceptual framework and examples of country* practices. https://www.oecd.org/education/school/44568106.pdf

Özdemir, S., Bülbül, M., & Acar, M. (2010, May 14–16). Challenges associated with administrative and professional accountability in the Turkish educational system. In J. Nemec & B. G. Peters (Eds.), *State and administration in a changing world: NISPAcee Annual Conference* (pp. 271–282). https://ssrn.com/abstract=1992399

Özdemir, S. (2021). Türk eğitim sistemin yapısı, eğilimleri ve sorunları. In S. Özdemir (Ed.), *Türk eğitim sistemi ve okul yönetimi* (pp. 7–46). Pegem Akademi Yayıncılık.

Özen, F. (2011). *İlköğretim okulu yönetici ve öğretmenlerinin görüşlerine göre okul geliştirme aracı olarak hesap verebilirlik.* [Unpublished doctoral dissertation, Ankara University]. Council of Higher Education Thesis Center.

P21. (2019). *Framework for 21st century learning.* https://www.battelleforkids.org

Perie, M., Park, J., & Klau, U. K. (2007). *Key elements for educational accountability models.* https://www.wyoleg.gov/InterimCommittee/2011/SelectAccountability/Key%20elements%20final2.pdf

Range, B. G., Scherz, S., Holt, C. R., & Young, S. (2011). Supervision and evaluation: The Wyoming perspective. *Educational Assessment, Evaluation and Accountability, 23*(3), 243–265. http://dx.doi.org/10.1007/s1092-011-9123-5

Reinhorn, S., & Johnson, S. M. (2015). Can teacher evaluation provide both accountability and development? Learning from six schools' implementation of evaluation policy. Retrieved March 30, 2024, from https://projectngt.gse.harvard.edu/files/gse-projectngt/files/can_evaluation_provide_accountability_and_development_1016.pdf

Republic of Turkey Ministry of Finance Strategy Development Unit. (2013). *Public Financial Management and Control Law No. 5018.* https://ms.hmb.gov. tr/uploads/2019/01/Public-Financial-Management-and-Control-Law-No.-5018.pdf

Resmi Gazete. (1973). *Milli Eğitim Temel Kanunu.* https://www.resmigazete.gov.tr/arsiv/14574.pdf

Resmi Gazete. (2004). *Regulation on the principles of ethical behavior of public officials and application procedures and essentials.* https://ms.hmb.gov.tr/uplo ads/2019/02/etik_regulation.pdf

Resmi Gazete. (2017). *Milli Eğitim Bakanlığı Teftiş Kurulu Yönetmeliği* https:// www.resmigazete.gov.tr/eskiler/2017/08/20170820-1.htm

Resmi Gazete. (2022). *Milli Eğitim Bakanlığı Eğitim Müfettişleri Yönetmeliği.* https://www.resmigazete.gov.tr/eskiler/2022/03/20220301-9.htm

Romzek, B.S. (2000). Dynamics of public sector accountability in an era of reform. *International Review of Administrative Sciences, 66,* 21-44. https://doi.org/10.1177/0020852300661004

Ryan, K. E. (2004). Serving public interests in educational accountability: Alternative approaches to democratic evaluation. *American Journal of Evaluation, 25*(4), 457–460. http://dx.doi.org/10.1177/109821400402500403

Sabancı, A., & Yücel, E. (2014). Öğretmenlerin görüşlerine göre denetmenlerin etik dışı davranma düzeyleri. *e-International Journal of Educational Research, 5*(2), 1–19. https://www.e-ijer.com/tr/pub/issue/8026/105467

Şanlı, Ö., Altun, M., & Tan, Ç. (2015). Okul müdürlerinin denetmenlik görevlerindeki yeterlik düzeylerinin değerlendirilmesi. *Elektronik Eğitim Bilimleri Dergisi, 4*(7), 82–99.

Taymaz, H. (2011). *İlköğretim ve ortaöğretim okul müdürleri için okul yönetimi.* Pegem Akademi.

Taymaz, H. (2015). *Eğitim sisteminde teftiş.* Pegem Akademi

TED. (2007). *Türkiye'de okul öncesi eğitim ve ilköğretim sistemi,* Özet Rapor. Turkish Education Association.

Tonbul, Y., & Baysülen, E. (2017). Ders denetimi ile ilgili yönetmelik değişikliğinin maarif müfettişlerinin, okul yöneticilerinin ve öğretmenlerin görüşleri açısından değerlendirilmesi. *İlköğretim Online, 16*(1), 299–311. https://dergipark.org.tr/tr/pub/ilkonline/issue/28825/308461

Uzun, O. N. (2019). *Okul müdürlerinin ders denetim etkinliklerinin hesap verebilirlik çerçevesinde incelenmesi* [Unpublished master's thesis, Tokat Gaziosmanpaşa University]. Council of Higher Education Thesis Center.

Ünal, A., & Şentürk, R. (2011, September 8–10). *İlköğretim okul müdürlerinin ders denetimi uygulamaları.* [Paper Presentation]. The 20th National Educational Sciences Congress, Burdur, Turkey

World Bank. (2004). *State-society synergy for accountability: Lessons for the World Bank.* [World Bank Working Paper; No. 30]. http://hdl.handle.net/10986/14944

Yaman, A. (2008). *İç denetim modelinin Milli Eğitim Bakanlığı'nda benimsenme ve uygulanabilirliğine ilişkin yönetici ve denetçi görüşleri* [Unpublished master's thesis, Ankara University]. Council of Higher Education Thesis Center.

Yeşil, D., & Kış, A. (2015). Okul müdürlerinin ders denetimlerine ilişkin öğretmen görüşlerinin incelenmesi. *İnönü Üniversitesi Eğitim Bilimleri Enstitüsü Dergisi, 2*(3), 27–45.

Yılmaz, K. (2009). Okul müdürlerinin denetim görevi. *İnönü Üniversitesi Eğitim Fakültesi Dergisi, 10*(1), 19–35.

Yılmaz, Y. (2018). *Okul müdürleri tarafından ders denetimi yapılmasına ilişkin yönetici ve öğretmen görüşleri.* [Unpublished master's thesis, Pamukkale University]. Council of Higher Education Thesis Center.

Yüksel, B. (2005). *Devlette etikten etik devlete: Kamu yönetiminde etik kavramsal çerçeve ve uluslararası uygulamalar.* TÜSİAD Yayınları.

Dr. Evrim Eveyik-Aydın

Dr. Ece Genç-Yöntem

Chapter 10 Reflective Practices and Teacher Research for Pre-service Teachers' Professional Development in Language Teacher Education

Abstract: This chapter explores the concepts of *reflectivity* and *teacher research* in the field of language teacher education. This exploration involves defining these concepts, unraveling their interconnections, examining their nature and scopes, and assessing the effectiveness of such reflective practices in language teacher education. Besides, the chapter concludes by providing suggestions supported by empirical evidence to enhance the implementation of these critical practices for pre-service teachers' professional development in the ITE programs. The aspiration is that the knowledge gained from this chapter not only supports the development of prospective teachers' reflective mindset, an essential 21st century skill, through key tasks and research, but also provides guidance for teacher educators and practitioners in their ongoing learning and professional growth.

Keywords: reflectivity, teacher research, language teacher education, professional development

The professional development journey of teachers commences during their time as students in initial teacher education (ITE) programs, wherein they cultivate practical theories to plan, implement, and assess their future teaching practices and instructional strategies (Körkkö et al., 2016; Levin & He, 2008). An inherent difficulty for pre-service teachers in these programs is to build a connection between the theoretical content and pedagogical knowledge attained in courses and the practical teaching knowledge gained during micro-teaching and practicum experiences. In other words, putting theoretical knowledge into practice proves challenging for pre-service teachers (Çelik & Eveyik-Aydın, 2023; Zaragoza et al., 2021). To fortify this connection, various tasks, such as keeping reflective journals (Bain, et al., 2002; Francis, 1995; Karpava, 2023; Nuraeni & Heryatun, 2021), engaging in observational learning (Karpava, 2023; Young & Bender-Slack, 2011), participating in micro-teachings and collaborative teaching practices, coupled with subsequent self-evaluation and peer-evaluation reports (Korthagen, 2001; Reddy, 2019; Shuwen & Yui, 2023;Taggart & Wilson, 2005; Zeichner & Liston, 1996) play a crucial role. These reflective tasks enable pre-service teachers to critically evaluate their strengths and weaknesses, explore their decision-making processes, and attain skills to plan lessons and create ideal learning environments for their students, all while adopting a teacher's perspective by consistently scrutinizing the underlying assumptions during their actions (Chien, 2014; Nuraeni & Heryatun, 2021; Jay & Johnson, 2002). It is also important to support pre-service teachers' engagement in research to foster their development as prospective reflective practitioners and researchers (Borg, 2013; Burns, 2009b; Cabaroglu, 2014; Cochran-Smith & Lytle, 1999; Dikilitaş & Bostancıoğlu, 2019).

With that said, this chapter aims to provide the stakeholders of education with a deep understanding of the concepts of *reflectivity* and *teacher research* in the field of language teacher education, while uncovering the toolkit for professional development.

Historical Roots of Reflective Teaching

The concept of *reflection* was introduced in the early 20th century. In the 1930s, John Dewey was one of the pioneering progressive educational theorists in the United States who perceived teachers as reflective practitioners with significant roles in shaping decisions that could impact curriculum development, educational reform, and the society at large (Zeichner & Liston, 1996). He perceived schools with reflective teachers as the agents of social change. According to Dewey, reflective thought involves *"Active, persistent, and careful consideration of any belief or supposed form of knowledge in the light of the grounds that support it, and the further conclusions to which it tends"* (1933, p. 9), and begins when teachers encounter challenging experiences. While reflective teachers deliberately engage in critical thinking about these experiences, whether during or after the course of their teaching, unreflective teachers operate based on routine actions and the collective codes of their schools without critically questioning their experiences, thus becoming "merely the agents of others" (Zeichner & Liston, 1996, p. 9).

Dewey's emphasis on the fundamental role of teachers in reforming education considerably influenced Kurt Lewin, a social psychologist who developed the action research method in response to the problems in social action in the mid-1940s and provided the theoretical groundwork for teacher research. During the tumultuous era of World War II, Lewin actively pursued democratic inquiry within the social sciences believing that social challenges should be the driving force for public inquiry within democratic communities. His organizational action research which prioritized reflection involved a circle of activities, namely problem analysis, fact-finding, conceptualization, planning, implementation, more fact-finding and evaluation (Dickens & Watson, 1999). The aim of this cyclical process of taking action and reflecting on the outcomes was to cause positive changes in organizations, engaging all of its members in the process. Lewin and his followers also classified the action research as *diagnostic, participant, empirical* and *experimental* (for their descriptions and more detail on the origins of action research see Adelman, 1993). While action research was introduced to the field of education in the 1950s by Stephen Corey, a professor of education at Teachers' College, who highlighted the experiential knowledge teachers acquired through inquiry, it did not gain popularity until the 1980s (Efron & Ravid, 2020). In the 1970s, Lawrence Stenhouse, a professor of education in the United Kingdom, initiated the Humanities Curriculum Project and urged teachers to become *practitioner researchers* by systematically examining and scrutinizing their teaching practices for professional development. He advocated for testing and questioning educational theories through practical application and fostering a willingness to openly share and discuss one's work with others (Hammersley, 1993). His work encouraged teachers to engage in research in the United States, Canada, Australia, and New Zealand in the 1980s (Efron & Ravid, 2020).

In the 1980s, fifty years after Dewey, Donald Schön (1983, 1988) extended the concept of reflection by making a distinction between the two types of reflective practices teachers could undertake: *reflection-in-action* and *reflection-on-action*. During teaching, professionals frequently encounter uncertain and unique situations that demand spontaneous action based on their intuitive feelings and implicit knowledge. According to Schön, this knowledge in action is not rooted in prior intellectual operation but is accumulated through experience in practice. When this "intuitive performance leads to surprises, pleasing and promising or unwanted" (1983, p. 56), teachers start explicitly thinking about the situation at hand during the course of action and hence *reflection-in-action* occurs. *Reflection-on-action*, however, takes place when teachers critically think about their decisions and teachings after they have occurred. Hence, they consider the implications of their actions, evaluate the effectiveness of their decisions, and learn from their experiences to improve future performance. This reflective process contributes to teachers' ongoing professional development, refining their skills and knowledge over time.

Building upon Schön's concept of reflection, Wallace (1991) introduced reflective practice to the field of second language teaching. He proposed a teacher training model that integrates received knowledge, acquired through observing and imitating an experienced master teacher (the craft model), research-based knowledge relying on empirical science (the applied science model) and experiential knowledge acquired through an ongoing reflective practice. In his reflective model, he emphasized the importance of continuous reflective and critical analysis of teaching facilitated by diverse professional development practices to achieve professional competence. Before we proceed with the reflective practices that were integrated into ITE programs in second language teaching ever since, let us explore teacher research as a significant means for professional development.

Teacher Research as a Professional Development Tool

A promising yet still critiqued change in teacher education has been a growing interest in teacher research, which was resulted from published papers in the late 80s aiming at improving teaching, learning and curriculum through a shift in the roles of teachers towards being "knower and agent for change" and "researcher, who did not need more findings from university-based researchers, but more dialogue with other teachers that would generate theories grounded in practice" (Cochran-Smith & Lytle, 1999, p. 15). As the new roles such as "decision maker, consultant, curriculum developer, analyst, activist, school leader" have been added to teachers in education, the scope of teacher research has been enhanced (Cochran-Smith & Lytle, 1999, p. 17) to include the understanding of different contexts and educational dimensions. Therefore, some teacher educators and researchers questioned the knowledge of practical implications and implementation of the results of university-based research studies in the real classroom settings, which was obviously due to the unique and dynamic nature of each classroom setting and various factors involved in students' learning. Another reason that has led to the revival of teacher research especially in the U.S. was the published papers based on "intellectual movement" which encouraged teachers' being involved in the research community to engage in research "as a form of social action and change" (Beyer, 1988 in Cochran-Smith & Lytle, 1999, p. 15). Teacher research in the form of action research was described by Burns (2009b) as follows:

> As the researcher plans and undertakes actions to enhance the current situation, she also deliberately observes and documents what happens as a result of these actions. Often, the results of changes are unpredictable and reveal new or unexpected avenues for further action, which is then observed and documented further (p. 290).

According to this description, teacher researchers induce change to enhance teaching and learning in their classrooms by actively taking actions, observing, taking notes, and evaluating. Lastly, the ideas that support teachers as "expert knowers of their students" and "teaching as research" (Duckworth, 1987 in Cochran-Smith & Lytle, 1999, p. 16) have been influential in the teacher research movement in the U.S. Thus, the idea that research is a part of teaching has been supported by distinguished scholars such as Zeichner (2015), who consider teacher research to be a reflective mindset that involves questioning and exploring one's teaching practices as well as the settings in which they occur.

Teacher research have encountered criticism until it firmly established its position within the field of education. University-based researchers have often viewed "teacher stories as insufficiently systematic, too local, and too little connected to broader academic and social issues" while teacher researchers have perceived academic researchers as "too removed from the everyday concerns of practitioners" and their technical language "too inaccessible" (Fishman & McCarthy, 2000, p. 6). Additional critiques include concerns about the reliability of data collection instruments used by teachers (Huberman, 1996) and inadequate quality of research in addressing educational problems (Brown, 2005). Moreover, Borg (2013, p. 18) has identified various reasons for teachers' reluctance to engage in research, including "non-collaborative school cultures, limitations in teachers' awareness, beliefs, skills, and knowledge, limited resources, lack of teacher motivation, economic considerations, and unsupportive leadership, along with political issues". Despite all these criticisms and challenges, teacher research has been linked to professional development and teacher education programs. By adopting an inquiry stance or exploratory attitude, these programs can serve as crucial and insight-producing undertakings that contribute to teachers' professional development (Cochran-Smith & Lytle, 1990). While teachers may engage in different forms of teacher research, such as action research (Burns, 2009a), collaborative action research (Arefian, 2022; Burns, 1999) and/or exploratory practice (Allwright, 2003; Dikilitaş & Bostancıoglu, 2019), the objectives are shared: To foster teaching and learning and to develop professionally. Therefore, engaging pre-service teachers in the research process should be a goal of teacher education, aiming to spark a passion for learning and teaching. However, Zeichner (2015) suggests that teachers and university faculty should work collaboratively to produce new knowledge beneficial to both stakeholders in teacher education. He emphasizes the importance of universities and schools collectively constructing shared environments where both parties recognize and appreciate the knowledge and abilities, they each bring.

While teacher research holds promise for prospective teachers' professional development, its integration into ITE programs varies in terms of its form, duration, and requirements. In some teacher education programs, teacher research is structured as a final term project, while in others, it is incorporated within a lesson study approach, a Japanese approach to professional development (Yalcin Arslan, 2019). As a final term project, teacher research starts with the identification of a puzzle or an inquiry that problematizes teaching and learning in the practicum schools. For instance, some puzzling situations for trainee teachers may involve the observation of students' first language use in pair/group work activities, their persistent mispronunciation despite repeated corrections, difficulty in expressing themselves in the target language, or consistent grammatical errors even after multiple explanations and practice activities. These situations prompt them to explore the puzzle or inquiry, search for possible solutions or explanations, implement the solutions, collect evidence and evaluate the results by reflecting on the process. Similarly, pre-service teachers may explore different aspects of their own practices as part of their teacher research projects. On the other hand, teacher research as a part of the lesson study approach enables groups of teacher candidates to collaborate to plan a lesson, conduct teaching, observe the lesson, and analyze a specific aspect (e.g. a teaching technique, skill, or appropriateness of an activity type with a specific group of learners) to report their findings. Using these inquiry-based practices, teacher candidates take the responsibility of their own learning, improve their problem-solving skills, and increase their self-efficacy (Cabaroglu, 2014). In a nutshell, the complementary nature of reflection and teacher research showcases the interplay between them in that teacher research is mostly initiated through teachers' reflection on their teaching practices to identify a puzzle, a problem, or an inquiry relevant to teaching and learning in their immediate contexts with the aim of improving teaching and learning of students. Subsequently the process is completed by re-engaging in reflective practices to evaluate the research results.

Reflective Practice in Language Teacher Education

The literature on reflective teaching extensively details tasks that facilitate the development of reflectivity in both in-service and preservice teachers by providing evidence for their contribution. Richards and Farrell (2005) categorize these reflective tasks, which can be undertaken individually, one-to-one with another colleague, collaboratively in groups, or in accordance with the institutional directives, for in-service teacher development (p. 14). These tasks include "self-monitoring, journal writing, critical incidents, teaching portfolios, action research, peer coaching, peer observation of teaching, critical friendships, team teaching, case studies, teacher support groups, and workshops." Similarly, for the professional development of preservice teachers, ITE programs often integrate diverse reflective tasks including task-based observational learning practices, peer/micro-teaching and practicum teaching practices in real classrooms accompanied by peer-and self-evaluation reports, reflective journals, practicum portfolio, technology-enhanced reflective practices, examination of critical incidents and case studies, and teacher research. Engaging in these activities enables prospective teachers to develop a significant understanding of their teaching practices and the dynamic nature of teaching. This, in turn, empowers them to make well-informed decisions to enhance their effectiveness in the classroom. Those shown to be beneficial in language teacher education to cultivate reflectivity are summarized below with a focus on their nature and scope:

Reflective journals: A journal functions as teachers' and prospective teachers' written response to teaching events. Pre-service teachers are often tasked with keeping reflective journals or writing reports as they observe mentor teachers in real classes adopting a critical perspective to understand the reasons behind their teaching decisions. They record events and ideas for later reflection and act as a catalyst for insights into teaching, serving as a discovery process (Richards & Lockart, 1996). It is a common practice in ITE programs to guide prospective teachers with focused and guided observation tasks during practicum. In focused observations, trainee teachers receive weekly assignments with some guiding questions to explore various aspects of teaching, such as teaching skills and strategies, lesson planning, classroom management, and resource and materials utilization (Wajnryb, 1992). Through meticulous notetaking and evidence collection, teacher candidates reflect on what they observe and draw conclusions. Journal writing allows them to express personal reactions, pose questions and articulate observations about classroom challenges. In other words, this approach facilitates the description of significant issues that are likely to be encountered in real classrooms, fosters critical thinking, questioning and problem-solving skills, promoting metacognition, and enhances creativity (Moon, 2007). Besides, journal keeping fosters continuous learning by providing pre-service teachers with the opportunity to derive insights from their experiences and become more aware of their inner thoughts (Lee, 2007; Tican & Taspinar, 2015; Afzali, 2018; Bain et al., 2002). Hence, the entries become the record of their professional growth.

Evaluative tasks that follow (micro)teaching practices: Pre-service teachers engage in micro-teaching or peer-teachings as part of their ITE courses, preparing for language skills instruction in real practicum settings. Before these teachings, they are expected to create comprehensive lesson plans, aligning teaching objectives with activities appropriate for the age and proficiency levels of the target students. Following these teaching practices, they evaluate

and reflect on their own and peers' performances through oral and/or written tasks of *self-evaluation* and *peer evaluation* reports. These evaluative tasks
allow them to explore how they translate theoretical knowledge into practice with a focus on the strengths and weaknesses of their teaching and help
them make decisions and develop strategies for their prospective teachings.
Developing a critical eye in these aspects fosters reflective mindset (Comoglu
& Dikilitas, 2020; Guney, 2008; İsmail, 2011; Karpava, 2023; Shuwen & Rui,
2023; Yalcin Arslan, 2019), enhances assessment skills (Dymoke & Harrison,
2008), and boosts self-efficacy Goker (2006).

The lesson plans, along with self and peer evaluation reports, as well as the
video recording of teaching (Alamri & Alfayez, 2023; Karakaş & Yükselir,
2021; Osmanoglu, 2016) and reports written by the supervisors, constitute the
pre-service teachers' teaching portfolio, providing valuable sources of constructive feedback, which facilitates professional development and strengthens the connection between theory and practice (Tican & Taspinar, 2015;
Winsor et al., 1999). With the advancement of technology, these reflective
portfolios often take the form of blogging (Muncy, 2014; Tang & Lam, 2014),
e-portfolios (Oakley et al., 2014), and e-journals (Tavil, 2014).

*Self-monitoring/self-observation (with lesson reports & audio/video record-
ings):* Self-monitoring or self-observation aims to collect systematic data on
ones' teaching, enabling the teacher-initiated objective evaluation and judgment of instructional practices (Richards & Farrell, 2005). In language classes
this can be achieved through lesson reports and audio/video recordings of
teachings. Unlike lesson plan created before the teachings, lesson report is
completed after the lesson either to document or to evaluate issues including the success of the activities, deviations from the plan, and difficulties
encountered both by the teacher and the learners to guide future teachings. Lesson reports can take the form of a narrative account detailing these
issues or be presented in the form of a checklist or questionnaire. Engaging
in self-monitoring through lesson reports and recordings not only promotes
self-affirmation and assurance but also facilitates problem identification, pin-
pointing areas for improvement. Thus, it serves as a starting point for planning professional development (Richards & Farrell, 2005).

Research-based tasks: Pre-service teachers can be tasked to do research as a
reflective practice in language teacher education programs. They may engage
in conducting action or teacher research in collaboration with their university supervisors and cooperating teachers in practicum schools. Within action
research, pre-service teachers may identify and explore an inquiry or a real
classroom problem by collecting evidence through lesson observations or

interviews with mentor teachers, students, and their supervisors in order to find some solutions for better teaching and learning practices (Val Madin & Swanto, 2019). This inquiry-based task improves their self-efficacy and boosts their reflectivity (Cabaroglu, 2014).

Critical incidents: A critical incident is an unforeseen event that occurs in class which prompts reflection on the meaning and implications of that event (Farrell, 2008). An event becomes a critical incident based on "the interpretation and meaning attributed to an incident" (Richards & Farrell, 2005, p. 115). Critical analysis of such events involves the documentation of teaching incidents, whether in written or spoken form, following the steps of self-observation, detailing the events, self-awareness, and self-evaluation (Thiel, 1999), which offers several benefits for teachers' and pre-service teachers' professional development. Teachers become more self-aware by reconsidering assumptions and beliefs about language teaching, and they enhance their teaching repertoire by evaluating their established routines and instructional strategies. While these tasks foster critical questioning about various dimensions of teaching and develop reflectivity, they boost professional dialogue (Farrell, 2008; Griffin, 2003; Harrison & Lee, 2011; Richards & Farrell, 2005). Harrison and Lee (2011, p. 203) also explain that critical incidents.

> ... provide an opportunity for questioning the way things in school normally operate (How did you act in the incident? What lessons do you learn from it? Why did you make that judgment?). Such questions form the basis of diagnostic teaching and interpretative approaches that can develop professional judgment.

When trainee teachers are tasked to analyze their critical incidents during micro and practicum teachings, they can progress beyond a descriptive account of what happened, developing a more critical perspective on the events. Additionally, critical incident analysis can serve as a foundation for action research, contribute to building a community of critical practitioners, and provide a valuable resource for both new and experienced teachers (Richards & Farrell, 2005).

Case Analyses: Cases are "accounts of practical or strategic dilemmas that confront a teacher" (Shulman, 1999, p. 92). They involve information collected over time about a teaching situation, examined to derive principles based on how teachers handled them (Richards & Farrell, 2005). While cases stimulate dialogue among experienced teachers involved in peer coaching, they also establish a valuable foundation for reflective discussions in ITE programs, aiding in the training of inexperienced pre-service teachers and providing sources for their consultation. Analyzing real-life teaching cases with peers and teacher trainers enhances pre-service teachers' awareness of classroom situations and dilemmas and provides them with an opportunity to reflect on possible solutions, which also refine their problem-solving skills. Besides, they develop an understanding of how experienced teachers think and respond to challenging classroom situations.

Suggestions for Effective Implementation of Reflective Practices in Language Teacher Education

Drawing on the mentioned contributions of reflective tasks to teachers' professional development, let's now provide evidence-based recommendations for integrating these practices into language teacher education. The development of reflectivity and research engagement among pre-service teachers can be facilitated through various strategies employed by teacher educators, mentor teachers, practitioners, and curriculum developers in the field of education.

Offering Explicit Instruction to Guide and Encourage Critical Reflection

Critical reflection goes beyond merely listing and describing what happened during teaching; it involves developing an awareness of socio-cultural, socio-political, or historical factors and diverse viewpoints that influence actions, events, or problems (Hatton & Smith, 1995). Similarly, in Taggart and Wilson's (2005) reflection model, the critical level is referred to as the dialectical level in which teachers consider ethical and political matters related to instructional planning, maintaining an openness to cultural, social, and moral values in evaluating teaching. Although prospective teachers are encouraged to reflect on their classwork or teaching practices especially during practicum, the examination of their reflective journals including peer and self-evaluation reports, which mostly involve descriptions rather than reflections (Çelik & Eveyik-Aydın, 2023; Seban, 2009), raises questions about whether they are adequately taught how to reflect or develop critical reflection skills. In fact, the research indicates that reflecting at critical level is challenging for inexperienced or novice teachers, primarily because they tend to focus on technical issues, driven by immediate instructional concerns, due to their limited schemata in addressing educational challenges (Taggart & Wilson, 2005; Valli, 1997), lack of teaching experience, lack of time to acquire reflective thinking skills (Tuncer & Ozkan, 2018) and their unfamiliarity with the features of critical reflection (Luk, 2008). To address this issue, Afzali (2018) recommends explicit instruction for reflective journal writing in order to foster critical reflections rather than descriptive ones. Evidence suggests that pre-service teachers, when provided with explicit training on reflectivity, demonstrate increased scores in reflection at higher levels (Weber, 2013). Similarly, the tasks should also explicitly induce critical reflection with the guiding questions (Çelik & Eveyik-Aydın, 2023). Pre-service teachers are very likely to benefit from such explicit focus on reflectivity, but it should be integrated into courses as of the first year of the ITE programs, because time is a crucial factor that contributes to changes in reflectivity (Lee, 2005).

Providing Opportunities for Cooperative Learning Environment and Dialogic Feedback

As emphasized by Farrell (2019, p. 38), reflective practices "should be viewed from a collaborative, cooperative, sharing, personal experience and peer-feedback dialoguing position rather than practiced in isolation". This implies that reflective practices should be implemented hand in hand to have the best practices (Dewey, 1933, cited in Farrell, 2019). To illustrate, research engagement requires pre-service teachers as researchers to work cooperatively and engage in a dialogue with their peers, other teachers as practitioners, mentor teachers and/or teacher educators as their university supervisors. The feedback provided by teacher educators during this process facilitates the development of critical reflective practice (Asregid et al., 2023). Given that there is growing evidence supporting the role of collaborative learning, teacher educators should provide opportunities to effectively incorporate it together with a feedback loop into teacher education.

Encouraging Research-based Practices and Engagement with Teacher Research

There is empirical evidence suggesting that research-engaged pre-service teachers improve their critical reflection (Lambe, 2011; Hagevik et al., 2012). However, despite the recognized importance of research in educational practices and the endorsement of evidence-based practice as a government initiative in the U.K., Borg (2013, p. 4) highlights the alien nature of research for many language teachers worldwide. This lack of research engagement among language teachers is unfortunate and may indicate inadequacies in faculties and teacher education programs, as well as a lack of a supportive research culture for classroom-based research. To address this issue, there is a need to integrate research-based activities, such as teacher research and lesson study, more extensively into Initial Teacher Education (ITE) programs.

Adopting an Eclectic Approach to Developing Reflectivity Throughout ITE

A comprehensive and eclectic approach to developing reflectivity is essential throughout the entire ITE process, as each reflective practice, whether conducted online or face-to-face, offers unique benefits for pre-service teachers. Relying solely on critical incidents, for example, has been shown to be insufficient for professional development (Francis, 1997). Similarly, integrating technology-enhanced reflective practices has proven highly practical in enhancing the reflective thinking of teacher candidates. Instead of limiting reflective tasks to a singular approach, teacher educators should assign prospective teachers a variety of reflective tasks.

Conclusion

In this chapter, we explored the concepts of reflection and teacher research by critically assessing their role in language teacher education. With this purpose, the roots and nature of these concepts have been described, and practical implications have been provided for the effective preparation of language teachers for the educational landscape of the 21ˢᵗ century. Throughout the chapter we emphasize that teacher researchers naturally embrace reflective practices, ranging from keeping a teaching portfolio, writing reflective journals, conducting small-scale classroom research, and evaluating their own and peers' teaching practices to analyzing critical incidents and case studies. As the research supporting reflection in language teacher education continues to grow (Farrell, 2019, p. 47), it is hoped that the collection of reflective and critical thinking ideas presented in this chapter benefits language teacher educators and teacher trainers in raising reflective language teachers, who value their professional development by engaging in teacher research, cooperative and collaborative learning activities, dialogic feedback, and other reflective practices.

References

Adelman, C. (1993). Kurt Lewin and the origins of action research. *Educational Action Research, 1*(1), 7–24. https://doi.org/10.1080/0965079930010102

Afzali, K. (2018). Evaluating recall and reflection journals written by pre-service teachers in EFL practicum courses. *Iranian Journal of Applied Linguistics, 21*(1), 1–27. http://ijal.khu.ac.ir/article-1-2851-en.html

Alamri, H. A., & Alfayez, A. A. (2023). Preservice teachers' experiences of observing their teaching competencies via self-recorded videos in a personalized learning environment. *Humanities and Social Sciences Communications,* *10*(1). https://doi.org/10.1057/s41599-023-02260-2

Allwright, D. (2003). Exploratory practice: Rethinking practitioner research in language teaching. *Language Teaching Research, 7*(2), 113–141. https://doi.org/10.1191/1362168803lr118oa

Arefian, M. H. (2022). Collaborative action research as a reflective tool for pre-service EFL, *Reflective Practice, 22,* 651–662. https://doi.org/10.1080/14623943.2022.2103107

Asregid, D., Mekonnen, M. D., & Kassa, S.A. (2023). Teacher educators' use of feedback to facilitate reflective practice among pre-service teachers during microteaching, *Cogent Education, 10*(2), 1–13. https://doi.org/10.1080/2331186X.2023.2257121

Bain, J. D., Mills, C., Ballantyne, R., & Packer, J. (2002). Developing reflection on practice through journal writing: Impacts of variations in the focus and level of feedback. *Teachers and Teaching: Theory and Practice, 8*(2), 171–196. https://doi.org/10.1080/13540600220127368

Borg, S. (2013). *Teacher research in language teaching: A critical analysis.* Cambridge University Press.

Brown, S. (2005). How can research inform ideas of good practice in teaching? The contributions of some official initiatives in the UK. *Cambridge Journal of Education, 35*(3), 383–406. https://doi.org/10.1080/03057640500319073

Burns, A. (1999). *Collaborative action research for English language teachers.* Cambridge University Press.

Burns, A. (2009a). *Doing action research in English language teaching: A guide for practitioners.* Routledge.

Burns, A. (2009b). Action research in second language teacher education. In A. Burns & J. C. Richards (Eds.), *The Cambridge guide to second language teacher education* (pp. 289–297). Cambridge University Press. https://doi.org/10.1017/9781139042710.038

Cabaroglu, N. (2014). Professional development through action research: Impact on self-efficacy. *System, 44,* 79–88. https://doi.org/10.1016/j.system.2014.03.003

Chien, C. W. (2014). Pre-service elementary school English teachers' learning and reflection through simulated teaching practice and oral interviews. *Reflective Practice: International and Multidisciplinary Perspectives, 15*(6), 821–835. https://doi.org/10.1080/14623943.2014.944139

Cochran-Smith, M., & Lytle, S. (1999). The teacher research movement: A decade later. *Educational Research, 28*(7), 15–25. https://doi.org/10.3102/0013189X028007015

Comoglu, I., & Dikilitas, K. (2020). Learning to become an English language teacher: Navigating the self through peer practicum. *Australian Journal of Teacher Education (Online)*, *45*(8), 23–40. https://doi.org/10.14221/ajte.2020v45n8.2

Çelik, S., & Eveyik-Aydın, E. (2023). Preservice EFL teachers' reflectivity levels on evaluation tasks assigned during practicum. *Innovational Research in ELT*, *4*(2), 17–27. https://doi.org/10.29329/irelt.2023.623.2

Dewey, J. (1933). *How we think: A restatement of the relation of reflective thinking to the educative process*. Heath and Company.

Dickens, L., & Watkins, K. (1999). Action Research: Rethinking Lewin. *Management Learning*, *30*(2), 127–140. https://doi.org/10.1177/135050769 9302002

Dikilitaş, K., & Bostancıoğlu, A. (2019). *Inquiry and research skills for language teachers*. Springer Nature.

Dymoke, S., & Harrison, J. (2008). *Reflective teaching and learning*. SAGE Publications Ltd.

Efron, S. E., & Ravit, R. (2020). *Action research in education: A practical guide* (2nd ed.). The Guilford Press.

Fishman, S. M., & McCarthy, L. (2000). *Unplayed tapes: A personal history of collaborative teacher research. The Practitioner Inquiry Series*. National Council of Teachers of English, Urbana, IL.

Francis, D. (1995). The reflective journal: A window to preservice teachers' practical knowledge. *Teaching and Teacher Education*, *11*(3), 229–241. https://doi.org/10.1016/0742-051X(94)00031-Z

Farrell, T. S. (2008). Critical incidents in ELT initial teacher training. *ELT journal*, *62*(1), 3–10. https://doi.org/10.1093/elt/ccm072

Farrell, T. S. (2019). Reflective practice in L2 teacher education. In S. Walsh & S. Mann (Eds.), *The Routledge handbook of English language teacher education* (pp. 38–51). Routledge Handbooks Online. https://doi.org/10.4324/978131 5659824

Goker, S. D. (2006). Impact of peer coaching on self-efficacy and instructional skills in TEFL teacher education. *System*, *34*(2), 239–254. https://doi.org/10.1016/j.system.2005.12.002

Griffin, M. L. (2003). Using critical incidents to promote and assess reflective thinking in preservice teachers. *Reflective Practice*, *4*(2), 207–220. https://doi.org/10.1080/14623940308274

Guney, K. (2008). *Mikro-yansıtıcı öğretim yönteminin öğretmen adaylarının sunu performansı ve yansıtıcı düşünmesine etkisi* [The Effect of Micro-Reflective Teaching Method in Accordance with the presentation performance and reflective thinking activities-teachers]. [Unpublished PhD Thesis]. Firat University.

Hagevik, R., Aydeniz, M., & Rowell, C. G. (2012). Using action research in middle level teacher education to evaluate and deepen reflective practice. *Teaching and Teacher Education* 28(5), 675–684. https://doi.org/10.1016/j.tate.2012.02.006

Hammersley, M. (1993). On the teacher as researcher. *Educational Action Research, 1*(3), 425–445. http://dx.doi.org/10.1080/0965079930010308

Harrison, J. K., & Lee, R. (2011). Exploring the use of critical incident analysis and professional learning conversation in an initial teacher education programme. *Journal of Education for Teaching, 37*(2), 199–217. https://doi.org/10.1080/02607476.2011.558285

Hatton, N., & Smith, D. (1995). Reflection in teacher education: Towards definition and implementation. *Teaching and teacher education, 11*(1), 33–49. https://doi.org/10.1016/0742-051X(94)00012-U

Huberman, M. (1996). Focus on research moving mainstream: Taking a closer look at teacher research. Language Arts, 73(2), 124–140. https://www.jstor.org/stable/41482267

Ismail, S. A. A. (2011). Student teachers' microteaching experiences in a pre-service English Teacher Education Program. *Journal of Language Teaching & Research, 2*(5). https://doi.org/10.4304/jltr.2.5.1043-1051

Jay, J. K., & Johnson, K. L. (2002). Capturing complexity: A typology of reflective practice for teacher education. *Teaching and Teacher Education, 18*(1), 73–85. https://doi.org/10.1016/S0742-051X(01)00051-8

Karakaş, A., & Yükselir, C. (2021). Engaging pre-service EFL teachers in reflection through video-mediated team micro-teaching and guided discussions. *Reflective Practice, 22*(2), 159–172. https://doi.org/10.1080/14623943.2020.1860927

Karpava, S. (2023). Reflection, professional development and underlying psychological dimensions of teaching. In I. Papadopoulos & E. Papadopoulou (Eds.), *Pedagogical and research perspectives on language education* (pp. 81–105). Nova Science Publishers. https://doi.org/10.52305/YZWI6174

Kelch, K., & Malupa-Kim, M. (2014). Implementing Case Studies in Language Teacher Education and Professional Development. *Ortesol Journal*, 31, 10-18.

Korthagen, F. A. J. (2001, April). *Linking practice and theory: The pedagogy of realistic teacher education.* [Paper presentation]. Annual meeting of the American Educational Association, Seattle, WA. https://www.academia.edu/1935777/Linking_practice_and_theory_The_pedagogy_of_realistic_teacher_education

Körkkö, M., Kyrö-Ämmälä, O., & Turunen, T. (2016). Professional development through reflection in teacher education. *Teaching and Teacher Education, 55,* 198–206. https://doi.org/10.1016/j.tate.2016.01.014

Lambe, J. (2011). Developing pre-service teachers' reflective capacity through engagement with classroom-based research. *Reflective Practice, 12*(1), 87–100. https://doi.org/10.1080/14623943.2011.541098

Lee, H. J. (2005). Understanding and assessing preservice teachers' reflective thinking. *Teaching and Teacher Education, 21*(6), 699–715. https://doi.org/10.1016/j.tate.2005.05.007

Lee, I. (2007). Preparing pre-service English teachers for reflective practice. *ELT Journal, 61,* 321–329. https://doi.org/10.1093/elt/ccm022

Levin, B., & He, Y. (2008). Investigating the content and sources of teacher candidates' personal practical theories (PPTs). *Journal of Teacher Education, 59*(1), 55–68. https://doi.org/10.1177/0022487107310749s

Luk, J. (2008). Assessing teaching practicum reflections: Distinguishing discourse features of the "high" and "low" grade reports. *System, 36*(4), 624–641. https://doi.org/10.1016/j.system.2008.04.001

Moon, J. (2007). *Learning journals: A handbook for reflective practice and professional development* (2nd ed.). Routledge.

Muncy, J. A. (2014). Blogging for reflection: The use of online journals to engage students in reflective learning. *Marketing Education Review, 24*(2), 101–114. https://doi.org/10.2753/MER1052-8008240202

Nuraeni, N., & Heryatun, Y. (2021). Reflective practice strategies of pre-service English teachers during teaching practicum to promote professional development. *Studies in English Language and Education, 8*(3), 1144–1157. https://doi.org/10.24815/siele.v8i3.20221

Oakley, G., Pegrum, M., & Johnston, S. (2014). Introducing e-portfolios to pre-service teachers as tools for reflection and growth: Lessons learnt. *Asia-Pacific Journal of Teacher Education 42*(1), 36–50. https://doi.org/10.1080/1359866X.2013.854860

Osmanoglu, A. (2016). Prospective teachers' teaching experience: Teacher learning through the use of video. *Educational Research, 58*(1), 39–55. https://doi.org/10.1080/00131881.2015.1117321

Placio, E. D. C., Vargas, D. S., & Estigoy, M. A. (2021). Virtual call-out: The aggressions and advantages of cancel culture. *Innovations, 67,* 538-554. https://www.researchgate.net/profile/Maria_Adrielle_Estigoy/publication/358283905_Virtual_Call-Out_The_Aggressions_and_Advantages_of_Cancel_Culture/links/61fb5c861e98d168d7e912c9/Virtual-Call-Out-The-Aggressions-and-Advantages-of-Cancel-Culture.pdf

Reddy, K. (2019). Teaching how to teach: Microteaching (A way to build up teaching skills). *Journal of Gandaki Medical College-Nepal, 12*(1), 65–71. https://doi.org/10.3126/jgmcn.v12i1.22621

Richards, J. C., & Farrell, T. S. C. (2005). *Professional development for language teachers: Strategies for teacher learning*. Cambridge University Press.

Richards, J. C., & Lockhart, C. (1996). *Reflective teaching in second classrooms*. Cambridge University Press.

Sailofsky, D. (2022). Masculinity, cancel culture and woke capitalism: Exploring Twitter response to Brendan Leipsic's leaked conversation. *International review for the sociology of sport*, 57(5), 734-757. https://doi.org/10.1177/10126902211039768

Schön, D. A. (1983). *The reflective practitioner: How professionals think in action*. Basic Books.

Schön, D. A. (1988). *Educating the reflective practitioner*. Jossey-Bass.

Seban, D. (2009). Researching reflective field practices of elementary pre-service teachers: Two-dimensional analysis of teacher narratives. *Reflective Practice, 10*(5), 669–681, https://doi.org/10.1080/14623940903290745

Shuwen, L., & Rui, Y. (2023). Probing pre-service language teachers' emotional experiences through lesson study: A Macau study. *Language Learning Journal, 51*(5), 636–648. https://doi.org/10.1080/09571736.2023.2242869

Taggart, G. L., & Wilson, A. P. (2005). *Promoting reflective thinking in teachers: 50 action strategies*. Corwin Press.

Tang, E. L.-Y., & Lam, C. (2014). Building an effective online learning community (OLC) in blog-based teaching portfolios. *The Internet and Higher Education, 20*, 79–85. https://doi.org/10.1016/j.iheduc.2012.12.002

Tavil, Z. M. (2014). The effect of self-reflections through electronic journals (e-journals) on the self-efficacy of pre-service teachers. *South African Journal of Education, 34*, 1–20. https://files.eric.ed.gov/fulltext/EJ1136416.pdf

Thiel, T. (1999). Reflections on critical incidents. *Prospect 14*(1), 44–52. https://eric.ed.gov/?id=EJ597464

Tuncer, H., & Ozkan, Y. (2018). A case study on assessing reflectivity levels of preservice language teachers through journals. *Novitas-ROYAL, 12*(2), 173–186. https://files.eric.ed.gov/fulltext/EJ1195278.pdf

Tican, C., & Taspinar, M. (2015). The effects of reflective thinking-based teaching activities on pre-service teachers' reflective thinking skills, critical thinking skills, democratic attitudes, and academic achievement. *The Anthropologist, 20*(1–2), 111–120. https://doi.org/10.1016/j.iheduc.2012.12.002

Wallace, M. J. (1991). *Training foreign language teachers: A reflective approach.* Cambridge University Press.

Wajnryb, R. (1992). *Classroom observation tasks. A resource book for language teachers and trainers.* Cambridge University Press.

Weber, S. S. S. (2013). Can preservice teachers be taught to become reflective thinkers during their first internship experience? (Publication No. 1355761839). [Doctoral dissertation, Liberty University]. ProQuest Dissertations & Theses Global.

Winsor, P. J. T., Richard, L. B., & Reeves, H. (1999). Portraying professional development in preservice teacher education: Can portfolios do the job? *Teachers and Teaching, 5*(1), 9–31. https://doi.org/10.1080/1354060990050102

Val Madin, C., & Swanto, S. (2019). An inquiry approach to facilitate reflection in action research for ESL pre-service teachers. *TEFLIN Journal: A Publication on the Teaching & Learning of English, 30*(1). http://dx.doi.org/10.15639/teflin journal.v30i1/1-21

Valli, L. (1997). Listening to other voices: A description of teacher reflection in the United States. *Peabody Journal of Education, 72*(1), 67–88. https://doi.org/10.1207/s15327930pje7201_4

Yalcin Arslan, F. (2019). The role of lesson study in teacher learning and professional development of EFL teachers in Turkey: A case study. *TESOL Journal, 10*(2). https://doi.org/10.1002/tesj.409

Young, T., & Bender-Slack, D. (2011). Scaffolding pre-service teachers' observations: Eye on the future. *Teaching Education, 22*(3), 325–337. https://doi.org/10.1080/10476210.2011.593166

Zaragoza, A., Seidel, T., & Hiebert, J. (2021). Exploring preservice teachers' abilities to connect professional knowledge with lesson planning and observation. *European Journal of Teacher Education.* https://doi.org/10.1080/02619768.2021.1996558

Zeichner, K. M., & Liston, D. P. (1996). *Reflective teaching: An introduction.* Lawrence Erlbaum Associates.

Zeichner, K. (2015). Commentary: A candid look at teacher research and teacher education today. *LEARNing Landscapes, 8*(2), 49–57. https://doi.org/10.36510/learnland.v8i2.695

Dr. Berna Güloğlu

Chapter 11 School Counseling in New Normal: Improving Cognitive Flexibility and Self-Regulation in Students

Abstract: The Covid-19 pandemic has caused the world to undergo rapid and fundamental changes. Notions of normalcy, stability, and certainty have been crushed by rising levels of anxiety and stress around the world. It is thought that its effects will continue for a while by changing many social norms. A new concept which was called the "new normal" has emerged. In the new normal which was dominated by uncertainty, it is thought that crises will continue, and it will be important for individuals' mental health to adapt quickly to crises and take actions to solve the crisis. In addition, it is important for students to have self-regulation skills in the education system where new teaching methods such as online education and distance education are emerging. Thus, self-regulation and cognitive flexibility appear to be important factors in protecting individuals' mental health. Therefore, the goal of this paper was to understand the role of school counseling services in crisis times and to improve the level of cognitive flexibility and self-regulation of students.

Keywords: Cognitive flexibility, Self-regulation, "New normal", "Old normal", education

Traumatic events such as pandemics, natural disasters, economic crises, wars, and terrorist attacks have become a part of an individual's life. All kinds of traumatic experiences negatively affect the mental health of individuals of all age groups. However, some groups, such as children and adolescents, are more sensitive to the negative effects of traumatic experiences. The reactions of children and adolescents, who are a vulnerable group to traumatic events, are more distressing and their development is negatively affected in the long-term. In a systemic review study, 18 articles investigated and found that pandemics cause stress, worry, helplessness, and social and risky behavioral problems such as substance abuse, suicide, and absenteeism from work among children and adolescents (Meherali et al., 2021). In another study, the results indicated that between 2.2 % and 9.9 % of participants reported emotional and behavioral problems. Moreover, it was concluded that there was an increase in oppositional-challenging behaviors in preschool children (1–6 years old), and in emotional problems in adolescents. Adolescents experienced significantly greater reductions in emotional and behavioral problems than both preschool and school children (Schmidt et al., 2021).

Besides pandemics, it is estimated that about 175 million children are impacted by natural disasters every year due to climate change (Codreanu et al., 2014). A study conducted following the earthquake in China in 2008 that caused the death of 70,000 people and injured 375,000 found the relationship between PTSD and depressive symptoms (Cheng et al., 2018). Moreover, after studying 300 children over 4 years and collecting data four times, they concluded that the causal relationship between PTSD and depressive symptoms changes over time. While the effects of PTSD tended to decrease over time, depression tended to increase over time. To understand the long-term health impacts of natural disasters in individual's health, Hlodversdottir et al. (2018) conducted a study aftermath the eruption of the Eyjafjallajökull volcano in Iceland in 2010. Adults who were and were not exposed to volcanic eruptions in 2010 and 2013 were asked questions about the psychological and physical health of their children. The results indicated that the respiratory symptoms and anxiety levels of children exposed to the explosion increased. These problems were more common in those whose houses were damaged, and the problems did not decrease 3 years after the explosion. Sepahvand et al. (2019) examined the prevalence of PTSD in Iranians following disasters and wars using a meta-analytic method. The findings revealed that the prevalence of PTSD about 74 %, 58 %, 47 %, 40 %, 25 %, and 11 % caused by rape, earthquake, war, burning, childbirth, and accident, respectively.

Covid-19 pandemic has once again revealed the importance of schools and school counselors in protecting the mental health of students. School counselors, who helped children and families manage their fears, worries, anxieties during the pandemic, were their biggest supporters in helping students adapt to school after the pandemic. Uncertainty emerged as the most serious challenge for individuals during the pandemic period. The best way to cope with uncertainty was considered to enhance cognitive flexibility and self-regulation skills of students. Cognitive flexibility is the ability to adapt to changes in environmental stimuli (Dennis and Vander Wal, 2010) in order to meet situational demands (Goldfarb et al., 2017). However, while doing this, it does not deviate from its own value system (Kashdan & Rottenberg, 2010). Individuals with high cognitive flexibility have low levels of PTSD symptoms and high levels of posttraumatic growth and optimism (Keith et al., 2015). Similarly, high level of cognitive flexibility may lead to enhance resilience to change, self-regulation, and self-efficacy (Kim & Omizo, 2005; Nakhostin-Khayyat et al., 2024. Furthermore, the results of Odacı et al.'s study (2021) indicated that cognitive flexibility had partial mediating effect on the relationship between childhood trauma (physical abuse and physical neglect, emotional abuse and emotional neglect, and sexual abuse) and substance abuse tendency.

Self-regulation was described as the ability to manage individual's own emotions, cognitions, and behaviors to achieve specific goals (Baumeister and Tierney 2011; Diamond, 2013) and is positively associated with a range of desirable life outcomes such as physical and emotional health, academic performance, and welfare (Moffitt et al., 2011; Tangney et al., 2004). On the other hand, deficits in self-regulatory capacity are correlated with a range of personal and social problems, such as depression, aggression, overeating and alcohol use, and criminal behavior (Robson et al., 2020). Therefore, it is no coincidence that several psychological interventions aim to improve individuals' skills in managing their own behavior. With these interventions, individuals are asked to maintain their gains by instilling personal resources, knowledge, and skills and to overcome the problems they will encounter in the future.

School counselors are positioned in schools to provide students with access to social, emotional, and academic support that enables them to improve their mental health and to succeed academically. Hence, the aim of this study is to show the role of cognitive flexibility and self-regulation in coping with traumatic experiences in children and adolescents. It also emphasizes the role of school psychological counseling and guidance services in the preparation and implementation of intervention programs that will contribute to the development of cognitive flexibility and self-regulation skills of children and adolescents.

Impacts of Traumatic Experiences on Mental Health of Students

As one of the biggest disasters of the 21st century, Covid-19 pandemic has changed the lives of individuals and societies rapidly and fundamentally. Although humanity has been exposed to numerous disasters before, their effects remained in a limited area due to the regional nature of these disasters. However, for the first time in many years, the world has been subjected to a disaster that affects everyone in the same way. In a preliminary study conducted by China-EPA-UNEPSA group in Shaanxi provience during Covid-19 (Jiao et al., 2020), it was found that more than 30 % of children and adolescents aged 3–18 in China experienced symptoms of inattention, irritability, and clinginess. In particular, symptoms of clinginess and fear about the health of relatives were significantly more severe in preschool children compared to children aged 6 to 18 years. The latter group showed more signs of inattention and was obsessed with asking for updates on the pandemic. A study of preschool children aged 4–6 years (Liu et al., 2020) found evidence of sleep disturbances. In addition to the problems of children going to bed and waking up later, it was yielded that their sleep duration was longer at night and their naps were shorter. Changes in eating habit, stress, less exposure to sunlight and increased use of technology during quarantine may have had such a negative impact on children's sleep patterns (Becker & Gregory, 2020). A study conducted in China with children and adolescent indicated that 12.33% and 6.26% of participants reported depression and anxiety after lockdown. Suicidal ideation and insomnia were positively related to depression and anxiety (Liu et al., 2021). Studies conducted with adolescents (Buzzi et al., 2020; Guessoum et al., 2020; Oosterhoff & Palmer, 2020) found high rates of moderate to severe depression, anxiety, helplessness, worry, fear, and dysfunctional attitudes towards the pandemic. The findings of the meta-analysis study, which examined 23 studies conducted with children and adolescents in Turkey and China, showed that during the Covid-19 pandemic period, 29 % of children and adolescents had depression, 26 % had anxiety, 44 % had sleep disorders and 48 % had PTSD (Ma et al., 2020).

As Turkey was still trying to overcome the psychological aftermath of the Covid-19 pandemic, an even greater challenge presented itself in the form of an earthquake. A devastating earthquake ravaged Turkey on February 6, 2023, claiming the lives of 53,000,537 individuals, and causing injuries to 107,000,213 more. Approximately 4 million students and 220 thousand teachers were impacted by the earthquake. Following the earthquake that occurred during the two-week school break and affected 10 provinces, the break was extended for another two weeks throughout the country. As a result, the large-scale earthquake experienced in the country caused students to be away from education for almost one month. In the earthquake region, education was started gradually, and this process was completed almost two months after the earthquake. However, most of the schools were destroyed in the earthquake, and some of the teachers and school counselors lost their lives or were seriously affected by the earthquake. There were teachers, school counselors and students who were trapped under the rubble, lost their relatives, had their homes destroyed, and were disabled. Education, which started 1.5 months after the earthquake, was taking place in tents and in such an environment. For teachers and students trying to return to their schools after the pandemic, losing their schools due to this disaster was another factor that had a negative impact on their mental health.

Schools in Crises Times

Trauma and disasters happen all over the world and students experience mental health issues during and after traumatic events because of social isolation (Pincus et al., 2020), fear of getting sick or witnessing the illness of others, and post-bereavement grief (Stevenson et al., 2009). School closures have led to children spending more time at home with their parents. Thus, parents become a crucial factor in the mental health of children and adolescents throughout the pandemic. Strong family relationships support children's mental health (Yuen et al., 2019) and are related to lower rates of self-harm and suicide (Law & Shek, 2016). However, in many cases, spending all time under the same roof has been shown to increase tension within the family and lead to more depression and anxiety during pandemics (Liu et al. (2021).

The Covid-19 epidemic, described as the disaster of the century, once again showed the importance of schools. Firstly, the closure of schools and playgrounds has damaged the social networks of students. Peer relations, especially during adolescence, are a crucial source of support for mental health problems. Therefore, adolescents emerged as the most vulnerable group to the challenges caused by social distancing measures. During the stormiest period of their lives, they had to stay away from their friends. They were alone, struggling with the challenges of being adolescents as well as the challenges of the disaster of the century. Indeed, they showed high levels of loneliness, depression, and anxiety during and after enforced social isolation (Loades et al., 2020; Sharma et al., 2020). Secondly, children and parents faced new challenges due to school closures and the start of distance learning. These challenges were even worse for families experiencing economic uncertainty, where parents were required to work remotely, were unemployed or had low incomes, and had limited opportunities. All these difficulties may have led to discomfort in the parent-child relationship, burnout on the part of the parent, and neglect of the child (Cluver et al., 2020; Griffith, 2020; Russell et al., 2020) Thus, a negative parent-child relationship impacts children and adolescents' mental health negatively. A study indicated that while quarreling with parents was positively correlated with depression and anxiety, not living with parent was positively related to depression (Liu et al., 2021). Additionally, school closures may have triggered or increased concerns in students and their families about their academic performance. The loss of stability in the lives of children and adolescents with the disappearance of school routines and loss of access to mental health services may have increased existing mental health problems (Fegert & Schulze, 2020; Fegert et al., 2020; Lee, 2020). Thirdly, very young children may have difficulty understanding changes to their daily routines (for example, the absence of regular caregivers) and processing complex information about Covid-19 due to their limited cognitive and verbal capacities. Given that some parents' concerns about the pandemic (e.g. fear of death of relatives, financial loss) and its consequences is quite high, having young children deal with it can be especially challenging given their limited reasoning and coping skills.

School counselors are called to take action during the school closure, and they were at the forefront of providing support for students and their families. Since, they have the potential to help them with their issues and meet their needs (Pincus et al., 2020). However, schools have faced enormous challenges when trying to support the mental health of their students and families (Reimers & Schleicher, 2020). Indeed, the pandemic has changed the scope and quality of counseling services provided by schools, including in the relationship between school counselor and parent. For instance, a study employed by 948 school counselors (Savitz-Romer et al., 2020) indicated that school closures impacted the time counselors spent in their duties. School counselors failed to work with students on social-emotional issues. They reported that they were often struggling to meet logistical and administrative needs. Although counselors found these duties important, they noted that spending time for logical and administrative duties harmed their ability to connect with their students. Another problem was that school administrations were not clear about their expectations from school counselors.

Throughout this process, the crucial fact that teachers and school counselors were also victims seems to be forgotten. Like everyone else in the world, they were experiencing the fears, concerns and anxieties caused by the Covid-19 epidemic. While they were taking care of their children at home, they were striving to fulfill their work responsibilities. They also had fears such as losing their families, infected Covid-19, or losing their jobs. However, the emotions and thoughts of teachers and school counselors were ignored by school administrators and parents. Thus, a study showed that counselors find themselves caught between the personal stressors of the pandemic and the urgent needs of the school and students (Heled & Davidovitch, 2022).

With the return to school after the pandemic, teachers and counselors faced the challenges of preparing students for life after the pandemic. School counselors, who thought that everything would be fine at the end of the pandemic, confronted with the reality that the situation was not as they expected. It was not a circumstance that a school counselor anticipated to encounter students whose anxiety during the pandemic period continued, whose success in distance education decreased, who had difficulty in complying with the classroom rules of in-person education, and who even forgot how to communicate with their friends. The other side of the coin was that there were declines in some of the skills of not only the students, but also the teachers and school counselors.

The Role of Cognitive Flexibility in Mental Health of Students

Traumas experienced at national and global levels have shown that uncertainty is the main problem of our age. Individuals believe that they should live with the thought that anything can happen at any time. This view is also supported by social and political actors, and a view such as "get used to living this way" is adopted. Faced with the fact that the world will now be full of uncertainties and living this way is the new normal, human beings have begun to investigate how to cope with uncertainty. After the pandemic, educators, and students, like everyone else, are trying to create their own normal. While some are trying to redefine themselves in the new normal, others are trying to return to the old normal before the covid 19 pandemic. Even whether it will adapt to the new normal or return to the old normal involves uncertainty in itself. Individuals' reaction to uncertainty might influence the degree to which they experience psychological distress. At that point, the concept of cognitive flexibility emerged.

Cognitive flexibility was described as the ability of an individual to view circumstances under his or her own control, to be able to provide different explanations for situations and the behavior of others, and to produce multiple solutions to problems (Dennis & Vander Wal, 2010). Individuals indicate flexibility by changing their mindsets when the strategies they use to maintain balance in their lives do not work (Kashdan and Rottenberg, 2010). Cognitive flexibility may include attributional structures as well as cognitive styles (Palm ve Follette 2011). In the face of difficult conditions, individuals with high cognitive flexibility tend to have a more flexible approach to make attributions to events.

Cognitive flexibility was considered as an important characteristic that may play a role in stronger protection against trauma-related psychological and behavioral health problems (Johnson et al., 2011). Cognitive flexibility includes acceptance of lived experiences and the values-based actions taken after experiences. These two processes are mutually dependent on each other. Individuals with low cognitive flexibility might create stricter rules regarding the need to control or avoid experiences that are evaluated negatively. Accordingly, individuals with high cognitive flexibility face difficult life events rather than avoiding, controlling, or changing them. Taking actions in line with their personal values can contribute to supporting this perspective (Hayes et al. 2006). Therefore, individuals exposed to trauma can avoid mental disorders if they perceive the difficulties they experience as manageable and use more compatible explanations after encountering traumatic events.

The findings of a study conducted with individuals who were exposed to at least one traumatic event throughout their lives demonstrated that the cognitive flexibility levels of individuals with PTSD are lower than those of individuals without PTSD (Daneshvar et al., 2022). A study employed by Ben-Zion et al. (2018) revealed that shortly after trauma exposure, cognitive flexibility may emerge as a significant predictor of PTSD symptom severity. Higher levels of cognitive flexibility at 1-month post-trauma predict less severe PTSD symptoms at 6- and 14-months post-trauma. Another study with earthquake-exposed adolescents attending three different middle schools in Sichuan showed that cognitive flexibility had a moderating role in the relationship between injury during the earthquake and psychological well-being. (Fu & Chow, 2017). Moreover, cognitive flexibility was a negative and significant predictor of self-harming behaviors in adolescents (Mashalpoure fard et al., 2023). To conclude, cognitive flexibility may play an important role in mitigating the development of mental health issues for traumatized children and adolescents.

The Role of Self-regulation in Mental Health of Students

Traumatic experiences leave traces that might last for many years on children and adolescence. One of the factors that are effective in helping individuals recover from the traumatic experience with the least impact is self-regulation (SR). SR which combines executive functioning and emotion processing encompasses several important competencies, such as the capacity to monitor one's emotions, the ability to interact positively with others, the capacity to avoid inappropriate or offensive actions, and the ability to self-learn (Bronson, 2000). In a broader perspective, SR refers to the ability to monitor and manage cognition, emotion, and behavior, to achieve one's goals and/or adapt to the cognitive and social demands of particular situations (Berger et al., 2007). Cognitive processes that contribute to SR are often referred to as executive functions which include the ability to direct or focus attention, adapt to changes flexibly by changing perspective, retain information, inhibit automatic and impulsive responses to achieve goals, such as problem solving (Hoffman et al., 2012; Hughes & Ensor, 2011).

Self-regulation may enhance mental health, in three ways. Firstly, setting, planning and actively pursuing an individual's goal can strengthen mental health because the sense of autonomy of the individual who directs her behavior towards a specific goal can increase (Sheldon & Elliot,1999; Sheldon et al., 2002). Secondly, goal achievement has a positive impact. Research indicated that successfully achieving personal goals leads to satisfaction, a sense of meaning, competence, and well-being (Carver & Scheier,1990; Heckhausen et al., 2010). Thirdly, emotional and behavioral problems or poor mental health may result from unsuccessful or insufficient efforts to achieve the goal. However, the effect of disappointment over goal failure might be prevented by using the right (emotional) coping strategies or by disengaging and re-engaging in the goal at the right time (Massey et al., 2009; Wrosch et al., 2003). Thus, striving to achieve the goal, eventually achieving the goal, or processing the failed goal contributes to mental health.

It is through self-regulation that psychobiological capacities are activated that enable the individual and his/her essential relationships to maintain security, integrity, development, well-being, and goal achievement. However, childhood traumas negatively impact the development of SR skills (Ford, 2005; Ford et al., 2013), and so risky behaviors increase during adolescence (Blood, 2011; Song & Qian, 2020). For instance, a study of 88,815 high school adolescents indicated that there was a strong relationship between traumatic adverse childhood experiences (ACEs) and various sexual and reproductive health (SRH) risk behaviors and outcomes, such as unplanned pregnancy (Song & Qian, 2020). SR, which was the mediating variable in the relationship between interpersonal trauma and executive functioning, affects depression and behaviors that reduce tension (Blood, 2011).

Self-regulation is correlated with several crucial issues throughout life, such as physical and mental health, social and emotional well-being, and educational and economic success (Galla & Duckworth, 2015; Murray et al. (2016). Students whose level of cognitive flexibility and self-regulation was high indicated low level of test anxiety (Korhan et al., 2021). In conclusion, self-regulation, like cognitive flexibility, has an important role in the mental health of children and adolescents.

The Role of Schools to Improve Cognitive Flexibility and Self-regulation

Schools have an important role for improving students' mental health during and after traumatic events. The contribution of school psychological counselors is important in the development of cognitive flexibility and self-regulation, which emerge as an important protective factor in mental health in children and adolescents. Because cognitive flexibility and self-regulation can be heightened through interventions, in childhood or adolescence.

Increasing evidence pointing to the importance of cognitive flexibility and self-regulation in the mental health of children and adolescence has led to the creation and application of a range of interventions to improve cognitive flexibility and self-regulation skills. A study (Altunkol, 2017) revealed that the cognitive flexibility levels of high school students who participated in the Cognitive Flexibility Psychoeducation Program based on Cognitive Behavioral Therapies increased compared to those who did not participate. However, follow-up measurement showed that there was no difference in cognitive flexibility between the two groups. Similarly, Latorre-Román et al. (2021) investigated the effectiveness of an active recess programme in school setting on cognitive flexibility in children. The program, implemented three times a week for 10 weeks, included moderate to vigorous intensity physical exercises with cognitive engagement. The findings showed that there was a significant difference between experimental and control groups in terms of cognitive flexibility. In other words, children being active during recess increases their cognitive flexibility.

Similar to cognitive flexibility, SR interventions that focus on improving SR skills may have positive impacts on adolescents' mental health by enhancing their emotional regulation and helping them achieve personally important goals (MacLeod et al., 2008; Wrosch et al., 2003). The basic component of K12 education is the development of SR skills. At this point, Ryan et al. (2017) described the basic development of SR in kindergarten students. Sharing common space, resources, and even the teacher's attention is the most obvious example. Play, which occurs in strength-based, supported by adults and led by children environment, provides children with opportunities for safe eye contact, physical and relational closeness in a fun atmosphere. This encourages the growth of neural pathways, leading to more adaptive attachments, regulatory abilities, and overall neural plasticity (Gaskill & Perry, 2014). As students mature in SR skills, their internal neural plasticity develops and their capacity to adapt these skills to deeper functioning grows. Acquiring this habit of self-regulation can be beneficial when facing the challenges of trauma. Since, children have been experiencing chronic stress that can impair their brain function and overall development (Swick et al., 2013).

SR is particularly promising as an intervention approach because it is a learned skill that can be taught, practiced, and reinforced across different life stages (Murray et al., 2014). Due to brain development during adolescence, that period may be the most critical time for the development of SR skills (Casey et al., 2019). A meta-analysis of 50 SR programs for youth found consistent evidence that the programs were effective in improving self-regulation overall, as well as improving a variety of health, behavioral, and academic outcomes (Pandey et al., 2018).

For instance, Plant et al. (2023) developed a widely implemented program which is called Practice Self-Regulation (PS-R). This program is a trauma-focused, neuroscience-based therapeutic intervention enhancing mental health of youth exposed to trauma. The PS-R is based on the theory of change in which youth become aware of how their personal experiences of trauma, including those related to sexual and reproductive health, impact their current decision-making and behavior. Individuals participating in this program will learn self-regulation skills, prioritize their personal values and self-worth, and match their knowledge of safe sex practices with their goals of making healthy decisions about their sexual health. The program consists of 10 in person meetings with a PS-R trained helper as well as a workbook that participants complete on their own. Participants receive medically accurate sexual health information and discuss what they have learned about themselves. They also engage in neuroscience-based multi-sensory activities (such as values clarification, guided imagery, and mindfulness practices) to reinforce program content, improve memory retention, and reduce impulsivity.

Later on, a hybrid learning adaptation of PS-R which combined online, and in-person learning was developed and called as e-Practice Self-Regulation (e-PS-R). The original 10 PS-R in-person meetings have been reduced to four. Moreover, the program's in-person sessions are designed to be delivered by trained, non-clinical staff. Hence, organizations that do not have licensed mental health professionals are more likely to be able to implement the intervention. The content of the PS-R workbook was rearranged and turned into e-learning that youth can complete in eight weeks using a smartphone, tablet, or computer. e-PS-R sessions include a mixture of videos, audio stories, and text. Each session includes a wide range of questions that get youth thinking about their experiences, goals, and learning. The program specifically focuses on how past traumatic experiences may impact participants' sexual behavior and how they can practice healthier decision-making. Additionally, participants are asked to state their values and dreams.

In order to examine the effects of self-regulation-based interventions on children and adolescents, Pandley et al. (2018) conducted a systematic and meta-analysis study. The findings of the study indicated that the SR interventions were classified as curriculum based, mindfulness and yoga, family based, exercise based, and other social and personal skills–based intervention strategies/ delivery methods. The most common intervention type was curriculum-based interventions, that are especially used for the age groups younger than 10 years. 42 % of this intervention was implemented in the classroom, usually with teachers. These interventions, which were applied predominantly to preschool and primary school children, involved a combination of teacher professional training and classroom-based activities based on a predefined curriculum. The strategies used in preschool and kindergarten included circle-time games, storytelling, book reading, and self-talk. For older children, the curriculum included activities such as role play, cognitive modeling, and psychoeducational group therapeutic lessons. Compared to curriculum interventions, mindfulness and yoga interventions were shorter in duration (6 months or less) and required trained yoga and exercise instructors. These interventions were especially effective for pre-adolescents and adolescents. Interventions that use physical activity or exercise to improve SR include high-intensity interval training, martial arts, and team games. These interventions were delivered during school or after-school times and were administered by trained professionals. Family-based interventions used parents and/or siblings to enhance SR. Interventions that aimed social and personal skills training in small groups; a framework of personal responsibility, exemplary behavior, and conflict resolution, etc. were used. This framework was particularly useful for aspects of SR such as delay of gratification, control with effort, and attention. To conclude, the results revealed that the SR interventions were effective for both children and adolescents in community and schools.

Van Genugten et al. (2017) conducted a meta-analysis to identify effective self-regulation techniques (SRTs) in the interventions of primary prevention and secondary prevention on mental well-being in adolescents. Primary prevention is for the general population and aims to prevent emotional and behavioral problems and improve mental health. Secondary prevention, which targets individuals with subclinical problems, aims to prevent the development of serious dysfunction (Haney & Durlak, 1998). The results demonstrated that primary intervention was carried out in 25 studies. All of the programs were implemented in schools, 11 of them were implemented by teachers, and the majority of the remaining programs were implemented by a health professional. The mean length of the intervention was 11 weeks. It was found that the most popular SRTs were *coping planning* (21 times) and *management of stress and emotions* (20 times). Only three interventions used *rewarding*. However, the most effective skills were found as *asking for social support* and *management of stress and emotions*.

Out of 16 interventions of the secondary interventions, 8 of them were delivered in schools, other locations were community centers and training programmes. Ten interventions were delivered by a health professional, two by a teacher. Eight interventions had more than eight intervention sessions. One of the interventions consisted of 90 sessions. In 5 interventions, there were homework assignments for participants, while in 9 interventions, there was a manual or training for healthcare promoter.

Secondary interventions had statistically significant effects on internalizing behavior and self-esteem. The most popular SRTs were *coping planning and skills* (11 studies) and *management of stress and emotions* (9 studies). The intervention that includes *asking for social support* was more effective on internalizing behavior. Interventions that included *monitoring and evaluation* had a stronger effect on self-esteem. In conclusion, primary interventions had a small-to-medium effect on self-esteem and internalizing behavior. Secondary interventions had a medium-to-large short-term effect on internalizing behavior and self-esteem.

As a result, the Covid-19 global pandemic has undoubtedly brought professional and personal challenges to all educators. But some ways to cope with difficulties were offered, such as cognitive flexibility and self-regulation. School counselors who play an active role in the mental health of students have a major responsibility in developing cognitive flexibility and self-regulation. The impact of intervention programs prepared and implemented by school counseling services in raising children and adolescents who can look at the difficulties they experience from different perspectives and produce alternative solutions and regulate themselves cannot be ignored.

References

Altunkol, F. (2017). The effects of cognitive flexibility education program on high school students' cognitive flexibility, perceived stress levels and coping styles. (Unpublished doctoral dissertation), University of Çukurova, Adana, Turkey.

Baumeister, R., & Tierney, J. (2011). Willpower: Rediscovering the greatest human strength. New York: Penguin Press.

Becker, S. P., & Gregory, A. M. (2020). Editorial perspective: Perils and promises for child and adolescent sleep and associated psychopathology during the COVID-19 pandemic. *Journal of Child Psychology and Psychiatry, 61*(7), 757–759. https://doi.org/10.1111/jcpp. 13278

Berger, A., Kofman, O., Livneh, U., & Henik, A. (2007). Multidisciplinary perspectives on attention and the development of self-regulation. *Progress in Neurobiology, 82*(5), 256–286. https://doi.org/10.1016/j.pneurobio.2007.06.004

Ben-Zion, Z., Fine, N.B., Keynan, N.J., Admon, R., Green, N., Halevi, M., Fonzo, G.A., Achituv, M., Merin, O., Sharon, H., Halpern, P., Liberzon, I., Etkin, A., Hendler, T. & Shalev, A.Y. (2018). Cognitive flexibility predicts PTSD symptoms: Observational and interventional Studies. Frontiers in Psychiatry, 9(477), 1-9. https://doi.org/10.3389/fpsyt.2018.00477

Bloch, L., Moran, E. K., & Kring, A. M. (2010). On the need for conceptual and definitional clarity in emotion regulation research on psychopathology. In A. M. Kring & D. M. Sloan (Eds.), *Emotion regulation and psychopathology: A transdiagnostic approach to etiology and treatment* (pp. 88–104). The Guilford Press.

Blood, R. (2011). *The relationship among self-regulation, executive functioning, coping resources, and symptomatology resulting from traumatic events* [Unpublished doctoral dissertation], Georgia State University.

Bluhm, R. L., Frewen, P. A., Coupland, N. C., Densmore, M., Schore, A. N., & Lanius,R. A. (2012). Neural correlates self-reflection in post-traumatic stress disorder. *Acta Psychiatrica Scandinavica, 125*(3), 238–246.

Bronson, M. B. (2000). Recognizing and supporting the development of self-regulation in young children. *Young Child, 55*(2), 32–37. https://eric.ed.gov/?id=EJ605513

Buzzi, C., Tucci, M., Ciprandi, R., Brambilla, I., Caimmi, S., Ciprandi, G., & Marseglia, G. L. (2020). The psychosocial effects of COVID-19 on Italian adolescents' attitudes and behaviors. *Italian Journal of Pediatrics, 46*(1), 69. https://doi.org/10.1186/s13052-020-00833-4.

Casey, B.J., Heller, A.S., Gee, D.G., & Cohen, A.O. (2019). Development of the emotional brain. Neuroscience Letters, 693, 29-34. https://doi.org/10.1016/j.neulet.2017.11.055

Carver, C. S., & Scheier, M. F. (1990). Origins and functions of positive and negative affect: A control-process view. *Psychological Review, 97*(1), 19–35. https://doi.org/10.1037/0033-295X.97.1.19

Cheng, J., Liang, Y., Fu, L., & Liu, Z. (2018). Posttraumatic stress and depressive symptoms in children after the Wenchuan earthquake. *European Journal of Psychotraumatology, 9*(1), 1472992. https://doi.org/10.1080/20008198.2018.1472992

Cluver, L., Lachman, J. M., Sherr, L., Wessels, I., Krug, E., Rakotomalala, S., … McDonald, K. (2020). Parenting in the time of COVID-19. *The Lancet, 395*(10231), e64. https://doi.org/10.1016/S0140-6736(20)30736-4

Codreanu, T. A., Celenza, A., & Jacobs, I. (2014). Does disaster education of teenagers translate into better survival knowledge, knowledge of skills, and adaptive behavioral change? A systematic literature review. *Prehospital and Disaster Medicine, 29*(6), 629–642. https://doi.org/10.1017/S1049023X14001083

Daneshvar, S., Basharpoor, S., & Shafiei, M. (2022). Self-compassion and cognitive flexibility in trauma-exposed individuals with and without PTSD. *Current Psychology, 41*, 2045–2052. https://doi.org/10.1007/s12144-020-00732-1.

Dennis, J. P., & Vander Wal, J. S. (2010). The cognitive flexibility inventory: Instrument development and estimates of reliability and validity. *Cognitive Therapy and Research, 34*(3), 241–253. https://doi.org/10.1007/s10608-009-9276-4

Fegert, J. M., Vitiello, B., Plener, P. L., & Clemens, V. (2020). Challenges and burden of the Coronavirus 2019 (COVID-19) pandemic for child and adolescent mental health: A narrative review to highlight clinical and research needs in the acute phase and the long return to normality. *Child and Adolescent Psychiatry and Mental Health, 14*(1), 20. https://doi.org/10.1186/s13034-020-00329-3

Fegert, J. M., & Schulze, M. E. (2020). COVID-19 and its impact on child and adolescent psychiatry – A German and personal perspective. *Irish Journal of Psychological Medicine, 37*(3), 243–245. https://doi.org/10.1017/ipm.2020.43

Ford, J.D. (2005). Treatment implications of altered affect regulation and information processing following child maltreatment. Psychiatric Annals, 35(5), 410-419.

Ford, J.D. (2013). How Can Self-Regulation enhance our understanding of trauma and dissociation?, Journal of Trauma & Dissociation, 14:3, 237-250. https://doi.org/10.1080/15299732.2013.769398

Fu, F., & Chow, A. (2017). Traumatic exposure and psychological wellbeing: The moderating role of cognitive flexibility. *Journal of Loss and Trauma, 22*(1), 24–35. https://doi.org/10.1080/15325024.2016.1161428

Galla, B. M., & Duckworth, A. L. (2015). More than resisting temptation: Beneficial habits mediate the relationship between self-control and positive life outcomes. Journal of Personality and Social Psychology, 109(3), 508–525. https://doi.org/10.1037/pspp0000026

Gaskill, R.L. & Perry, B.D. (2014). The neurobiological power of play: Usimg the neurosequential model of therapeutics to guide play in the healing process. In C.A. Malchiodi & D.A. Crenshaw (Ed.), Creative arts and play therapy for attachment problems (pp. 178-194).

Goldfarb, E.V., Frobösei M.I., Cools, R., & Phelps, E.A. (2017). Stress and cognitive flexibility: Cortisol increase are associated with enhanced updating but impaired switching. Journal of Cognitive Neuroscience, 29(1), 14-24. https://doi.org/10.1162/jocn_a_01029

Griffith, A. K. (2020). Parental burnout and child maltreatment during the COVID-19 pandemic. *Journal of Family Violence, 37,* 725–731 https://doi.org/10.1007/s10896-020-00172-2.

Guessoum, S. B., Lachal, J., Radjack, R., Carretier, E., Minassian, S., Benoit, L., & Moro, M. R. (2020). Adolescent psychiatric disorders during the COVID-19 pandemic and lockdown. *Psychiatry Research, 291,* 113264. https://doi.org/10.1016/j.psychres.2020.113264

Haney, P., & Durlak, J. A. (1998). Changing self-esteem in children and adolescents: A meta-analytical review. Journal of Clinical Child Psychology, 27(4), 423–4

Hayes, S. C., Luoma, J. B., Bond, F. W., Masuda, A., & Lillis, J. (2006). Acceptance and commitment therapy: Model, processes, and outcomes. *Behavior Research and Therapy, 44*(1), 1–25. https://doi.org/10.1016/j.brat.2005.06.006

Heckhausen, J., Wrosch, C., & Schulz, R. (2010). A motivational theory of life-span development. *Psychological Review, 117*(1), 32–60. https://doi.org/10.1037/a0017668

Heled, E., & Davidovitch, N. (2022). School counseling during the COVID-19 crisis – From crisis to growth. *Journal of Education and Learning, 11*(1), 28–39. https://doi.org/10.5539/jel.v11n1p28.

Hlodversdottir, H., Thorsteinsdottir, H., Thordardottir, E. B., Njardvik, U., Petursdottir, G., & Hauksdottir, A. (2018). Long-term health of children following the Eyjafjallajökull volcanic eruption: A prospective cohort study. *European Journal of Psychotraumatology, 9*(Suppl 2), 1442601. https://doi.org/10.1080/20008198.2018.1442601

Hofmann, W., Schmeichel, B. J., & Baddeley, A. D. (2012). Executive functions and self-regulation. *Trends in Cognitive Sciences, 16*(3), 174–180. https://doi.org/10.1016/j.tics.2012.01.006

Hughes, C. (2011). Changes and challenges in 20 years of research into the development of executive functions. *Infant Child Development, 20*(3), 251–271. https://doi.org/10.1002/icd.736

Hughes, C., & Ensor R. (2011). Individual differences in growth in executive function across the transition to school predict externalizing and internalizing behaviors and self-perceived academic success at 6 years of age. *Journal of Experimental Child Psychology, 108*(3), 663–676. https://doi.org/10.1016/j.jecp. 2010.06.005

Jiao, W.Y., Wang, L.N., Liu, J., Feng-Fang, S., Jiao, F.Y., Pettoello-Mantovani, M., Somekh, E. (2020). Behavioral and emotional disorders in children during the Covid-19 epidemic. Journal of Pediatrics, 221, 264- 266e1. https://doi.org/10.1016/j.jpeds.2020.03.013

Johnson, D. C., Polusny, M. A., Erbes, C. R., King, D., King, L., Litz, B. T., Schnurr, P. P., Friedman, M., Pietrzak, R. H., & Southwick, S. M. (2011). Development and initial validation of the response to stressful experiences scale. *Military Medicine, 176*(2), 161–169. https://doi.org/10.7205/MILMED-D-10-00258

Kashdan, T.B., & Rottenberg, J. (2010). Psychological flexibility as a fundamental aspect of health. Clinical Psychology Review, 30, 865–878. https://doi.org/10.1016/j.cpr.2010.03.001

Keith, J., Velezmoro, R., & O'Brien, C. (2015). Correlates of cognitive flexibility in veterans seeking treatment for posttraumatic stress disorder. Journal of Nervous and Mental Disease, 203(4), 287–293.

Kim, B. S. K., & Omizo, M. M. (2005). Asian and European American Cultural Values, Collective Self-Esteem, Acculturative Stress, Cognitive Flexibility, and General Self-Efficacy Among Asian American College Students. Journal of Counseling Psychology, 52(3), 412–419. https://doi.org/10.1037/0022-0167.52.3.412

Latorre-Román, P. Á., Berrios-Aguayo, B., Aragón-Vela, J., & Pantoja-Vallejo, A. (2021). Effects of a 10-week active recess program in school setting on physical fitness, school aptitudes, creativity, and cognitive flexibility in elementary school children. A randomized-controlled trial. Journal of Sports Sciences, 39(11), 1277–1286. https://doi.org/10.1080/02640414.2020.1864985

Law, B.M.F., & Shek, D.T.L. (2016). A 6 year logitudinal study of self-harm and suicidal behaviors among Chinese adolescents in Hong Kong. Journal of Pediatric and Adolescent Gynecology, 29, S38-S48. http://dx.doi.org/10.1016/j.jpag.2015.10.007

Lee, J. (2020). Mental health effects of school closures during COVID-19. The Lancet Child & Adolescent Health, 4(6), 421. https://doi.org/0.1016/S2352-4642(20)30109-7

Liu, Y., Yue, S., Hu, X., Zhu, J., Wu, Z., Wang, J., & Wu, Y. (2021). Associations between feelings/behaviors during Covid-19 pandemic lockdown and depression/anxiety after lockdown in a sample of Chinese children and adolescent. Journal of Affective Disorders, 284, 98-103. https://doi.org/10.1016/j.jad.2021.02.001

Liu, Z., Tang, H., Jin, Q., Wang, G., Yang, Z., Chen, H., … & Owens, J. (2020). Sleep of preschoolers during the coronavirus disease 2019 (COVID-19) outbreak. Journal of Sleep Research, 30(1), e13142. https://doi.org/10.1111/jsr.13142

Loades, M. E., Chatburn, E., Higson-Sweeney, N., Reynolds, S., Shafran, R., Brigden, A., … Crawley, E. (2020). Rapid systematic review: The impact of social isolation and loneliness on the mental health of children and adolescents in the context of COVID-19. Journal of the American Academy of Child and Adolescent Psychiatry, 59(11), 1218–1239.e3. https://doi.org/10.1016/j.jaac.2020.05.009

Ma, L., Mazidi, M., Li, K., Li, L., Chen, S., Kirwan, R., Zhou, H., Yan, N., Rahman, A., Wang, W., & Wang, Y. (2021). Prevalence of mental health problems among children and adolescents during the COVID-19 pandemic: A systematic review and meta-analysis. Journal of Affective Disorders, 293, 78–89. https://doi.org/10.1016/j.jad.2021.06.021

MacLeod, A.K., Coates, E., & Hetherton, J. (2008). Increasing well-being through teaching goal-setting and planning skills: results of a brief intervention.

Journal of Happiness Studies, 9, 185-196. htpps://doi.org/10.1007/s10902-007-9057-2

Massey, E. K., Garnefski, N., & Gebhardt, W. A. (2009). Goal frustration, coping and well-being in the context of adolescent headache: A self-regulation approach. *European Journal of Pain, 13*(9), 977–984. https://doi.org/10.1016/j.ejpain.2008.11.012

Meherali, S., Punjani, N., Louie-Poon, S., Abdul Rahim, K., Das, J. K., Salam, R. A., & Lassi, Z. S. (2021). Mental health of children and adolescents amidst covid-19 and past pandemics: A rapid systematic review. *International Journal of Environmental Research and Public Health, 18*(7), 1–16. https://doi.org/10.3390/ijerph18073432.

Moffitt, T. E., Arseneault, L., Belsky, D., Dickson, N., Hancox, R. J., Harrington, H., et al. (2011). A gradient of childhood self-control predicts health, wealth, and public safety. Proceedings of the National Academy of Sciences, 108(7), 2693–2698. https://doi.org/10.1073/ pnas.1010076108.

Murray, D. W., Rosanbalm, K., & Christopoulos, C. (2016). *Self-regulation and toxic stress report 3: A comprehensive review of self-regulation interventions from birth through young adulthood.* OPRE Report #2016-34. Office of Planning, Research, and Evaluation, Administration for Children and Families, U.S. Department of Health and Human Services. https://www.acf.hhs.gov/opre/report/self-regulation-and-toxic-stress-report-3-comprehensive-review-self-regulation

Nakhostin-Khayyat, M., Borjali, M., Zeinali, M., Fardi, D., & Montazeri, A. (2024). The relationship between self-regulation, cognitive flexibility, and resilience among students: A structural equation modeling. BMC Psychology, 12(337), 1-8. https://doi.org/10.1186/s40359-024-01843-1

Odacı, H., Bulbul, K., & Turkkan, T. (2021). The mediating role of cognitive flexibility in the relationship between traumatic experiences in the childhood period and substance abuse proclivity. Journal of Rational Emotive and Cognitive Behavioral Therapy, 39, 538-554. https://doi.org/10.1007/s10942-020-00385-w

Oosterhoff, B., & Palmer, C. (2020). Attitudes and psychological factors associated with news monitoring, social distancing, disinfecting, and hoarding behaviors among US adolescents during the Coronavirus disease 2019 pandemic. *JAMA Pediatrics, 174*(12), 1184–1190. https://doi.org/10.1001/jamapediatrics.2020.1876

Pincus, R., Hannor-Walker, T., Wright, L.S. & Justice J. (2020). Covid-19's effect on students: How school counselors rise to the rescue. NASSP Bulletin, 104(4), 241-256. https://doi.org/10.177/019263520975866

Palm, K. M., & Follette, V. M. (2011). The roles of cognitive flexibility and experiential avoidance in explaining psychological distress in survivors of interpersonal victimization. *Journal of Psychopathology and Behavioral Assessment, 33*(1), 79–86. https://doi.org/10.1007/s10862-010-9201-x

Pandey, A., Hale, D., Das, S., Goddings, A. L., Blackmore, S. J., & Viner, R. M. (2018). Effectiveness of universal self-regulation–based interventions in children and adolescents: A systematic review and meta-analysis. *JAMA Pediatry, 72*(6), 566–575. https://doi.org/10.1001/jamapediatrics.2018.0232

Plant, A., Schladale, J., Neffa-Greech, D., Qaragholi, N., Miller, M., & Montaya, J. (2023). Development, acceptability, and perceived effectiveness of a trauma-informed adolescent self-regulation intervention. *Evaluation and Program Planning, 97*(2023), 102232. https://doi.org/10.1016/j.evalprogplan.2023.102232

Reimers., F. M., & Schleicher, A. (2020). A framework to guide an education response to the COVID-19 pandemic of 2020. Retrieved from https://read. oecd-ilibrary.org/view/?ref=126_126988-t63lxosohs&title=A- framework-to-guide-an-education-response-to-the-Covid-19-Pandemic-of-2020. Accessed: 25.01.2024

Robson, D., Allen, M.S., & Howard, S.J. (2020). Self-regulation in childhood as a predictor of future outcomes: A meta-analytic review. Faculty of Social Sciences - Papers. 4656. https://ro.uow.edu.au/sspapers/4656

Russell, B. S., Hutchison, M., Tambling, R., Tomkunas, A. J., & Horton, A. L. (2020). Initial challenges of caregiving during COVID-19: Caregiver burden, mental health, and the parent-child relationship. *Child Psychiatry and Human Development, 51*(5), 671–682. https://doi.org/10.1007/s10578-020-01037-x

Ryan, K., Lane, S. J., & Powers, D. (2017). A multidisciplinary model for treating complex trauma in early childhood. *International Journal of Play Therapy, 26*(2), 111–123. https://doi.org/10.1037/pla0000044

Savitz-Romer, M., Rowan-Kenyon, H. T., Nicola, T. P., Carroll, S., & Hecht, L. (2020). *Expanding support beyond the virtual classroom: Lessons and recommendations from school counselors during the COVID-19 crisis.* Harvard Graduate School of Education & Boston College Lynch School of Education and Human Development. http://hgse.me/schoolcounselors-covid19

Sepahvand, H., Mokhtari Hashtjini, M., Salesi, M., Sharei, H. & Pirzad Jahromi, G. (2019). Prevalence of post-traumatic stress disorder (PTSD) in Iranian population following disasters and wars: A systematic review and meta-analysis. Iran Journal of Psychiatry Behavior Science, 13(1), e66124. https://doi. org/10.5812/ijpbs.66124

Sbarra, D. A., & Hazan, C. (2008). Coregulation, dysregulation, self-regulation: An integrative analysis and empirical agenda for understanding adult attachment,

Dr. Berna Güloğlu

separation, loss, and recovery. *Personality & Social Psychology Review, 12*(2), 141–167. https://doi.org/10.1177/108886830831570

Sheldon, K. M., & Elliot, A. J. (1999). Goal striving, need satisfaction, and longitudinal well-being: The self-concordance model. *Journal of Personality and Social Psychology, 76*(3), 482–497. https://doi.org/10.1037/0022-3514.76.3.482

Sheldon, K. M., Kasser, T., Smith, K., & Share, T. (2002). Personal goals and psychological growth: Testing an intervention to enhance goal attainment and personality integration. *Journal of Personality, 70*(1), 5–31. https://doi.org/10.1111/1467-6494.00176

Song, W., & Qian, X. (2020). Adverse childhood experiences and teen sexual behaviors: The role of self-regulation and school-related factors. *Journal of School Health, 90*(11), 830–841. https://doi.org/10.1111/josh.12947

Schmidt, S. J., Barblan, L. P., Lory, I., & Landolt, M. A. (2021). Age-related effects of the COVID-19 pandemic on mental health of children and adolescents. *European Journal of Psychotraumatology, 12*(1). https://doi.org/10.1080/20008198.2021.1901407

Swick, K. J., Knopf, H, Williams, R., & Fields, M. E. (2013). Family school strategies for responding to the needs of children experiencing chronic stress. *Early Childhood Education Journal, 41*, 181–186. https://doi.org/10.1007/s10643-012-0546-5

Tangney, J. P., Baumeister, R. F., & Boone, A. L. (2004). High self-control predicts good adjustment, less pathology, better grades, and interpersonal success. Journal of Personality, 72, 271–324. doi:10.1111/j.0022-3506.2004.00263.x

Van Genugten, L., Dusseldorp, E., Massey, E. K., & Van Empelen, P. (2017). Effective self-regulation change techniques to promote mental wellbeing among adolescents: A meta-analysis. *Health Psychology Review, 11*(1), 53–71 http://dx.doi.org/10.1080/17437199.2016.1252934

Wrosch, C., Scheier, M. F., Miller, G. E., Schulz, R., & Carver, C. S. (2003). Adaptive self-regulation of unattainable goals: Goaldisengagement, goal reengagement, and subjective well-being. *Personality and Social Psychology Bulletin, 29*(12), 1494–1500. https://doi.org/10.1177/0146167203256921

Yuen, W.W.Y., Liu, L.L., & Tse, S. (2019). Adolescent mental health problems in Hong Kong: A critical review on prevalence, psychosocial correlates, and prevention. Journal of Adolescent Health, 64, S73-S85. https://doi.org/10.1016/j.jadohealth.2018.10.005

www.ingramcontent.com/pod-product-compliance
Lightning Source LLC
La Vergne TN
LVHW050142060326
832904LV00004B/129